Capital Structure and Firm Performance

Capital Structure and Firm Performance

Dr. Sanjeev Kumar Singh

RANDOM PUBLICATIONS

NEW DELHI - 110 002 (INDIA)

Capital Structure and Firm Performance

ISBN 978-93-51114-57-4

Published in 2014 in India by

RANDOM PUBLICATIONS

4376-A/4B, Gali Murari Lal, Ansari Road
New Delhi-110 002
Phone: +9111-43580356, 23289044
E-mail: randomexports@gmail.com; sales@randompublications.com; info@randompublications.com

Type Setting by: Friends Media, Delhi-110089
Printed at : Thomson Press (India) Ltd.

Preface

Capital structure refers to the way a corporation finances its assets through some combination of equity, debt, or hybrid securities. A firm's capital structure is then the composition or 'structure' of its liabilities. For example, a firm that sells $20 billion in equity and $80 billion in debt is said to be 20% equity-financed and 80% debt-financed. The firm's ratio of debt to total financing, 80% in this example, is referred to as the firm's leverage. In reality, capital structure may be highly complex and include dozens of sources. Gearing Ratio is the proportion of the capital employed of the firm which come from outside of the business finance, e.g. by taking a short term loan etc. Consider a perfect capital market (no transaction or bankruptcy costs; perfect information); firms and individuals can borrow at the same interest rate; no taxes; and investment returns are not affected by financial uncertainty. Modigliani and Miller made two findings under these conditions. Their first 'proposition' was that the value of a company is independent of its capital structure. Their second 'proposition' stated that the cost of equity for a leveraged firm is equal to the cost of equity for an unleveraged firm, plus an added premium for financial risk. That is, as leverage increases, while the burden of individual risks is shifted between different investor classes, total risk is conserved and hence no extra value created.

A subjective measure of how well a firm can use assets from its primary mode of business and generate revenues. This term is also used as a general measure of a firm's overall financial health over a given period of time, and can be used to compare similar firms across the same industry or to compare industries or sectors in aggregation. There are many different ways to measure financial performance, but all measures should be taken in aggregation. Line items such as revenue from operations, operating income or cash flow from operations can be used, as well as total unit sales. Furthermore, the analyst or investor may wish to look deeper into financial statements and seek out margin growth rates or any declining debt. Corporate performance management is the area of business intelligence (BI) involved with monitoring and managing an organization's performance, according to key performance indicators (KPIs) such as revenue, return on investment (ROI), overhead, and operational costs. CPM is also known as business performance management (BPM) or enterprise performance management (EPM). The relationship existing between the capital structure and performance of listed firms have been a debate existing in corporate finance.

This valuable resource takes a practical approach to capital structure by discussing why various theories make sense and how firms use them to solve problems and create wealth. In the wake of the recent financial crisis, the insights found here are essential to excelling in today's volatile business environment.

I thank all members of my team who have helped in the preparation of the book. My special thanks go to "Random Publications" who have published the book.

— Dr. Sanjeev Kumar Singh

Contents

1

Introduction Capital Structure Theory: An Overview

Capital (Economics)

In economics, capital goods, real capital, or capital assets are already-produced durable goods or any non-financial asset that is used in production of goods or services. Additionally, some accounting systems recognise the concept of a Triple bottom line which takes into account natural capital and social capital, thus including ecosystems and social relations in the definition of capital.

Control and protection of capital obtained through jobs is the primary means of accumulating wealth in the modern economy. If a broader definition of wealth is used (say including health, employability, or well-being) then a broader definition of capital is appropriate.

In all systems of accounting and in all definitions of asset types, the capital goods are not significantly consumed, though they may depreciate in the production process. How a capital good or asset is maintained or regrown or returned to its pre-production state varies based on the type of capital involved.

Manufactured or physical capital is distinct from land (or natural capital) in that capital must itself be produced by human labour before it can be a factor of production. At any given moment in time, total physical capital may be referred to as the capital stock (which is not to be confused with the capital stock of a business entity.)

In a fundamental sense, capital consists of any produced thing that can enhance a person's power to perform economically useful work—a stone or an arrow is capital for a caveman who can use it as a hunting instrument, and roads are capital for inhabitants of a city. Capital is an input in the production function. Homes and personal autos are not usually defined as capital but as durable goods because they are not used in a production of saleable goods and services. The division between capital and durable good is set in an accounting regime and depends on the types or styles of capital that are recognised as capital assets and the types of goods and services that are recognised as economic. For instance natural capital produces one yield of agricultural output and social capital substitutes significantly for financial in developing economies, and triple bottom line accounting recognises this.

In classical economic schools of thought, particularly in Marxist political economy, capital is money used to buy something only in order to sell it again to realise a financial profit. For Marx capital only exists within the process of economic exchange—it is wealth that grows out of the process of circulation itself, and for Marx it formed the basis of the economic system of capitalism. In more contemporary schools of economics, this form of capital is generally referred to as "financial capital" and is distinguished from "capital goods".

In Narrow and Broad Uses

Classical and neoclassical economics regard capital as one of the factors of production (alongside the other factors: land and labour). All other inputs to production are called intangibles in classical economics. This includes organisation, entrepreneurship, knowledge, goodwill, or management (which some characterize as talent, social capital or instructional capital).

Capital includes goods with the following features:

- The good can be used in the production of other goods (this is what makes it a factor of production).
- The good is not used up immediately in the process of production unlike raw materials or intermediate goods. (The significant exception to this is depreciation allowance, which like intermediate goods, is treated as a business expense.)
- The good is produced (in contrast to "land", which refers to naturally occurring resources such as geographical locations and minerals). *This last condition is removed and replaced with looser conditions such as the capital asset being fungible, clearly defined in right by a deed or patent, or transferrable between persons, or some such. The requirement that it be produced by a production process similar to a durable good is*

relatively arbitrary, extremely hotly debated and in any case changes as production processes differ. For instance, it is possible to produce genetic material in a lab or in an organism - thus organisms themselves can be understood as being produced.

These distinctions of convenience have carried over to contemporary economic theory. There was the further clarification that capital is a stock. As such, its value can be estimated at a point in time. By contrast, investment, as production to be added to the capital stock, is described as taking place over time ("per year"), thus a flow.

Marxian economics distinguishes between different forms of capital:

- constant capital, which refers to capital goods
- variable capital, which refers to labour-inputs, where the cost is "variable" based on the amount of wages and salaries are paid throughout the duration of an employee's contract/ employment,
- fictitious capital, which refers to intangible representations or abstractions of physical capital, such as stocks, bonds and securities (or "tradable paper claims to wealth")

Earlier illustrations often described capital as physical items, such as tools, buildings, and vehicles that are used in the production process. Since at least the 1960s economists have increasingly focused on broader forms of capital. For example, investment in skills and education can be viewed as building up human capital or knowledge capital, and investments in intellectual property can be viewed as building up intellectual capital. These terms lead to certain questions and controversies discussed in those articles.

Modern Types of Capital

Detailed classifications of capital that have been used in various theoretical or applied uses generally respect the following division:

- Financial capital, which represents obligations, and is liquidated as money for trade, and owned by legal entities. It is in the form of capital assets, traded in financial markets. Its market value is not based on the historical accumulation of money invested but on the perception by the market of its expected revenues and of the risk entailed.
- Natural capital, which is inherent in ecologies and protected by communities to support life, e.g., a river that provides farms with water.

- Social capital, which in private enterprise is partly captured as goodwill or brand value, but is a more general concept of inter-relationships between human beings having money-like value that motivates actions in a similar fashion to paid compensation.
- Instructional capital, defined originally in academia as that aspect of teaching and knowledge transfer that is not inherent in individuals or social relationships but transferrable. *Various theories use names like knowledge or intellectual capital to describe similar concepts but these are not strictly defined as in the academic definition and have no widely agreed accounting treatment.*
- Human capital, a broad term that generally includes social, instructional and individual human talent in combination. *It is used in technical economics to define balanced growth which is the goal of improving human capital as much as economic capital. A far less common term, spiritual capital, refers to the power, influence and dispositions created by a person or an organisation's spiritual belief, knowledge and practice, which is also an aspect of human capital that may not be easily captured as a component social, instructional or individual element.*

Public and private sector accounting differ in goals, time scales and accordingly in accounting. The ownership and control of some forms of capital may accordingly justify differentiating it in an economic theory. A blanket term that attempts to characterize all that clearly physical capital that is considered infrastructure and which supports production in unclear or poorly accounted ways is public capital.

This encompasses the aggregate body of all government-owned assets that are used to promote private industry productivity, including highways, railways, airports, water treatment facilities, telecommunications, electric grids, energy utilities, municipal buildings, public hospitals and schools, police, fire protection, courts and still others. However it is a problematic term insofar as many of these assets can be either publicly or privately owned.

Separate literatures have developed to describe both natural capital and social capital. Such terms reflect a wide consensus that nature and society both function in such a similar manner as traditional industrial infrastructural capital, that it is entirely appropriate to refer to them as different types of capital in themselves. In particular, they can be used in the production of other goods, are not used up immediately in the process of production, and can be enhanced (if not created) by human effort.

There is also a literature of intellectual capital and intellectual property law. However, this increasingly distinguishes means of capital investment, and collection of potential rewards for patent, copyright (creative or individual capital), and trademark (social trust or social capital) instruments.

Endowment

Endowment is the natural state of something, before it is processed. The production turns an endowment into capital. Just as capital can be split into natural capital etcetera, so endowment can also be split into a country's natural endowment or a population's endowment.

Interpretations

Some thinkers, such as Werner Sombart and Max Weber, locate the concept of capital as originating in double-entry bookkeeping, which is thus a foundational innovation in capitalism, Sombart writing in "Medieval and Modern Commercial Enterprise" that:

The very concept of capital is derived from this way of looking at things; one can say that capital, as a category, did not exist before double-entry bookkeeping. Capital can be defined as that amount of wealth which is used in making profits and which enters into the accounts."

Within classical economics, Adam Smith (*Wealth of Nations*, Book II, Chapter 1) distinguished fixed capital from circulating capital. The former designated physical assets not consumed in the production of a product (e.g. machines and storage facilities), while the latter referred to physical assets consumed in the process of production (e.g. raw materials and intermediate products). For an enterprise, both were types of capital.

Karl Marx adds a distinction that is often confused with David Ricardo's. In Marxian theory, variable capital refers to a capitalist's investment in labour-power, seen as the only source of surplus-value. It is called "variable" since the amount of value it can produce varies from the amount it consumes, *i.e.*, it creates new value. On the other hand, constant capital refers to investment in non-human factors of production, such as plant and machinery, which Marx takes to contribute only its own replacement value to the commodities it is used to produce.

Investment or capital accumulation, in classical economic theory, is the production of increased capital. Investment requires that some goods be produced that are not immediately consumed, but instead used to produce other goods as capital goods. Investment is closely related to saving, though it is not the same. As Keynes pointed out, saving involves not spending all of one's income on current goods or services, while investment refers to spending on a specific type of goods, *i.e.*, capital goods.

Austrian School economist Eugen von Böhm-Bawerk maintained that capital intensity was measured by the roundaboutness of production processes. Since capital is defined by him as being goods of higher-order, or goods used to produce consumer goods, and derived their value from them, being future goods.

Human development theory describes human capital as being composed of distinct social, imitative and creative elements:

- Social capital is the value of network trusting relationships between individuals in an economy.
- Individual capital, which is inherent in persons, protected by societies, and trades labour for trust or money. Close parallel concepts are "talent", "ingenuity", "leadership", "trained bodies", or "innate skills" that cannot reliably be reproduced by using any combination of any of the others above. In traditional economic analysis individual capital is more usually called *labour*.
- Instructional capital in the academic sense is clearly separate from either individual persons or social bonds between them.

This theory is the basis of triple bottom line accounting and is further developed in ecological economics, welfare economics and the various theories of green economics. All of which use a particularly abstract notion of capital in which the requirement of capital being produced like durable goods is effectively removed.

The Cambridge capital controversy was a dispute between economists at Cambridge, Massachusetts based MIT and University of Cambridge in the UK about the measurement of capital.

The Cambridge, UK economists, including Joan Robinson and Piero Sraffa claimed that there is no basis for aggregating the heterogeneous objects that constitute 'capital goods.'

Political economists Jonathan Nitzan and Shimshon Bichler have suggested that capital is not a productive entity, but solely financial and that capital values measure the relative power of owners over the broad social processes that bear on profits.

Financial Capital

Financial capital is money used by entrepreneurs and businesses to buy what they need to make their products or to provide their services to the sector of the economy upon which their operation is based, i.e. retail, corporate, investment banking, etc.

Three Concepts of Capital Maintenance Authorized in IFRS

Financial capital or just capital in finance and accounting, is funds provided by lenders (and investors) to businesses to purchase real capital equipment for producing goods/services. Real capital or economic capital comprises physical goods that assist in the production of other goods and services, e.g. shovels for gravediggers, sewing machines for tailors, or machinery and tooling for factories.

Financial capital generally refers to saved-up financial wealth, especially that used to start or maintain a business. A financial concept of capital is adopted by most entities in preparing their financial reports. Under a financial concept of capital, such as invested money or invested purchasing power, capital is synonymous with the net assets or equity of the entity. Under a physical concept of capital, such as operating capability, capital is regarded as the productive capacity of the entity based on, for example, units of output per day. Financial capital maintenance can be measured in either nominal monetary units or units of constant purchasing power.

There are thus three concepts of capital maintenance in terms of International Financial Reporting Standards (IFRS): (1) Physical capital maintenance (2) Financial capital maintenance in nominal monetary units (3) Financial capital maintenance in units of constant purchasing power.

Financial capital is provided by lenders for a price: interest.

Furthermore, financial capital, is any liquid medium or mechanism that represents wealth, or other styles of capital. It is, however, usually purchasing power in the form of money available for the production or purchasing of goods, etcetera. Capital can also be obtained by producing more than what is immediately required and saving the surplus.

Financial capital can also be in the form of purchasable items such as computers or books that can contribute directly or indirectly to obtaining various other types of capital.

Financial capital has been subcategorized by some academics as economic or "productive capital" necessary for operations, signaling capital which signals a company's financial strength to shareholders, and regulatory capital which fulfills capital requirements.

Sources of Capital

- Long term - usually above 7 years
  - Share Capital
  - Mortgage loan
  - Retained Profit
  - Venture Capital
  - Debenture
  - Project Finance
- Medium term - usually between 2 and 7 years
  - Term Loans
  - Leasing
  - Hire Purchase
- Short term - usually under 2 years
  - Bank Overdraft
  - Trade Credit
  - Deferred Expenses
  - Factoring

Capital Market

- Long-term funds are bought and sold:
  - Shares
  - Debentures
  - Long-term loans, often with a mortgage bond as security
  - Reserve funds
  - Euro Bonds
  - Law Firms

Money Market

- Financial institutions can use short-term savings to lend out in the form of short-term loans:
  - Credit on open account
  - Bank overdraft

- o Short-term loans
- o Bills of exchange
- o Factoring of debtors

Differences between Shares and Debentures

- Shareholders are effectively owners; debenture-holders are creditors.
- Shareholders may vote at AGMs (Annual General Meetings) and be elected as directors; debenture-holders may not vote at AGMs or be elected as directors.
- Shareholders receive profit in the form of dividends; debenture-holders receive a fixed rate of interest.
- If there is no profit, the shareholder does not receive a dividend; interest is paid to debenture-holders regardless of whether or not a profit has been made.
- In case of dissolution of firms debenture holders are paid first as compared to shareholder.

Fixed Capital

This is money which is used to purchase assets that will remain permanently in the business and help it to make a profit

Factors Determining Fixed Capital Requirements

- Nature of business
- Size of business
- Stage of development
- Capital invested by the owners
- location of that area

Working Capital

Working capital is that part of capital invested which is used for running the business such like money which is used to buy stock, pay expenses and finance credit.

Factors Determining Working Capital Requirements

- Size of business
- Stage of development
- Time of production
- Rate of stock turnover ratio
- Buying and selling terms

- Seasonal consumption
- Seasonal product
- profit level
- growth and expansion
- production cycle
- general nature of business
- business cycle

Instruments

A contract regarding any combination of capital assets is called a financial instrument, and may serve as a

- medium of exchange,
- standard of deferred payment,
- unit of account, or
- store of value.

Most indigenous forms of money (wampum, shells, tally sticks and such) and the modern fiat money is only a "symbolic" storage of value and not a real storage of value like commodity money.

Own and Borrowed Capital

Capital contributed by the owner or entrepreneur of a business, and obtained, for example, by means of savings or inheritance, is known as own capital or equity, whereas that which is granted by another person or institution is called borrowed capital, and this must usually be paid back with interest. The ratio between debt and equity is named leverage. It has to be optimized as a high leverage can bring a higher profit but create solvency risk.

Borrowed Capital

This is capital which the business borrows from institutions or people, and includes debentures:

- Redeemable debentures
- Irredeemable debentures
- Debentures to bearer
- Ordinary debentures
- bonds
- deposits
- loans

Own Capital

This is capital that owners of a business (shareholders and partners, for example) provide:

- Preference shares/hybrid source of finance
  - o Ordinary preference shares
  - o Cumulative preference shares
  - o Participating preference shares
- Ordinary shares
- Bonus shares
- Founders' shares

These have preference over the equity shares. This means the payments made to the shareholders are first paid to the preference shareholder(s) and then to the equity shareholders.

Issuing and Trading

Like money, financial instruments may be "backed" by state military fiat, credit (i.e. social capital held by banks and their depositors), or commodity resources. Governments generally closely control the supply of it and usually require some "reserve" be held by institutions granting credit. Trading between various national currency instruments is conducted on a money market. Such trading reveals differences in probability of debt collection or store of value function of that currency, as assigned by traders.

When in forms other than money, financial capital may be traded on bond markets or reinsurance markets with varying degrees of trust in the social capital (not just credits) of bond-issuers, insurers, and others who issue and trade in financial instruments. When payment is deferred on any such instrument, typically an interest rate is higher than the standard interest rates paid by banks, or charged by the central bank on its money. Often such instruments are called fixed-income instruments if they have reliable payment schedules associated with the uniform rate of interest. A variable-rate instrument, such as many consumer mortgages, will reflect the standard rate for deferred payment set by the central bank prime rate, increasing it by some fixed percentage. Other instruments, such as citizen entitlements, e.g. "U.S. Social Security", or other pensions, may be indexed to the rate of inflation, to provide a reliable value stream.

Trading in stock markets or commodity markets is actually trade in underlying assets which are not wholly financial in themselves, although they often move up and down in value in direct response to the trading in more purely financial derivatives. Typically commodity markets depend on politics that affect international trade, e.g. boycotts and embargoes, or factors that influence natural capital, e.g. weather that affects food crops. Meanwhile, stock markets are more influenced by trust in corporate leaders, i.e. individual capital, by consumers, i.e. social capital or "brand capital" (in some analyses), and internal organisational efficiency, i.e. instructional capital and infrastructural capital.

Some enterprises issue instruments to specifically track one limited division or brand. "Financial futures", "Short selling" and "financial options" apply to these markets, and are typically pure financial bets on outcomes, rather than being a direct representation of any underlying asset.

Broadening the Notion

The relationship between financial capital, money, and all other styles of capital, especially human capital or labour, is assumed in central bank policy and regulations regarding instruments as above.

Such relationships and policies are characterized by a political economy - feudalist, socialist, capitalist, green, anarchist or otherwise. In effect, the means of money supply and other regulations on financial capital represent the economic sense of the value system of the society itself, as they determine the allocation of labour in that society.

So, for instance, rules for increasing or reducing the money supply based on perceived inflation, or on measuring well-being, reflect some such values, reflect the importance of using (all forms of) financial capital as a stable store of value. If this is very important, inflation control is key - any amount of money inflation reduces the value of financial capital with respect to all other types.

If, however, the medium of exchange function is more critical, new money may be more freely issued regardless of impact on either inflation or well-being.

Marxian Perspectives

It is common in Marxian theory to refer to the role of "Finance Capital" as the determining and ruling class interest in capitalist society, particularly in the latter stages.

Valuation

Normally, a financial instrument is priced accordingly to the perception by capital market players of its expected return and risk.

Unit of account functions may come into question if valuations of complex financial instruments vary drastically based on timing. The "book value", "mark-to-market" and "mark-to-future" conventions are three different approaches to reconciling financial capital value units of account.

Economic Role

Socialism, capitalism, feudalism, anarchism, other civic theories take markedly different views of the role of financial capital in social life, and propose various political restrictions to deal with that.

Finance capitalism is the production of profit from the manipulation of financial capital. It is held in contrast to industrial capitalism, where profit is made from the manufacture of goods.

Public Capital

Public capital is the aggregate body of government-owned assets that are used as the means for private productivity. Such assets span a wide range including: large components such as highways, airports, roads, transit systems, and railways; local, municipal components such as public education, public hospitals, police and fire protection, prisons, and courts; and critical components including water and sewer systems, public electric and gas utilities, and telecommunications. Often, public capital is defined as government outlay, in terms of money, and as physical stock, in terms of infrastructure.

Current State in the U.S.

In 1988, the U.S. infrastructure system including all public and private non-residential capital stock was valued at $7 trillion, an immense portfolio to operate and manage. And according to the Congressional Budget Office, in 2004 the U.S. invested $400 billion in infrastructure capital across federal, state, and local levels including the private sectors on transportation networks, schools, highways, water systems, energy, and telecommunications services. While public spending on infrastructure grew by 1.7% annually between 1956 and 2004, it has remained constant as a share of GDP since early 1980s. Despite the value and investment of public capital, growing delays in air and surface transportation, aging electric grid, an untapped renewable energy sector, and inadequate school facilities all have justified additional funding in public capital investment.

The American Society of Civil Engineers have continued to give low marks, averaging a D grade, for the nation's infrastructure since its inception of the Report Card in 1998. In 2009, each category of infrastructure varied from C+ to D- grades with an estimated $2.2 trillion of needed public capital investment. The aviation sector remains mired in continued delays in the reauthorization of federal programs and an outdated air traffic control system. One in four rural bridges and one in three urban bridges are structurally deficient. States are understaffed and underfunded to conduct safety inspections of dams. Texas alone has only seven engineers and an annual budget of $435,000 to oversee more than 7,400 dams. Electricity demand outpaces energy supply transmission and generation. Almost half of the water locks maintained by the U.S. Army Corps of Engineers are functionally obsolete. Drinking water faces an annual shortfall of $11 billion to manage their aging facilities and comply with federal regulations. Leaking pipes lose an estimated 7 billion US gallons (26,000,000 m^3) of clean drinking water a day. Under tight budgets, national, state, and local parks suffer neglect. Without adequate funding, rail cannot meet future freight tonnage load. Schools require a staggering $127 billion to bring facilities to decent operating condition. Billions of gallons of untreated sewage continue to be discharged into U.S.'s surface waters each year.

Economic Growth

One of the most classic macroeconomic inquiries is the effect of public capital investment on economic growth. While many analysts debate the magnitude, evidence has shown a statistically significant positive relationship between infrastructure investment and economic performance. U.S. Federal Reserve economist David Alan Aschauer asserted an increase of the public capital stock by 1% would result in an increase of the total factor productivity by 0.4%. Aschauer argues that the golden age of the 1950s and 1960s were partly due to the post-World War II substantial investment in core infrastructure (highways, mass transit, airports, water systems, electric/gas facilities). Conversely, the drop of U.S. productivity growth in the 1970s and 1980s was in response to the decrease of continual public capital investment and not the decline of technological innovation. Likewise, the European Union nations have declined public capital investment through the same years, also witnessing declining productivity growth rates. A similar situation emerges in developing nations. Analyzing OECD and non-OECD countries' real-GDP growth rates from 1960-2000 with public capital as an explanatory variable (not using public investment rates), Arslanalp, Borhorst, Gupta, and Sze (2010) show that increases in the public capital stock does correlate with increases in growth. However, this relationship depends on initial levels of public capital and income levels for the country. Thus, OECD countries witness a stronger positive link in the short term while non-OECD countries experience a stronger positive link in the long term. Hence, developing countries can benefit from non-concessional foreign borrowing to finance high-prospect public capital investments.

Given this relationship of public capital and productivity, public capital becomes a third input in the standard, neoclassical production function:

$$Y_t = A_t * (N_t, K_t, G_t)$$

where:

Y_t represents real aggregate output of goods and services of the private sector

A_t represents productivity factor or Hicks-Neutral technical change

N_t represents aggregate employment of labour services

K_t represents aggregate stock of nonresidential capital

G_t represents flow of public capital stock (assuming services of public capital are proportional to public capital)

In this form, public capital has a direct influence on productivity as a third variable. Additionally, public capital has an indirect influence on multifactor productivity as it affects the other two inputs of labour and private capital. Despite this unique nature, public capital investment, used in the production process of nearly every sector, is not sufficient on its own to generate sustained economic growth. Thus, rather than the ends, public capital is the means. That is, instead of being seen as intermediate goods used as resources by businesses, public capital should be seen as goods which are used to make the final goods and services to consumers-taxpayers. Nevertheless, high public capital investment usually leads to crowding out effects for private investment. Similarly, public capital levels should not be too high that it leads to financing costs and high tax rates issues which will negate the positive benefits of such investments. Moreover, infrastructure services carry the market-distorting features of pure, non-rival public goods; network externalities; natural monopolies; and the common resource problem such as congestion and overuse.

Empirical models that attempt to estimate the public investment and economic growth link involve a wide variety including: the Cobb-Douglas production function; a behavioural approach cost/profit function which includes public capital stock; Vector Auto Regression (VAR) models; and government investment growth regressions. These models nonetheless contend with reverse causality, heterogeneity, endogeneity, and nonlinearities in trying to capture the public capital and economic growth link. New Keynesian models, though, analyze the effect of government spending through the supply side rather than traditional Keynesian models that analyzes it through the demand side. Therefore, a temporary surge of infrastructure investment yields an expansion of output, and vice versa that dwindling infrastructure, like in the 1970s, hamper longer-term movement in productivity. Furthermore, new research on regional growth (as opposed to national growth with GDP) shows a strong positive relationship between public capital and productivity. Both fixed costs and transport costs lower with expanded infrastructure in localities and the resulting cluster of industries. As a result, economic activity grows along its pattern of trade. Therefore, the importance of regional clusters and metropolitan economies comes into effect.

Social Benefit

Beyond economic performance, public capital investment yields returns in quality of life indicators such as health, safety, recreation, aesthetics, and leisure time and activities. In example, highways provide better access and mobility for increased discretionary time and recreational outlets; mass transit can improve air quality with reduced number of private vehicles; improved municipal waste facilities reduces toxic groundwater contamination and better green space aesthetics such as parks; expanded water facilities aids in health and sanitation and environment such as reducing odor and sewer overflows. Furthermore, infrastructure adds to community ambience and quality of place with livelier downtowns, vibrant waterfronts, efficient land uses, compact spaces for commerce and recreation.

On the contrary, inadequate public capital impairs quality of life and social well-being. Over-capacity landfills lead to groundwater contamination, having deleterious effects on health. Deficient supply and quality of mass transit services impacts transit-dependents on their access to opportunity and resources. Increasing congestion in airports and roadways causes loss of discretionary time and recreational activities. The lack of efficient U.S. freight and passenger rail service will neither aid in handling the "perfect storm" of environmental and energy sustainability nor meet the global competitive need of transporting goods and services at heightened speeds and times. Also, the continued loss of footing in clean energy technology will contribute to U.S.'s future loss of prosperity on the global stage in terms of the carbon footprint and economy.

Public Capital Initiatives

United States: Perhaps the largest contribution to the public works system in the U.S. came out of President Franklin D. Roosevelt's New Deal initiatives particularly the creation of the Works Progress Administration (WPA) in 1935. At a time of a deep economic crisis, the WPA employed at its peak 3.35 millions unemployed heads-of-households to work in rebuilding the country. The program helped construct millions of roads, bridges, parks, schools, hospitals, and levees while also providing educational programs, childcare, job training, and medical services. The overall public spending level for the program, unprecedented at the time, was $4.8 billion ($76 billion in 2008 dollars), and helped to stimulate the economy through public works projects.

Since then, the U.S. has contributed to other large infrastructure programs including the Interstate Highway System, 1956-1990, with a dedicated financing system through the gas tax and a matching contribution between federal government and states at 90% to 10%. Also, the Environmental Protection Agency's (EPA) Clean Water Act of 1972 provided a public capital investment of $40 billion in constructing and upgrading sewage treatment facilities with "significant positive impacts on the Nation's water quality." Considered by the National Academy of Engineering to be the greatest engineering achievement of the 20th century, the North American electric grid carries electricity over 300,000 miles (480,000 km) on high-voltage transmission lines across the U.S. Though currently facing aging facilities and equipment, this public capital investment has ubiquitously reached millions of homes and businesses.

Recently, the American Recovery and Reinvestment Act (ARRA) is another example of large public capital investment. Of the $311 billion in appropriations, about $120 billion are set aside for crucial investment in Infrastructure and Science and Energy. Some of ARRA's aims include smart grid technology, retrofitting of homes and federal buildings, automated aviation traffic control, advancing freight and passenger rail services, and upgrading water and waste facilities.

Other Countries

Worldwide, transformative public capital investments are taking place. China's ambitious rapid high speed rail program is estimated to extend 18,000 km by 2020. By the end of 2008, the country had a fleet of over 24,000 locomotives, the most lines in the world, the fastest express train in service, and longest high speed track in the world. UK, Denmark, and other countries in northern Europe that surround the Baltic Sea and North Sea, continue to develop their rapid expansion of off-shore wind farms. With continued expansion of terminals and connection to nation's comprehensive transport system, the Hong Kong International Airport is one of the largest engineering and architectural projects in the world. In the last decade, Chile installed five combined cycle gas-turbined (CCGT) power plants to meet its nation's growing energy needs.

Liquid Capital

Liquid Capital, or Fluid capital is a readily convertible asset, such as money or other bearer economic instruments, as opposed to a long term asset like real estate. Liquid capital may be held by individuals, companies, or governments.

Globalization means that developing countries have easier access to liquid capital from around the world, but if a country becomes too dependent on foreign liquid capital any political or economic difficulties can be exacerbated by capital flight.

Patient Capital

Patient capital is another name for long term capital. With patient capital, the investor is willing to make a financial investment in a business with no expectation of turning a quick profit. Instead, the investor is willing to forgo an immediate return in anticipation of more substantial returns down the road.

Although patient capital can be considered a traditional investment instrument, it has gained new life with the rise in environmentally and socially responsible enterprises. In this case, it may take the form of equity, debt, loan guarantees or other financial instruments, and is characterized by a:

- Willingness to forgo maximum financial returns for social impact, and an unwillingness to sacrifice the interests of the end customer for the sake of shareholders
- Greater tolerance for risk than traditional investment capital
- Longer time horizons for return of capital
- Intensive support of management as they grow their enterprise

The source of capital may be philanthropy, investment capital, or some combination of the two. Patient capital is not a grant, it is an investment intended to return its principal plus (below market-rate) interest. It does not seek to maximize financial returns to investors; it seeks to maximize social impact and to catalyze the creation of markets to combat poverty. On the spectrum of capital available to both non-profits and for-profits, patient capital sits between traditional venture capital and traditional philanthropy, between development aid and foreign direct investment.

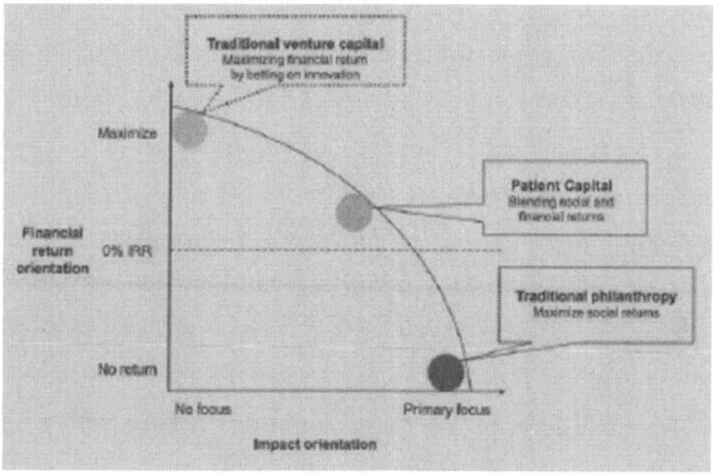

Figure: *Patient Capital*

Thomas Friedman of the New York Times describes patient capital as having "all the discipline of venture capital — demanding a return, and therefore rigor in how it is deployed — but expecting a return that is more in the 5 to 10 percent range, rather than the 35 percent that venture capitalists look for." Jacqueline Novogratz of Acumen adds patient capital, "takes the best of the markets as well as philanthropy and aid. Patient capital is money invested in entrepreneurs building companies and organisations that solve tough problems like healthcare, water, housing, alternative energy."

Constant Capital

Constant capital (c), is a concept created by Karl Marx and used in Marxian political economy. It refers to one of the forms of capital invested in production, which contrasts with variable capital (v). The distinction between constant and variable refers to an aspect of the economic role of factors of production in creating a new value.

Constant capital includes the outlay of money on (1) fixed assets, i.e. plant, machinery, land and buildings, (2) raw materials and ancillary operating expenses (including external services purchased), and (3) certain faux frais of production (incidental expenses). Variable capital by contrast refers to the capital outlay on labour costs insofar as they represent workers' earnings. The concept of constant vs. variable capital contrasts with that of fixed vs. circulating capital (used not only by Marx but by David Ricardo and other classical economists).

The latter distinction corresponds to the very common distinction in economics, between fixed inputs (and costs) and variable inputs (and costs). It distinguishes inputs from the point of view of their user (the capitalist), in terms of the degree of flexibility that the user has in using them.

On the other hand, constant capital refers to the non-human inputs into production, while variable capital refers to the human input (the hiring of labour power to do labour).

Measurement

Constant capital can be measured as a stock magnitude, i.e., the total value of means of production in use at a specific point in time. It can also be measured as a flow magnitude, i.e., the total value of raw materials and fixed means of production used up in an accounting period. Which measure is used depends on the purposes and assumptions of one's analysis, for example whether one is interested in the unit-costs of output or in the rate of return on capital invested.

The flow value divided by the stock value provides a measure of the number of rotations of the stock (the speed of turnover or turnover time) in an accounting period. It is strongly related to the actual depreciation rate of fixed capital. Alternatively, the stock value divided by the flow value is what Marx called the "turnover time."

The faster the turnover of constant capital (i.e., the shorter the turnover time), other things being equal, the higher the rate of profit.

Why "Constant"?

Marx calls the constant part of the capital outlay "constant" because according to his labour theory of value, constant capital inputs - once produced, purchased, withdrawn from the market and used to create new products - do not by themselves add new value to output, or increase in value in the production process. Instead, the value of equipment and materials being used in production is *conserved* and *transferred* to the new product by living labour.

It is true that the ruling *market prices* for constant capital inputs could change after they have been bought for use in production, but normally this cannot affect those inputs (having been withdrawn from the market for use in production), only the market valuation of the outputs created from those inputs.

Variable Capital

Constant capital contrasts with variable capital, v, the cost incurred in hiring labour power. Marx argues that only living labour creates new value. The higher value of output, compared to input costs, is (other things being equal) attributable to the exploitation of living labour-power only. Variable capital is "variable" because its value *changes* (varies) within the production process. Although most commentaries on Marx do not acknowledge this, these changes could be both positive or negative. A misapplication of labour, or the devaluation of types of labour activity by the market can mean the loss of part of the capital invested, or all of it. However, Marx does generally assume that labour will accomplish the valorisation of capital.

Criticism

Critics of Marxian value theory object that labour is not the only source of value-added goods.

Examples of such arguments:

- devaluations or revaluations of types of assets in response to changing demand conditions, which are influenced by price inflation. In national accounts and business accounts, for example, the change in the value of inventories held is adjusted for changes in their *current market prices*, affecting the profit calculation.
- Steve Keen argues that "Essentially, Marx reached the result that the means of production cannot generate surplus value by confusing depreciation, or the loss of value by a machine, with value creation" . His argument is, that a machine can add a value to new output in excess of the value of economic depreciation charged.
- Marxism asserts that capitalist production reduces all production to a combination of commodity inputs to complete the M...M' circuit. However, when one considers human labour to constitute a particular kind of activity among the many necessary to the production of goods, and when one considers that the price of other input factors like raw materials, machines, facilities, land or even other intermediate goods may *vary* based on the availability of such assets on a market, then the labour commodity is no more or less *variable* than any other, whether or not it is the sole source of surplus value, and hence profit. The dichotomy "fixed" vs. "variable" is thus a specious mathematicization of the actual "labour" vs. "non-labour" dichotomy.

Marxist Response

According to some Marxists, the first two types of objection above cut to the heart of the main dispute between Marx and mainstream economic theory—their different conceptions of value.

For Marx's critics, value, if it exists at all, is a technical feature of economic calculus or is simply another word for the price of a product.

For Marx, however, economic value is a social attribution, which expresses a social relation between people that is specific to certain historical conditions. Inanimate objects can only feature in value relations as tokens of prior human effort, since they are not social beings. Thus, it is not the machine with which new outputs are produced that itself adds value to those outputs, but rather the people operating the machine who permit its value to be conserved and who operate the transfer of part of its value to the new outputs.

Another clarification is that Marx may have used the terms fixed and variable capital to emphasize the idea that the input cost of compensation can be varied by the enterprise, which sets the compensation levels of its workers, whereas the price of the other input factors sold to the company is "fixed," insofar as it is set by external vendors.

Value and Price

Other Marxian economists note that, at any time, most of the stock of objects of value in a society has no actual market price, because those objects are *not being traded* (i.e. they are withdrawn from the market); they are either being used in production or consumption activities, or else stored for later use. This can be easily verified by striking a ratio between gross product and the *estimated* total asset wealth of a country in money units.

In other words, this stock of owned objects has, at best, an ideal price which is estimated or hypothesized (the price it might have, *if* it was traded in the market).

Nobody however will say that because this stock of objects has no actual market price, that it has no value; everybody knows that its exchange value could be expressed in money, within a certain *range* of probable prices; they may also know *approximately* that a quantity of one good is "worth" a certain quantity of another good.

This simple insight may help to clarify Marx's concept of value, because it shows that beyond prices there are also economic *value relations* referring to the changing relationships between objects of value which have no specific, defined or actual market price, and to the social outcome of the interactions between a myriad of prices. In turn, these value relations between objects reflect social relations between people.

The Particular Fetish of the Money Commodity as Capital

The fact that the productive force of labour appears within capitalism as the productive force of capital was for Marx an example of reification of the relations of production or of commodity fetishism. In other words, property (a "thing") is given human powers and characteristics which it does not truly have. Economists talk about the "productivity of capital" to describe the yield or return on capital, but capital itself "produces" nothing, people do that.

The fetish of capital is broken as soon as living labour is withdrawn; then it becomes clear that the constant part of capital produces nothing, and declines in value. Because of its role as a traditional money commodity some individuals give a reference display of this fetish by seeing gold as the only 'real' money, even in the current time when most money is lacking any substantial form whatsoever, even paper.

Critics object however that without the supply of means of production, labour also can produce nothing. That is, separated from means of production, workers are also nothing. This however raises the question of why and how workers come to be separated from the means of production which they have themselves created.

For Marx at least, the answer to this question is not "technical" but purely social, i.e. a matter of property relations which provides capital and its owners with a social power over people. But ownership by itself creates no net addition to new value produced, other than, perhaps, profit from speculation which redistributes existing asset values and claims to them.

Different Capital Compositions

The ratio, c/v is one measure of the organic composition of capital. As noted above, the distinction between constant and variable capital overlaps with the distinction between fixed capital and circulating capital. Constant capital has both fixed and circulating components: for example, the fixed constant capital would include a factory and the machinery in it, while the circulating constant capital would include the raw materials used and the intermediate inputs produced by the factory.

Variable capital is almost exclusively a component of circulating capital. However, the salaries of some "overhead" employees (who have long-term security from being fired or laid off) are in effect, fixed elements of variable capital.

Fictitious Capital

Fictitious capital is a concept used by Karl Marx in his critique of political economy. It is introduced in chapter 29 of the third volume of Capital. Fictitious capital contrasts with what Marx calls "real capital", which is capital actually invested in physical means of production and workers, and "money capital", which is actual funds being held. The market value of fictitious capital assets (such as stocks and securities) varies according to the expected return or yield of those assets in the future, which is at best only indirectly related to the growth of real production. Effectively, fictitious capital represents "accumulated claims, legal titles, to future production" and more specifically claims to the income generated by that production.

- Fictitious capital could be defined as a *capitalisation on property ownership*. Such ownership is real and legally enforced, as are the profits made from it, but the capital involved is fictitious; it is "money that is thrown into circulation as capital without any material basis in commodities or productive activity".
- Fictitious capital could also be defined as "tradeable paper claims to wealth", although tangible assets may themselves under certain conditions also be vastly inflated in price.
- In terms of mainstream financial economics, fictitious capital is the net present value of future cash flows.

Uses of the Term

Marx saw the origin of fictitious capital in the development of the credit system and the joint-stock system.

"The formation of a fictitious capital is called capitalisation." It represents a claim to property rights or income. Such claims can take many forms, for example, a claim on future government tax revenue or a claim issued against a commodity that remains, as yet, unsold. The stocks, shares and bonds issued by companies and traded on stock markets are also fictitious capital.

A company may raise (non-fictitious) capital by issuing stocks, shares and bonds. This capital may then be used to generate surplus value, but once this capital is set in motion, the claims held by the owners of the share certificate, etc., are simply "marketable claims to a share in future surplus value production". The stock market "is a market for fictitious capital. It is a market for the circulation of property rights as such".

Since the value of these claims does not function as capital, is merely a claim on future surplus, "the capital-value of such paper is...wholly illusory... The paper serves as title of ownership which represents this capital.

The stocks of railways, mines, navigation companies, and the like, represent actual capital, namely, the capital invested and functioning in such enterprises, or the amount of money advanced by the stockholders for the purpose of being used as capital in such enterprises...; but this capital does not exist twice, once as the capital-value of titles of ownership (stocks) on the one hand and on the other hand as the actual capital invested, or to be invested, in those enterprises." The capital "exists only in the latter form", while the stock or share "is merely a title of ownership to a corresponding portion of the surplus-value to be realised by it".

The formation of fictitious capital is, for Marx, linked to the wider contradiction between the financial system in capitalism and its monetary basis. Marx writes: "With the development of interest-bearing capital and the credit system, all capital seems to double itself, and sometimes treble itself, by the various modes in which the same capital, or perhaps even the same claim on a debt, appears in different forms in different hands. The greater portion of this 'money-capital' is purely fictitious. All the deposits, with the exception of the reserve fund, are merely claims on the banker, which, however, never exist as deposits." The expansion of the credit system can, in periods of capitalist expansion, be beneficial for the system; but in periods of economic crisis and uncertainty, capitalists tend, Marx argues, to look to the security of the "money-commodity" (gold) as the ultimate measure of value. Marx tends to assume the convertibility of paper money into gold. However, the modern system of inconvertible paper money, backed by the authority of states, poses greater problems. Here, in periods of crisis, "the capitalist class appears to have a choice between devaluing money or commodities, between inflation or depression. In the event that monetary policy is dedicated to avoiding both, it will merely end up incurring both".

Speculation and Fictitious Capital

Profit can be made purely from trading in a variety of *financial claims* existing only on paper. This is an extreme form of the fetishism of commodities in which the underlying source of surplus-value in exploitation of labour power is disguised. Indeed, profit can be made by using only *borrowed capital* to engage in (speculative) trade, not backed up by any tangible asset.

The price of fictitious capital is governed by a series of complex determinants. In the first instance they are governed by the "present and anticipated future incomes to which ownership entitles the holder, capitalised at the going rate of interest". But fictitious capital is also the object of speculation. The market value of such assets can be driven up and artificially inflated, purely as a result of supply and demand factors which can themselves be manipulated for profit. The inflated value can just as rapidly be punctured if large amounts of capital are withdrawn.

Illustrations

Banking: Marx cites the case of a Mr Chapman who testified before the British Bank Acts Committee in 1857:

"though in 1857 he was himself still a magnate on the money market, [Chapman] complained bitterly that there were several large money capitalists in London who were strong enough to bring the entire money market into disorder at a given moment and in this way fleece the smaller money dealers most shamelessly. There were supposed to be several great sharks of this kind who could significantly intensify a difficult situation by selling one or two million pounds worth of Consols and in this way taking an equivalent sum of banknotes (and thereby available loan capital) out of the market. The collaboration of three big banks in such a manoeuvre would suffice to turn a pressure into a panic."

Marx Added that: "The biggest capital power in London is of course the Bank of England, but its position as a semi-state institution makes it impossible for it to assert its domination in so brutal a fashion. Nonetheless, it too is sufficiently capable of looking after itself... Inasmuch as the Bank issues notes that are not backed by the metal reserve in its vaults, it *creates tokens of value that are not only means of circulation, but also forms additional - even if fictitious - capital for it,* to the nominal value of these fiduciary notes, and this extra capital yields it an extra profit."

Public Stocks

Marx Writes: "To the extent that the depreciation or increase in value of this paper is independent of the movement of value of the actual capital that it represents, the wealth of the nation is just as great before as after its depreciation or increase in value.

"The public stocks and canal and railway shares had already by the 23rd of October, 1847, been depreciated in the aggregate to the amount of £114,752,225." (Morris, Governor of the Bank of England, testimony in the Report on Commercial Distress, 1847-48 [No. 3800].)

"Unless this depreciation reflected an actual stoppage of production and of traffic on canals and railways, or a suspension of already initiated enterprises, or squandering capital in positively worthless ventures, the nation did not grow one cent poorer by the bursting of this soap bubble of nominal money-capital."

Instructional Capital

Instructional capital is a term used in educational administration after the 1960s, to reflect capital resulting from investment in producing learning materials.

Some have objected to this phrasing, which is an elaboration of referring to training as "human capital", either for the same reason that phrase is objectionable, or on the grounds that it implies that the human in which the knowledge is "invested" is a resource to be exploited.

Instructional capital can be used to guide or limit or restrict action by people (individual capital) or equipment (infrastructural capital) (if the learning materials are computer programs). It cannot generally make either individuals or infrastructure do what they are not trained or designed to do, but it can help prevent them from doing most stupid, destructive and dangerous things.

When people begin to trust instructions, they tend to associate social capital with them, as symbolized by a brand, flag or label. This usually opens up a possibility for those with power to start cheating and/or creating bad instructions that can no longer be trusted, but the good reputation of the brand, flag or label protects them from being caught for longer than would be the case without the symbol that is associated with good reputation.

Working Capital

Working capital (abbreviated WC) is a financial metric which represents operating liquidity available to a business, organisation or other entity, including governmental entity. Along with fixed assets such as plant and equipment, working capital is considered a part of operating capital. Gross working capital equals to current assets. Net working capital (NWC) is calculated as current assets minus current liabilities. It is a derivation of working capital, that is commonly used in valuation techniques such as DCFs (Discounted cash flows). If current assets are less than current liabilities, an entity has a working capital deficiency, also called a working capital deficit.

A company can be endowed with assets and profitability but short of liquidity if its assets cannot readily be converted into cash. Positive working capital is required to ensure that a firm is able to continue its operations and that it has sufficient funds to satisfy both maturing short-term debt and upcoming operational expenses. The management of working capital involves managing inventories, accounts receivable and payable, and cash.

Calculation

The basic calculation of the working capital is done on the basis of the gross current assets of the firm.

Basic Formula

- working capital = Gross Current assets
- Net working capital = Current assets – Current liabilities.

Inputs

Current assets and current liabilities include three accounts which are of special importance. These accounts represent the areas of the business where managers have the most direct impact:

- accounts receivable (current asset)
- inventory (current assets), and
- accounts payable (current liability)

The current portion of debt (payable within 12 months) is critical, because it represents a short-term claim to current assets and is often secured by long term assets. Common types of short-term debt are bank loans and lines of credit. An increase in net working capital indicates that the business has either increased current assets (that it has increased its receivables, or other current assets) or has decreased current liabilities—for example has paid off some short-term creditors, or a combination of both.

Working Capital Management

Decisions relating to working capital and short term financing are referred to as *working capital management*. These involve managing the relationship between a firm's short-term assets and its short-term liabilities. The goal of working capital management is to ensure that the firm is able to continue its operations and that it has sufficient cash flow to satisfy both maturing short-term debt and upcoming operational expenses.

A managerial accounting strategy focusing on maintaining efficient levels of both components of working capital, current assets and current liabilities, in respect to each other. Working capital management ensures a company has sufficient cash flow in order to meet its short-term debt obligations and operating expenses.

Decision Criteria

By definition, working capital management entails short-term decisions—generally, relating to the next one-year period—which are "reversible".

These decisions are therefore not taken on the same basis as capital-investment decisions (NPV or related, as above); rather, they will be based on cash flows, or profitability, or both.

- One measure of cash flow is provided by the cash conversion cycle—the net number of days from the outlay of cash for raw material to receiving payment from the customer. As a management tool, this metric makes explicit the inter-relatedness of decisions relating to inventories, accounts receivable and payable, and cash. Because this number effectively corresponds to the time that the firm's cash is tied up in operations and unavailable for other activities, management generally aims at a low net count.
- In this context, the most useful measure of profitability is return on capital (ROC). The result is shown as a percentage, determined by dividing relevant income for the 12 months by capital employed; return on equity (ROE) shows this result for the firm's shareholders. Firm value is enhanced when, and if, the return on capital, which results from working-capital management, exceeds the cost of capital, which results from capital investment decisions as above. ROC measures are therefore useful as a management tool, in that they link short-term policy with long-term decision making.
- Credit policy of the firm: Another factor affecting working capital management is credit policy of the firm. It includes buying of raw material and selling of finished goods either in cash or on credit. This affects the cash conversion cycle.

Management of Working Capital

Guided by the above criteria, management will use a combination of policies and techniques for the management of working capital. The policies aim at managing the *current assets* (generally cash and cash equivalents, inventories and debtors) and the short term financing, such that cash flows and returns are acceptable.

- Cash management. Identify the cash balance which allows for the business to meet day to day expenses, but reduces cash holding costs.
- Inventory management. Identify the level of inventory which allows for uninterrupted production but reduces the investment in raw materials—and minimizes reordering costs—and hence increases cash flow. Besides this, the lead times in production should be lowered to reduce Work in Process (WIP) and similarly, the Finished Goods should be kept on as low level as possible to avoid over production; Just In Time (JIT); Economic order quantity (EOQ); Economic quantity
- Debtors management. Identify the appropriate credit policy, i.e. credit terms which will attract customers, such that any impact on cash flows and the cash conversion cycle will be offset by increased revenue and hence Return on Capital (or *vice versa*)
- Short term financing. Identify the appropriate source of financing, given the cash conversion cycle: the inventory is ideally financed by credit granted by the supplier; however, it may be necessary to utilise a bank loan (or overdraft), or to "convert debtors to cash" through "factoring".

Capital Structure

In finance, capital structure refers to the way a corporation finances its assets through some combination of equity, debt, or hybrid securities. A firm's capital structure is then the composition or 'structure' of its liabilities. For example, a firm that sells $20 billion in equity and $80 billion in debt is said to be 20% equity-financed and 80% debt-financed. The firm's ratio of debt to total financing, 80% in this example, is referred to as the firm's leverage. In reality, capital structure may be highly complex and include dozens of sources. Gearing Ratio is the proportion of the capital employed of the firm which come from outside of the business finance, e.g. by taking a short term loan etc.

The Modigliani-Miller theorem, proposed by Franco Modigliani and Merton Miller, forms the basis for modern thinking on capital structure, though it is generally viewed as a purely theoretical result since it disregards many important factors in the capital structure process. The theorem states that, in a perfect market, how a firm is financed is irrelevant to its value. This result provides the base with which to examine real world reasons why capital structure *is* relevant, that is, a company's value is affected by the capital structure it employs. Some other reasons include bankruptcy costs, agency costs, taxes, and information asymmetry. This analysis can then be extended to look at whether there is in fact an optimal capital structure: the one which maximizes the value of the firm.

Capital Structure in a Perfect Market

Consider a perfect capital market (no transaction or bankruptcy costs; perfect information); firms and individuals can borrow at the same interest rate; no taxes; and investment returns are not affected by financial uncertainty. Modigliani and Miller made two findings under these conditions. Their first 'proposition' was that the value of a company is independent of its capital structure. Their second 'proposition' stated that the cost of equity for a leveraged firm is equal to the cost of equity for an unleveraged firm, plus an added premium for financial risk. That is, as leverage increases, while the burden of individual risks is shifted between different investor classes, total risk is conserved and hence no extra value created.

Their analysis was extended to include the effect of taxes and risky debt. Under a classical tax system, the tax deductibility of interest makes debt financing valuable; that is, the cost of capital decreases as the proportion of debt in the capital structure increases. The optimal structure, then would be to have virtually no equity at all, i.e. a capital structure consisting of 99.99% debt.

Capital Structure in the Real World

If capital structure is irrelevant in a perfect market, then imperfections which exist in the real world must be the cause of its relevance. The theories below try to address some of these imperfections, by relaxing assumptions made in the M&M model.

Theory of Capital Structure

Determination of an optimal capital structure has frustrated theoreticians for decades. The early work made numerous assumptions in order to simplify the problem and assumed that both the cost of debt and the cost of equity were independent of capital structure and that the relevant figure for consideration was the net income of the firm. Under these assumptions, the average cost of capital decreased with the use of leverage and the value of the firm (the value of the debt and equity combined) increased while the value of the equity remained constant.

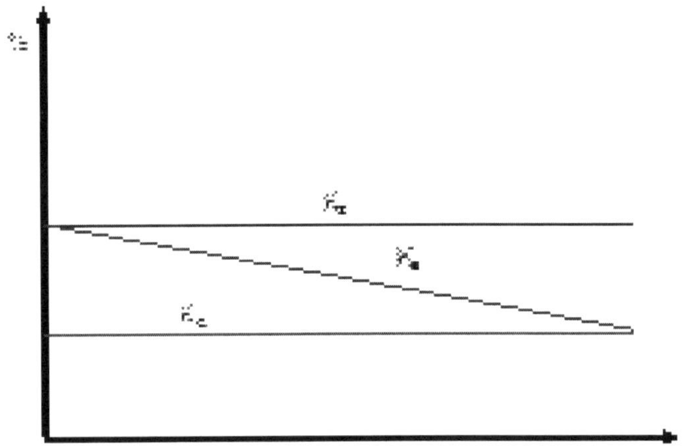

Debt/Equity

Modigliani and Miller showed that this could not be the case. Their contention was that two identical firms, differing only in their capital structure, must have identical total values. If they did not, individuals would engage in arbitrage and create the market forces that would drive the two values to be equal.

Their proof of this proposition was based upon several assumptions (many of which have subsequently been relaxed without changing the results):

- All investors have complete knowledge of what future returns will be
- All firms within an industry have the same risk regardless of capital structure
- No taxes (we will relax this assumption subsequently)
- No transactions costs
- Individuals can borrow as easily and at the same rate of interest as the corporation
- All earnings are paid out as dividends (thus, earnings are constant and there is no growth)
- The average cost of capital is constant

Since no taxes has been assumed, the operating income (EBIT) is equivalent to the net income which is all paid out as dividends. Thus, the value of the firm is equal to

$$V = \frac{EBIT}{k_a}$$

Since the value of the firm is equal to the sum of the value of the debt and equity,

$$V = D + E$$

then

$$k_a V = k_a(D + E)$$

and

$$k_a = k_s(\frac{E}{D+E}) + k_d(\frac{D}{D+E})$$

Substituting the last equation into the preceding equation and solving for K_s

$$k_s = k_a + (k_a - k_d)\frac{D}{E}$$

Thus, k_s must go up as debt is added to the capital structure.

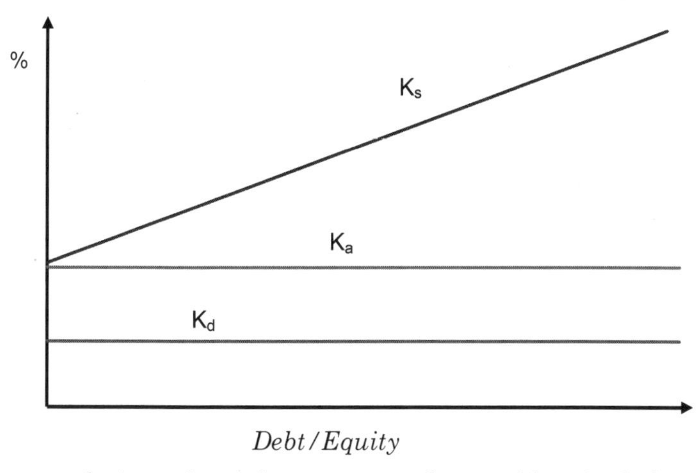

Debt/Equity

To prove their point, they assumed two identical firms, an unlevered firm (all equity) and a levered firm with $4 million of debt carrying an interest rate of 7.5%, both firms generating an operating income (EBIT) of $900,000 annually.

They adopted the assumption that stockholders of both firms would have the same required rate of return of 10% which, as previously mentioned, was the standard assumption at the time (that the cost of equity was constant regardless of capital structure).

	Unlevered Firm	Levered Firm
EBIT	\$ 900,000	\$ 900,000
-Interest	0	300,000
Income	\$ 900,000	\$ 600,000

Since the required rate of return of shareholders is 10% in both cases

	Unlevered Firm	Levered Firm
Value of Equity =	$\frac{\$900,000}{.10} = \$9,000,000$	$\frac{\$600,000}{.10} = \$\ 6,000,000$
Value of Debt =	\$ 0	\$ 4,000,000
Total Value of Firm =	\$9,000,000	\$10,000,000

If this were true, then someone who owns 10% of the levered firm would have income of \$60,000 (\$600,000 * 10%) and could sell it for \$600,000 (\$6 million * 10%). With this \$600,000 the individual could borrow another \$300,000 at 7.5% and buy 10% of the unlevered firm for \$900,000 (\$9 million * 10%). What would this individual's income be now?

EBIT	\$ 90,000	(\$900,000 * 10%)
-Interest	22,500	(\$300,000 * 7.5%)
Income	\$ 67,500	

Thus, the income would be greater by buying the unlevered firm's stock and borrowing money to finance the purchase. As other individuals see this opportunity, they also will sell the stock of the levered firm (driving its price down) and buy the stock of the unlevered firm (using some borrowed money) and thereby driving the value of the unlevered firm's stock up. As the price of the unlevered firm is bid up, the value of the unlevered firm increases above \$9 million dollars, while the selling of the levered firm's stock drives the equity value below \$6 million (which decreases the total firm value, including the \$4 million of debt, below \$10 million) until the two firms' values, in equilibrium, are equal and no opportunity to arbitrage the difference exists. Consequently, if the total value of the two firms is equal, then the average cost of capital must be equal. And if the average cost of capital is equal, then it must be true that the cost of equity rises in such a manner as to exactly offset the increased use of cheaper debt financing (and we end up with the previous graph showing this).

As we previously uncovered when we looked at financial leverage, this is not a surprising result. As a firm increases its use of debt, the risk to the stockholder increases and, as a consequence, the stockholder's required rate of return will increase. Modigliani and Miller simply defined *how* the stockholder's required rate of return should increase with increased financial leverage.

The lesson that is intended by this is that value cannot be created by simply substituting one form of financing for another.

Subsequent to this analysis, it was pointed out that corporate taxes have an impact on the valuation. Without going through the mathematics (which is in your textbook), suffice it to say that the result was that the value of the firm *increased* with increased leverage. Specifically,

$$V_L = V_U + t * D$$

The fact that the government is a "partner" in the business results in a subsidy when debt financing is used and a deductible expense (unlike equity payments). When corporate taxes were taken into account, the average cost of capital was found to *decrease* with increased leverage:

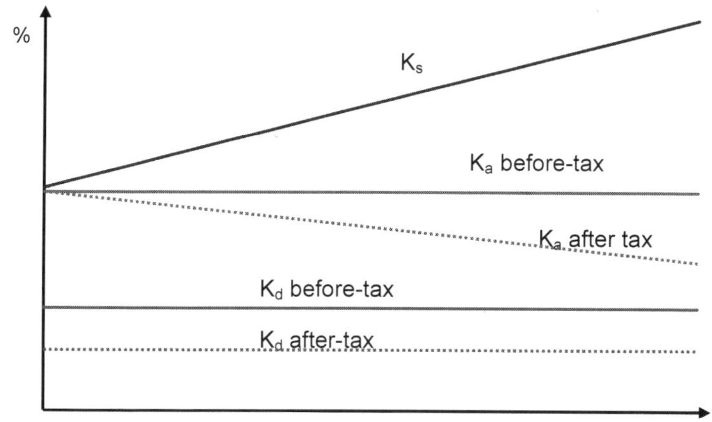

This implies that a firm should use as much debt as possible. Yet, we do not see companies using 100% debt. It might be pointed out that during the late 1980s there was a considerable amount of substitution of debt for equity among firms, particularly in the case of leveraged buyouts. However, many of those firms subsequently failed (for example, Unocal) and the typical debt/equity ratio today is similar to earlier levels.

So why do we not see more debt employed by companies? The answer to this question has been sought by many and two primary proposals have been put forth. First, bankruptcy costs were invoked as a factor. That is, the more debt a firm uses, the higher the probability that the firm would default and go into bankruptcy. Therefore, the present value of bankruptcy costs had to be deducted from the value of the firm. A second factor was that of "agency" costs, such as the necessity of reporting regularly to lenders (audited financial statements, bank "monitoring" fees, trustees for debt payments, etc.) that accompany the use of debt. Both of these costs increase in present value of expected costs terms as the proportion of debt increases. Another way of viewing these costs is that the *risk* of receiving full interest and principal payments increases and thus the required rate of return of lenders increases. (For example, "junk" bonds often yield higher rates of interest than the required rate of return on equity for companies with very little debt.) Consequently, the cost of debt increases and the average cost of capital will ultimately increase.

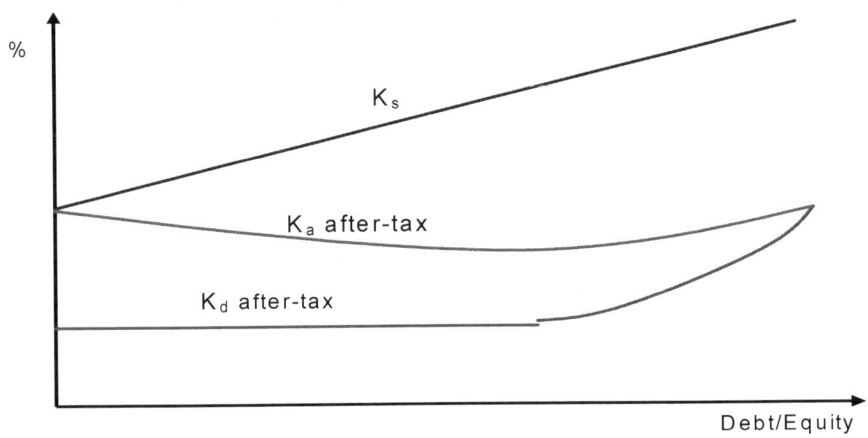

As can be observed from the graph, a minimum average cost of capital exists, but exactly where it should be has yet to be determined within a theoretical framework.

So what are the insights that we can gain from this theoretical view of capital structure? First, we should note that, while debt financing is "cheap" in the sense that required rates of return on equity will always be higher than the interest rate on debt, there is a "hidden" cost in that the cost of equity rises as we utilise more debt financing.

This is one reason that using the average cost of capital in valuing a project or company is more appropriate, even if we intend to borrow all of the money to finance it. While we may use cheap debt to finance a project, the increased risk to shareholders from increasing our financial leverage results in an increase in the cost of equity. The average cost of capital reflects both the cost of debt as well as the cost of equity and thus will reflect the increased cost of equity associated with the use of more debt financing.

The second important concept is that tax-deductible debt financing results in a tax subsidy by the government. This subsidy adds value to the firm. For example, what is the "advantage" of being a home owner with a mortgage rather than leasing a home? It is the taxes that you will save. The reason that Congress eliminated the deductibility of credit card interest is that it did not want to encourage, through a tax subsidy, the financing of purchases purely for consumption. On the other hand, the purchase of a home (which is still tax-deductible) is an "investment", not to mention the political consequences of voting to end the subsidy of the American Dream of home ownership.

Trade-off Theory of Capital Structure

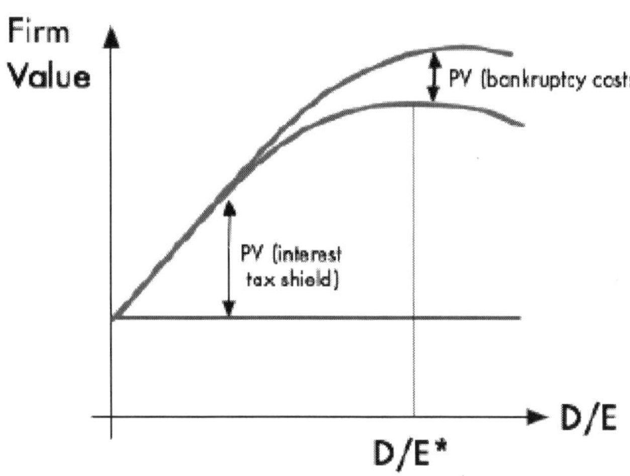

Figure: *As the Debt equity ratio (i.e. leverage) increases, there is a trade-off between the interest tax shield and bankruptcy, causing an optimum capital structure, D/E**

The trade-off theory of capital structure refers to the idea that a company chooses how much debt finance and how much equity finance to use by balancing the costs and benefits. The classical version of the hypothesis goes back to Kraus and Litzenberger who considered a balance between the dead-weight costs of bankruptcy and the tax saving benefits of debt. Often agency costs are also included in the balance. This theory is often set up as a competitor theory to the pecking order theory of capital structure. A review of the literature is provided by Frank and Goyal.

An important purpose of the theory is to explain the fact that corporations usually are financed partly with debt and partly with equity. It states that there is an advantage to financing with debt, the tax benefits of debt and there is a cost of financing with debt, the costs of financial distress including bankruptcy costs of debt and non-bankruptcy costs (e.g. staff leaving, suppliers demanding disadvantageous payment terms, bondholder/stockholder infighting, etc.). The marginal benefit of further increases in debt declines as debt increases, while the marginal cost increases, so that a firm that is optimizing its overall value will focus on this trade-off when choosing how much debt and equity to use for financing.

Evidence

The empirical relevance of the trade-off theory has often been questioned. Miller for example compared this balancing as akin to the balance between horse and rabbit content in a stew of one horse and one rabbit. Taxes are large and they are sure, while bankruptcy is rare and, according to Miller, it has low dead-weight costs. Accordingly he suggested that if the trade-off theory were true, then firms ought to have much higher debt levels than we observe in reality. Myers was a particularly fierce critic in his Presidential address to the American Finance Association meetings in which he proposed what he called "the pecking order theory". Fama and French criticized both the trade-off theory and the pecking order theory in different ways. Welch has argued that firms do not undo the impact of stock price shocks as they should under the basic trade-off theory and so the mechanical change in asset prices that makes up for most of the variation in capital structure.

Despite such criticisms, the trade-off theory remains the dominant theory of corporate capital structure as taught in the main corporate finance textbooks. Dynamic version of the model generally seem to offer enough flexibility in matching the data so, contrary to Miller's verbal argument, dynamic trade-off models are very hard to reject empirically.

The analysis of wide known trade off theory has been made within modern theory of capital structure and capital cost by Brusov-Filatova-Orekhova. It is shown that suggestion of risky debt financing (and growing credit rate near the bankruptcy) in opposite to waiting result does not lead to growing of weighted average cost of capital, WACC, which still decreases with leverage. This means the absence of minimum in the dependence of WACC on leverage as well as the absence of maximum in the dependence of company capitalization on leverage. Thus, it seems that the optimal capital structure is absent in famous trade off theory.

Financial Leverage and Capital Structure Policy - Modigliani and Miller's Capital Structure Theories

Modigliani and Miller, two professors in the 1950s, studied capital-structure theory intensely. From their analysis, they developed the capital-structure irrelevance proposition. Essentially, they hypothesized that in perfect markets, it does not matter what capital structure a company uses to finance its operations. They theorized that the market value of a firm is determined by its earning power and by the risk of its underlying assets, and that its value is independent of the way it chooses to finance its investments or distribute dividends.

The basic M&M proposition is based on the following key assumptions:

- No taxes
- No transaction costs
- No bankruptcy costs
- Equivalence in borrowing costs for both companies and investors
- Symmetry of market information, meaning companies and investors have the same information
- No effect of debt on a company's earnings before interest and taxes

Of course, in the real world, there are taxes, transaction costs, bankruptcy costs, differences in borrowing costs, information asymmetries and effects of debt on earnings. To understand how the M&M proposition works after factoring in corporate taxes, however, we must first understand the basics of M&M propositions I and II without taxes.

Modigliani and Miller's Capital-Structure Irrelevance Proposition

The M&M capital-structure irrelevance proposition assumes no taxes and no bankruptcy costs. In this simplified view, the weighted average cost of capital (WACC) should remain constant with changes in the company's capital structure. For example, no matter how the firm borrows, there will be no tax benefit from interest payments and thus no changes or benefits to the WACC. Additionally, since there are no changes or benefits from increases in debt, the capital structure does not influence a company's stock price, and the capital structure is therefore irrelevant to a company's stock price.

However, as we have stated, taxes and bankruptcy costs do significantly affect a company's stock price. In additional papers, Modigliani and Miller included both the effect of taxes and bankruptcy costs.

Modigliani and Miller's Tradeoff Theory of Leverage

The tradeoff theory assumes that there are benefits to leverage within a capital structure up until the optimal capital structure is reached. The theory recognises the tax benefit from interest payments - that is, because interest paid on debt is tax deductible, issuing bonds effectively reduces a company's tax liability. Paying dividends on equity, however, does not. Thought of another way, the actual rate of interest companies pay on the bonds they issue is less than the nominal rate of interest because of the tax savings. Studies suggest, however, that most companies have less leverage than this theory would suggest is optimal.

In comparing the two theories, the main difference between them is the potential benefit from debt in a capital structure, which comes from the tax benefit of the interest payments. Since the MM capital-structure irrelevance theory assumes no taxes, this benefit is not recognised, unlike the tradeoff theory of leverage, where taxes, and thus the tax benefit of interest payments, are recognised.

In summary, the MM I theory without corporate taxes says that a firm's relative proportions of debt and equity don't matter; MM I with corporate taxes says that the firm with the greater proportion of debt is more valuable because of the interest tax shield.

MM II deals with the WACC. It says that as the proportion of debt in the company's capital structure increases, its return on equity to shareholders increases in a linear fashion. The existence of higher debt levels makes investing in the company more risky, so shareholders demand a higher risk premium on the company's stock. However, because the company's capital structure is irrelevant, changes in the debt-equity ratio do not affect WACC. MM II with corporate taxes acknowledges the corporate tax savings from the interest tax deduction and thus concludes that changes in the debt-equity ratio do affect WACC. Therefore, a greater proportion of debt lowers the company's WACC.

2

Capital Structure: Tests of Optimality vs. Pecking Order Theory

Pecking Order Theory

In corporate finance, pecking order theory (or pecking order model) postulates that the cost of financing increases with asymmetric information. Financing comes from three sources, internal funds, debt and new equity. Companies prioritize their sources of financing, first preferring internal financing, and then debt, lastly raising equity as a "last resort". Hence: internal financing is used first; when that is depleted, then debt is issued; and when it is no longer sensible to issue any more debt, equity is issued. This theory maintains that businesses adhere to a hierarchy of financing sources and prefer internal financing when available, and debt is preferred over equity if external financing is required (equity would mean issuing shares which meant 'bringing external ownership' into the company). Thus, the form of debt a firm chooses can act as a signal of its need for external finance.

The pecking order theory is popularized by Myers and Majluf (1984) when they argue that equity is a less preferred means to raise capital because when managers (who are assumed to know better about true condition of the firm than investors) issue new equity, investors believe that managers think that the firm is overvalued and managers are taking advantage of this over-valuation. As a result, investors will place a lower value to the new equity issuance.

History

Pecking order theory was first suggested by Donaldson in 1961 and it was modified by Stewart C. Myers and Nicolas Majluf in 1984.

It states that companies prioritize their sources of financing (from internal financing to equity) according to the cost of financing, preferring to raise equity as a financing means of last resort. Hence, internal funds are used first, and when that is depleted, debt is issued, and when it is not sensible to issue any more debt, equity is issued.

Theory

Pecking order theory starts with asymmetric information as managers know more about their companies prospects, risks and value than outside investors. Asymmetric information affects the choice between internal and external financing and between the issue of debt or equity. There therefore exists a pecking order for the financing of new projects.

Asymmetric information favours the issue of debt over equity as the issue of debt signals the boards confidence that an investment is profitable and that the current stock price is undervalued (were stock price over-valued, the issue of equity would be favoured). The issue of equity would signal a lack of confidence in the board and that they feel the share price is over-valued. An issue of equity would therefore lead to a drop in share price. This does not however apply to high-tech industries where the issue of equity is preferable due to the high cost of debt issue as assets are intangible

Evidence

Tests of the pecking order theory have not been able to show that it is of first-order importance in determining a firm's capital structure. However, several authors have found that there are instances where it is a good approximation of reality. On the one hand, Fama and French, and also Myers and Shyam-Sunder find that some features of the data are better explained by the Pecking Order than by the trade-off theory. Goyal and Frank show, among other things, that Pecking Order theory fails where it should hold, namely for small firms where information asymmetry is presumably an important problem.

Profitability and Debt Ratios

The pecking order theory explains the inverse relationship between profitability and debt ratios:

1. Firms prefer internal financing.
2. They adapt their target dividend payout ratios to their investment opportunities, while trying to avoid sudden changes in dividends.

3. Sticky dividend policies, plus unpredictable fluctuations in profits and investment opportunities, mean that internally generated cash flow is sometimes more than capital expenditures and at other times less. If it is more, the firm pays off the debt or invests in marketable securities. If it is less, the firm first draws down its cash balance or sells its marketable securities, rather than reduce dividends.
4. If external financing is required, firms issue the safest security first. That is, they start with debt, then possibly hybrid securities such as convertible bonds, then perhaps equity as a last resort. In addition, issue costs are least for internal funds, low for debt and highest for equity. There is also the negative signaling to the stock market associated with issuing equity, positive signaling associated with debt.

Market Timing Hypothesis

The market timing hypothesis is a theory of how firms and corporations in the economy decide whether to finance their investment with equity or with debt instruments. It is one of many such corporate finance theories, and is often contrasted with the pecking order theory and the trade-off theory, for example. The idea that firms pay attention to market conditions in an attempt to time the market is a very old hypothesis.

Baker and Wurgler (2002), claim that market timing is the first order determinant of a corporation's capital structure use of debt and equity. In other words, firms do not generally care whether they finance with debt or equity, they just choose the form of financing which, at that point in time, seems to be more valued by financial markets.

Market timing is sometimes classified as part of the behavioural finance literature, because it does not explain why there would be any asset mis-pricing, or why firms would be better able to tell when there was mis-pricing than financial markets. Rather it just assumes these mis-pricing exists, and describes the behaviour of firms under the even stronger assumption that firms can detect this mis-pricing better than markets can. However, any theory with time varying costs and benefits is likely to generate time varying corporate issuing decisions. This is true whether decision makers are behavioural or rational.

The empirical evidence for this hypothesis is at best, mixed. Baker and Wurgler themselves show that an index of financing that reflects how much of the financing was done during hot equity periods and how much during hot debt periods is a good indicator of firm leverage over long periods subsequently. Alti studied issuance events. He found that the effect of market timing disappears after only two years.

Beyond such academic studies, a complete market timing theory ought to explain why at the same moment in time some firms issue debt while other firms issue equity. As yet nobody has tried to explain this basic problem within a market timing model. The typical version of the market timing hypothesis is thus somewhat incomplete as a matter of theory.

Capital Structure Substitution Theory

In finance, the capital structure substitution theory (CSS) describes the relationship between earnings, stock price and capital structure of public companies. The CSS theory hypothesizes that managements of public companies manipulate capital structure such that earnings per share (EPS) are maximized. Managements have an incentive to do so because shareholders and analysts value EPS growth. The theory is used to explain trends in capital structure, stock market valuation, dividend policy, the monetary transmission mechanism, and stock volatility, and provides an alternative to the Modigliani–Miller theorem that has limited descriptive validity in real markets. The CSS theory is only applicable in markets where share repurchases are allowed. Investors can use the CSS theory to identify undervalued stocks.

The Formula

The CSS theory assumes that company managements can freely change the capital structure of the company – substituting bonds for stock or vice versa – on a day-to-day basis and in small denominations without paying transaction costs. Companies can decide to buy back one single share for the current market price P and finance this by issuing one extra corporate bond with face value P or do the reverse. In mathematical terms these substitutions are defined as

$$\left[\frac{\partial D}{\partial n}\right]_{x,t} = -P_{x,t}$$

where D is the corporate debt and n the number of shares of company x at time t. The negative sign indicates that a reduction of the number of shares n leads to a larger debt D and vice versa. The earnings-per-share change when one share with price P is repurchased and one bond with face value P is issued:

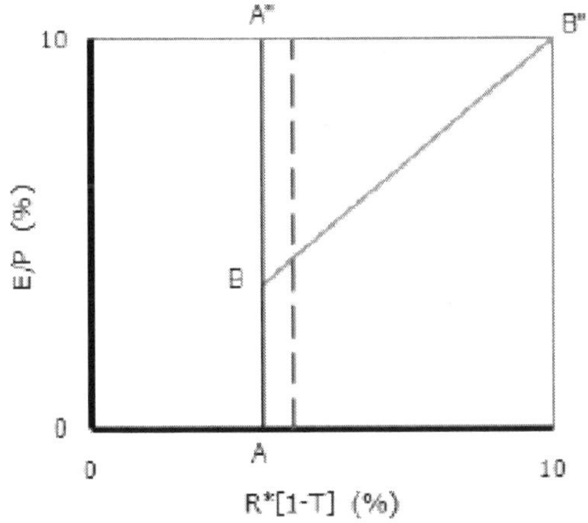

Figure: *CSS equilibrium conditions: (1) companies fulfilling the equilibrium condition are found on B-B", (2) companies cannot issue debt with interest rates below 'Aaa' rated bonds on line A-A", (3) high valued companies with E/P<R*[1-T] are not expected to hold long term debt, pay no dividends and are found on line A-B.*

1. The earnings that were 'allocated' to the one share that was repurchased are redistributed over the remaining outstanding shares, causing an increase in earnings per share of: E/n
2. The earnings are reduced by the additional interest payments on the extra bond. As interest payments are tax-deductible the real reduction in earnings is obtained by multiplying with the tax shield. The additional interest payments thus reduce the EPS by: $P \cdot R \cdot [1-T]/n$

Combining these two effects, the marginal change in EPS as function of the total number of outstanding shares becomes:

$$\left[\frac{\partial E}{\partial n}\right]_{x,t} = -\frac{E_{x,t}}{n} + \frac{P_{x,t}\, R_{x,t}\,[1-T]}{n}$$

where

- E is the earnings-per-share
- R is the nominal interest rate on corporate bonds
- T is the corporate tax rate

EPS is maximized when substituting one more share for one bond or vice versa leads to no marginal change in EPS or:

$$\frac{E_{x,t}}{P_{x,t}} = R_{x,t}\,[1-T]$$

This equilibrium condition is the central result of the CCS theory, linking stock prices to interest rates on corporate bonds.

Capital Structure

The two main capital structure theories as taught in corporate finance textbooks are the Pecking order theory and the Trade-off theory. The two theories make some contradicting predictions and for example Fama and French conclude:*"In sum, we identify one scar on the tradeoff model (the negative relation between leverage and profitability), one deep wound on the pecking order (the large equity issues of small low-leverage growth firms)..."*. The capital structure substitution theory has the potential to close these gaps. It predicts a negative relation between leverage and valuation (=reverse of earnings yield) which in turn can be linked to profitability. But it also predicts that high valued small growth firms will avoid the use of debt as especially for these companies the cost of borrowing ($R_{x,t}$) is higher than for large companies, which in turn has a negative effect on their EPS. This is consistent with the finding that *"...firms with higher current stock prices (relative to their past stock prices, book values or earnings) are more likely to issue equity rather than debt and repurchase debt rather than equity"*.

Asset Pricing

The equilibrium condition can be easily rearranged to an asset pricing formula:

$$P_{x,t} = \frac{E_{x,t}}{R_{x,t}[1-T]}$$

The CSS theory suggests that company share prices are not set by shareholders but by bondholders. As a result of active repurchasing or issuing of shares by company managements, equilibrium pricing is no longer a result of balancing shareholder demand and supply. In a way the CSS theory turns asset pricing upside-down, with bondholders setting share prices and shareholders determining company leverage. The asset pricing formula only applies to debt-holding companies. Some companies are offering stock screeners based on the CSS theory.

Fed Model Equilibrium

In the US, a positive relationship between the average earnings yield of the S&P 500 index and government bond yields has been present over the last several decades. This relationship has become popular as the Fed model and states in its strongest form an equality between the one year forward looking E/P ratio or earnings yield and the 10-year government bond yield. The CSS equilibrium condition suggests that the Fed model is misspecified: the S&P 500 earnings yield is not in equilibrium with the government bond yield but with the average after-tax interest rate on corporate bonds.

The CSS theory suggests that the Fed equilibrium was only observable after 1982, the year in which the United States Securities and Exchange Commission allowed open-market repurchases of shares.

Monetary Policy

An unanticipated 25-basis-point cut in the federal funds rate target is associated with a 1% increase in broad stock indexes in the US. The CSS theory suggests that the monetary policy transmission mechanism is indirect but straightforward: a change in the federal funds rate affects the corporate bond market which in turn affects asset prices through the equilibrium condition.

Beta

The CSS equilibrium condition can be used to deduct a relationship for the beta of a company x at time t:

$$Beta_{x,t} = \overline{R_t} \cdot \left[\frac{P}{E} \right]_{x,t} \cdot [1 - T]$$

where $\overline{R_t}$ is the market average interest rate on corporate bonds. The CSS theory predicts that companies with a low valuation and high leverage will have a *low* beta. This is counter-intuitive as traditional finance theory links leverage to risk, and risk to *high* beta.

Assumptions

- Managements of public companies manipulate capital structure such that earnings-per-share are maximized.
- Managements can freely change the capital structure of the company – substituting bonds for stock or vice versa – on a day-to-day basis and in small denominations.
- Shares can only be repurchased through open market buybacks. Information about share price is available on a daily basis.
- Companies pay a uniform corporate tax rate T.

Agency Costs

There are three types of agency costs which can help explain the relevance of capital structure.

- Asset substitution effect: As D/E increases, management has an increased incentive to undertake risky (even negative NPV) projects. This is because if the project is successful, share holders get all the upside, whereas if it is unsuccessful, debt holders get all the downside. If the projects are undertaken, there is a chance of firm value decreasing and a wealth transfer from debt holders to share holders.
- Underinvestment problem (or Debt overhang problem): If debt is risky (e.g., in a growth company), the gain from the project will accrue to debtholders rather than shareholders. Thus, management have an incentive to reject positive NPV projects, even though they have the potential to increase firm value.
- Free cash flow: unless free cash flow is given back to investors, management has an incentive to destroy firm value through empire building and perks etc. Increasing leverage imposes financial discipline on management.

Structural Corporate Finance

An active area of research in finance is that which tries to translate the models above as well as others into a structured theoretical setup that is time-consistent and that has a dynamic set up similar to one that can be observed in the real world. Managerial contracts, debt contracts, equity contracts, investment returns, all have long lived, multi-period implications. Therefore it is hard to think through what the implications of the basic models above are for the real world if they are not embedded in a dynamic structure that approximates reality. A similar type of research is performed under the guise of credit risk research in which the modelling of the likelihood of default and its pricing is undertaken under different assumptions about investors and about the incentives of management, shareholders and debt holders. Examples of research in this area are Goldstein, Ju, Leland (1998) and Hennessy and Whited (2004).

Capital Gearing Ratio

Capital gearing ratio = (Capital Bearing Risk) : (Capital not bearing risk)

- Capital bearing risk includes debentures (risk is to pay interest) and preference capital (risk to pay dividend at fixed rate).
- Capital not bearing risk includes equity share capital.

Therefore we can also say,

Capital gearing ratio= (Debentures+Preference share capital) : (shareholders' funds)

Arbitrage

Similar questions are also the concern of a variety of speculator known as a capital-structure arbitrageur.

A capital-structure arbitrageur seeks opportunities created by differential pricing of various instruments issued by one corporation. Consider, for example, traditional bonds and convertible bonds. The latter are bonds that are, under contracted-for conditions, convertible into shares of equity. The stock-option component of a convertible bond has a calculable value in itself. The value of the whole instrument *should* be the value of the traditional bonds *plus* the extra value of the option feature. If the spread (the difference between the convertible and the non-convertible bonds) grows excessively, then the capital-structure arbitrageur will bet that it will converge.

Modigliani–Miller Theorem

The Modigliani–Miller theorem (of Franco Modigliani, Merton Miller) is a theorem on capital structure, arguably forming the basis for modern thinking on capital structure. The basic theorem states that, under a certain market price process (the classical random walk), in the absence of taxes, bankruptcy costs, agency costs, and asymmetric information, and in an efficient market, the value of a firm is unaffected by how that firm is financed. It does not matter if the firm's capital is raised by issuing stock or selling debt. It does not matter what the firm's dividend policy is. Therefore, the Modigliani–Miller theorem is also often called the capital structure irrelevance principle.

Modigliani was awarded the 1985 Nobel Prize in Economics for this and other contributions.

Miller was a professor at the University of Chicago when he was awarded the 1990 Nobel Prize in Economics, along with Harry Markowitz and William Sharpe, for their "work in the theory of financial economics," with Miller specifically cited for "fundamental contributions to the theory of corporate finance."

Historical Background

Miller and Modigliani derived the theorem and wrote their groundbreaking article when they were both professors at the Graduate School of Industrial Administration (GSIA) of Carnegie Mellon University. The story goes that Miller and Modigliani were set to teach corporate finance for business students despite the fact that they had no prior experience in corporate finance. When they read the material that existed they found it inconsistent so they sat down together to try to figure it out. The result of this was the article in the *American Economic Review* and what has later been known as the M&M theorem.

Miller and Modigliani published a number of follow-up papers discussing some of these issues. The theorem was first proposed by F. Modigliani and M. Miller in 1958.

The Theorem

Consider two firms which are identical except for their financial structures. The first (Firm U) is unlevered: that is, it is financed by equity only. The other (Firm L) is levered: it is financed partly by equity, and partly by debt. The Modigliani–Miller theorem states that the value of the two firms is the same.

Without Taxes

Proposition I:

$$V_U = V_L$$

where

V_U *is the value of an unlevered firm* = price of buying a firm composed only of equity, and V_L *is the value of a levered firm* = price of buying a firm that is composed of some mix of debt and equity. Another word for levered is *geared*, which has the same meaning.

To see why this should be true, suppose an investor is considering buying one of the two firms U or L. Instead of purchasing the shares of the levered firm L, he could purchase the shares of firm U and borrow the same amount of money B that firm L does. The eventual returns to either of these investments would be the same. Therefore the price of L must be the same as the price of U minus the money borrowed B, which is the value of L's debt.

This discussion also clarifies the role of some of the theorem's assumptions. We have implicitly assumed that the investor's cost of borrowing money is the same as that of the firm, which need not be true in the presence of asymmetric information, in the absence of efficient markets, or if the investor has a different risk profile than the firm.

Proposition II

$$r_E = r_0 + \frac{D}{E}(r_0 - r_D)$$

where

- r_E *is the required rate of return on equity, or cost of equity.*
- r_0 *is the company unlevered cost of capital (ie assume no leverage).*
- r_D *is the required rate of return on borrowings, or cost of debt.*
- $\frac{D}{E}$ *is the debt-to-equity ratio.*

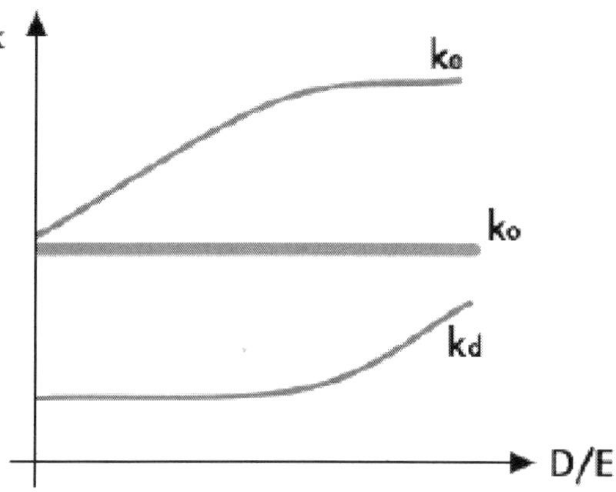

Figure: *Proposition II with risky debt. As leverage (D/E) increases, the WACC (k0) stays constant.*

A higher debt-to-equity ratio leads to a higher required return on equity, because of the higher risk involved for equity-holders in a company with debt. The formula is derived from the theory of weighted average cost of capital (WACC).

These propositions are true under the following assumptions:

- no transaction costs exist, and
- individuals and corporations borrow at the same rates.

These results might seem irrelevant (after all, none of the conditions are met in the real world), but the theorem is still taught and studied because it tells something very important. That is, capital structure matters precisely because one or more of these assumptions is violated. It tells where to look for determinants of optimal capital structure and how those factors might affect optimal capital structure.

With Taxes

Proposition I:

$$V_L = V_U + T_C D$$

where

- *V_L is the value of a levered firm.*
- *V_U is the value of an unlevered firm.*
- *$T_C D$ is the tax rate (T_C) x the value of debt (D)*
- the term $T_C D$ assumes debt is perpetual

This means that there are advantages for firms to be levered, since corporations can deduct interest payments. Therefore leverage lowers tax payments. Dividend payments are non-deductible.

Proposition II

$$r_E = r_0 + \frac{D}{E}(r_0 - r_D)(1 - T_C)$$

where:

- *r_E is the required rate of return on equity, or cost of levered equity = unlevered equity + financing premium.*
- *r_0 is the company cost of equity capital with no leverage (unlevered cost of equity, or return on assets with D/E = 0).*
- *r_D is the required rate of return on borrowings, or cost of debt.*
- *D / E is the debt-to-equity ratio.*
- *T_c is the tax rate.*

The same relationship as earlier described stating that the cost of equity rises with leverage, because the risk to equity rises, still holds. The formula, however, has implications for the difference with the WACC. Their second attempt on capital structure included taxes has identified that as the level of gearing increases by replacing equity with cheap debt the level of the WACC drops and an optimal capital structure does indeed exist at a point where debt is 100%.

The following assumptions are made in the propositions with taxes:

- corporations are taxed at the rate T_C on earnings after interest,
- no transaction costs exist, and
- individuals and corporations borrow at the same rate.

Capital Asset Pricing Model

In finance, the capital asset pricing model (CAPM) is used to determine a theoretically appropriate required rate of return of an asset, if that asset is to be added to an already well-diversified portfolio, given that asset's non-diversifiable risk. The model takes into account the asset's sensitivity to non-diversifiable risk (also known as systematic risk or market risk), often represented by the quantity beta (β) in the financial industry, as well as the expected return of the market and the expected return of a theoretical risk-free asset. CAPM "suggests that an investor's cost of equity capital is determined by beta."

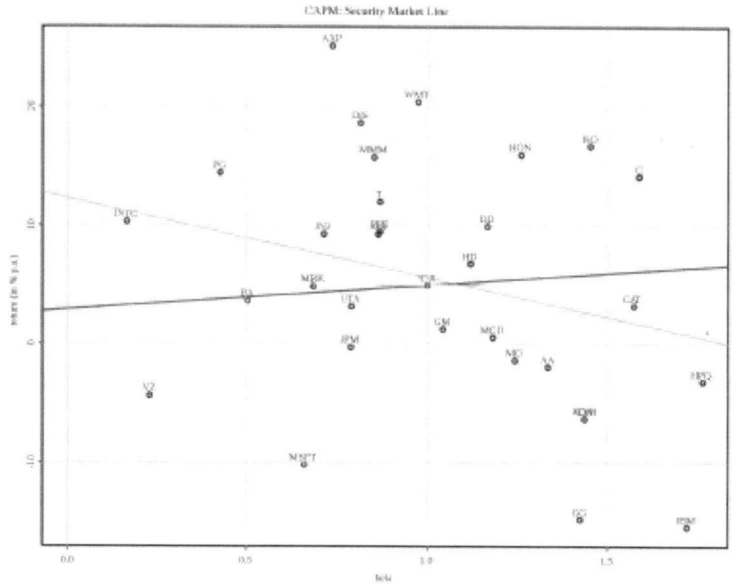

Figure: *An estimation of the CAPM and the security market line (purple) for the Dow Jones Industrial Average over 3 years for monthly data.*

The CAPM was introduced by Jack Treynor (1961, 1962), William Sharpe (1964), John Lintner (1965a,b) and Jan Mossin (1966) independently, building on the earlier work of Harry Markowitz on diversification and modern portfolio theory. Sharpe, Markowitz and Merton Miller jointly received the 1990 Nobel Memorial Prize in Economics for this contribution to the field of financial economics. Fischer Black (1972) developed another version of CAPM, called Black CAPM or zero-beta CAPM, that does not assume the existence of a riskless asset. This version was more robust against empirical testing and was influential in the widespread adoption of the CAPM.

Despite its empirical flaws and the existence of more modern approaches to asset pricing and portfolio selection (such as arbitrage pricing theory and Merton's portfolio problem), the CAPM still remains popular due to its simplicity and utility in a variety of situations.

Formula

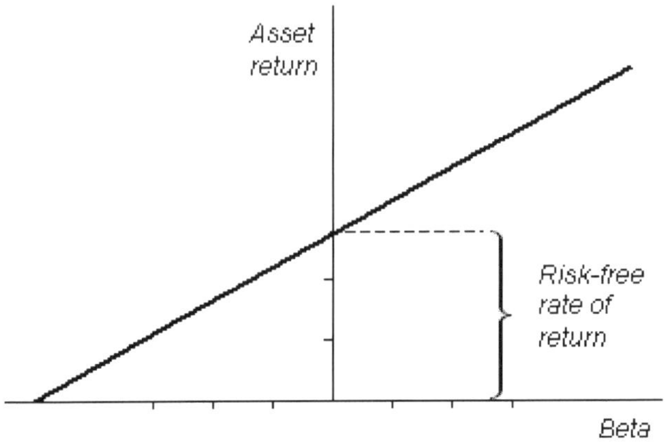

Figure: *The security market line, seen here in a graph, describes a relation between the beta and the asset's expected rate of return.*

The CAPM is a model for pricing an individual security or portfolio. For individual securities, we make use of the security market line (SML) and its relation to expected return and systematic risk (beta) to show how the market must price individual securities in relation to their security risk class. The SML enables us to calculate the reward-to-risk ratio for any security in relation to that of the overall market. Therefore, when the expected rate of return for any security is deflated by its beta coefficient, the reward-to-risk ratio for any individual security in the market is equal to the market reward-to-risk ratio, thus:

$$\frac{E(R_i) - R_f}{\beta_i} = E(R_m) - R_f$$

The market reward-to-risk ratio is effectively the market risk premium and by rearranging the above equation and solving for E(Ri), we obtain the capital asset pricing model (CAPM).

$$E(R_i) = R_f + \beta_i (E(R_m) - R_f)$$

where:

- $E(R_i)$ is the expected return on the capital asset
- R_f is the risk-free rate of interest such as interest arising from government bonds
- β_i (the *beta*) is the sensitivity of the expected excess asset returns to the expected excess market returns, or also

$$\beta_i = \frac{\text{Cov}(R_i, R_m)}{\text{Var}(R_m)},$$

- $E(R_m)$ is the expected return of the market
- $E(R_m) - R_f$ is sometimes known as the *market premium* (the difference between the expected market rate of return and the risk-free rate of return).
- $E(R_i) - R_f$ is also known as the *risk premium*

Restated, in terms of risk premium, we find that:

$$E(R_i) - R_f = \beta_i(E(R_m) - R_f)$$

which states that the *individual risk premium* equals the *market premium* times β.

Note 1: the expected market rate of return is usually estimated by measuring the Geometric Average of the historical returns on a market portfolio (e.g. S&P 500).

Note 2: the risk free rate of return used for determining the risk premium is usually the arithmetic average of historical risk free rates of return and not the current risk free rate of return.

Modified Formula

CAPM can be modified to include size premium and specific risk. This is important for investors in privately held companies who often do not hold a well-diversified portfolio. The equation is similar to the traditional CAPM equation "with the market risk premium replaced by the product of beta times the market risk premium:"

$$E(R_i) = R_f + \beta(RP_m) + RP_s + RP_u$$

"where:

$E(R_i)$ is required return on security i

R_f is risk-free rate

RP_m is general market risk premium

RP_s is risk premium for small size

RP_u is risk premium due to company-specific risk factor"

Security Market Line

The SML essentially graphs the results from the capital asset pricing model (CAPM) formula. The *x*-axis represents the risk (beta), and the y-axis represents the expected return. The market risk premium is determined from the slope of the SML.

The relationship between β and required return is plotted on the *securities market line* (SML), which shows expected return as a function of β. The intercept is the nominal risk-free rate available for the market, while the slope is the market premium, $E(R_m) - R_f$. The securities market line can be regarded as representing a single-factor model of the asset price, where Beta is exposure to changes in value of the Market. The equation of the SML is thus:

$$\text{SML}: E(R_i) = R_f + \beta_i (E(R_M) - R_f).$$

It is a useful tool in determining if an asset being considered for a portfolio offers a reasonable expected return for risk. Individual securities are plotted on the SML graph. If the security's expected return versus risk is plotted above the SML, it is undervalued since the investor can expect a greater return for the inherent risk. And a security plotted below the SML is overvalued since the investor would be accepting less return for the amount of risk assumed.

Asset Pricing

Once the expected/required rate of return $E(R_i)$ is calculated using CAPM, we can compare this required rate of return to the asset's estimated rate of return over a specific investment horizon to determine whether it would be an appropriate investment. To make this comparison, you need an independent estimate of the return outlook for the security based on either fundamental or technical analysis techniques, including P/E, M/B etc.

Assuming that the CAPM is correct, an asset is correctly priced when its estimated price is the same as the present value of future cash flows of the asset, discounted at the rate suggested by CAPM.

If the estimated price is higher than the CAPM valuation, then the asset is undervalued (and overvalued when the estimated price is below the CAPM valuation).

When the asset does not lie on the SML, this could also suggest mis-pricing. Since the expected return of the asset at time t is $E(R_t) = \frac{E(P_{t+1}) - P_t}{P_t}$, a higher expected return than what CAPM suggests indicates that P_t is too low (the asset is currently undervalued), assuming that at time $t+1$ the asset returns to the CAPM suggested price.

The asset price P_0 using CAPM, sometimes called the certainty equivalent pricing formula, is a linear relationship given by

$$P_0 = \frac{1}{1+R_f}\left[E(P_T) - \frac{\text{Cov}(P_T, R_M)(E(R_M) - R_f)}{\text{Var}(R_M)}\right]$$

where P_T is the payoff of the asset or portfolio.

Asset-Specific Required Return

The CAPM returns the asset-appropriate required return or discount rate—i.e. the rate at which future cash flows produced by the asset should be discounted given that asset's relative riskiness. Betas exceeding one signify more than average "riskiness"; betas below one indicate lower than average. Thus, a more risky stock will have a higher beta and will be discounted at a higher rate; less sensitive stocks will have lower betas and be discounted at a lower rate. Given the accepted concave utility function, the CAPM is consistent with intuition—investors (should) require a higher return for holding a more risky asset.

Since beta reflects asset-specific sensitivity to non-diversifiable, i.e. market risk, the market as a whole, by definition, has a beta of one. Stock market indices are frequently used as local proxies for the market—and in that case (by definition) have a beta of one. An investor in a large, diversified portfolio (such as a mutual fund), therefore, expects performance in line with the market.

Risk and Diversification

The risk of a portfolio comprises systematic risk, also known as undiversifiable risk, and unsystematic risk which is also known as idiosyncratic risk or diversifiable risk. Systematic risk refers to the risk common to all securities—i.e. market risk. Unsystematic risk is the risk associated with individual assets. Unsystematic risk can be diversified away to smaller levels by including a greater number of assets in the portfolio (specific risks "average out"). The same is not possible for systematic risk within one market. Depending on the market, a portfolio of approximately 30–40 securities in developed markets such as the UK or US will render the portfolio sufficiently diversified such that risk exposure is limited to systematic risk only. In developing markets a larger number is required, due to the higher asset volatilities.

A rational investor should not take on any diversifiable risk, as only non-diversifiable risks are rewarded within the scope of this model. Therefore, the required return on an asset, that is, the return that compensates for risk taken, must be linked to its riskiness in a portfolio context—i.e. its contribution to overall portfolio riskiness—as opposed to its "stand alone risk." In the CAPM context, portfolio risk is represented by higher variance i.e. less predictability. In other words the beta of the portfolio is the defining factor in rewarding the systematic exposure taken by an investor.

Efficient Frontier

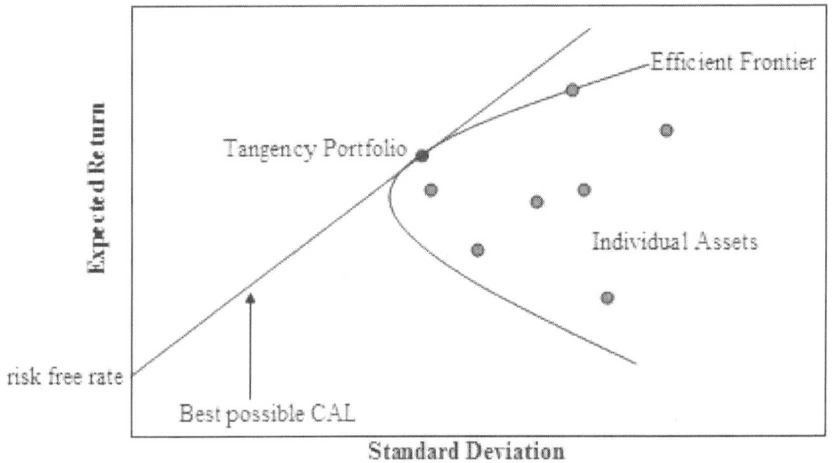

Figure: *The (Markowitz) efficient frontier. CAL stands for the capital allocation line.*

The CAPM assumes that the risk-return profile of a portfolio can be optimized—an optimal portfolio displays the lowest possible level of risk for its level of return. Additionally, since each additional asset introduced into a portfolio further diversifies the portfolio, the optimal portfolio must comprise every asset, (assuming no trading costs) with each asset value-weighted to achieve the above (assuming that any asset is infinitely divisible). All such optimal portfolios, i.e., one for each level of return, comprise the efficient frontier.

Because the unsystematic risk is diversifiable, the total risk of a portfolio can be viewed as beta.

Market Portfolio

An investor might choose to invest a proportion of his or her wealth in a portfolio of risky assets with the remainder in cash—earning interest at the risk-free rate (or indeed may borrow money to fund his or her purchase of risky assets in which case there is a negative cash weighting). Here, the ratio of risky assets to risk-free asset does not determine overall return—this relationship is clearly linear. It is thus possible to achieve a particular return in one of two ways:

1. By investing all of one's wealth in a risky portfolio,
2. or by investing a proportion in a risky portfolio and the remainder in cash (either borrowed or invested).

For a given level of return, however, only one of these portfolios will be optimal (in the sense of lowest risk). Since the risk-free asset is, by definition, uncorrelated with any other asset, option 2 will generally have the lower variance and hence be the more efficient of the two.

This relationship also holds for portfolios along the efficient frontier: a higher return portfolio plus cash is more efficient than a lower return portfolio alone for that lower level of return. For a given risk-free rate, there is only one optimal portfolio which can be combined with cash to achieve the lowest level of risk for any possible return. This is the market portfolio.

Assumptions of CAPM

All investors:

1. Aim to maximize economic utilities (Asset quantities are given and fixed).
2. Are rational and risk-averse.
3. Are broadly diversified across a range of investments.
4. Are price takers, i.e., they cannot influence prices.
5. Can lend and borrow unlimited amounts under the risk free rate of interest.
6. Trade without transaction or taxation costs.
7. Deal with securities that are all highly divisible into small parcels (All assets are perfectly divisible and liquid).
8. Have homogeneous expectations.
9. Assume all information is available at the same time to all investors.

Problems of CAPM

In their 2004 review, Fama and French argue that "the failure of the CAPM in empirical tests implies that most applications of the model are invalid".

- The model assumes that the variance of returns is an adequate measurement of risk. This would be implied by the assumption that returns are normally distributed, or indeed are distributed in any two-parameter way, but for general return distributions other risk measures (like coherent risk measures) will reflect the active and potential shareholders' preferences more adequately. Indeed risk in financial investments is not variance in itself, rather it is the probability of losing: it is asymmetric in nature. Barclays Wealth have published some research on asset allocation with non-normal returns which shows that investors with very low risk tolerances should hold more cash than CAPM suggests.

- The model assumes that all active and potential shareholders have access to the same information and agree about the risk and expected return of all assets (homogeneous expectations assumption).
- The model assumes that the probability beliefs of active and potential shareholders match the true distribution of returns. A different possibility is that active and potential shareholders' expectations are biased, causing market prices to be informationally inefficient. This possibility is studied in the field of behavioural finance, which uses psychological assumptions to provide alternatives to the CAPM such as the overconfidence-based asset pricing model of Kent Daniel, David Hirshleifer, and Avanidhar Subrahmanyam (2001).
- The model does not appear to adequately explain the variation in stock returns. Empirical studies show that low beta stocks may offer higher returns than the model would predict. Some data to this effect was presented as early as a 1969 conference in Buffalo, New York in a paper by Fischer Black, Michael Jensen, and Myron Scholes. Either that fact is itself rational (which saves the efficient-market hypothesis but makes CAPM wrong), or it is irrational (which saves CAPM, but makes the EMH wrong – indeed, this possibility makes volatility arbitrage a strategy for reliably beating the market).
- The model assumes that given a certain expected return, active and potential shareholders will prefer lower risk (lower variance) to higher risk and conversely given a certain level of risk will prefer higher returns to lower ones. It does not allow for active and potential shareholders who will accept lower returns for higher risk. Casino gamblers pay to take on more risk, and it is possible that some stock traders will pay for risk as well.

- The model assumes that there are no taxes or transaction costs, although this assumption may be relaxed with more complicated versions of the model.
- The market portfolio consists of all assets in all markets, where each asset is weighted by its market capitalization. This assumes no preference between markets and assets for individual active and potential shareholders, and that active and potential shareholders choose assets solely as a function of their risk-return profile. It also assumes that all assets are infinitely divisible as to the amount which may be held or transacted.
- The market portfolio should in theory include all types of assets that are held by anyone as an investment (including works of art, real estate, human capital...) In practice, such a market portfolio is unobservable and people usually substitute a stock index as a proxy for the true market portfolio. Unfortunately, it has been shown that this substitution is not innocuous and can lead to false inferences as to the validity of the CAPM, and it has been said that due to the inobservability of the true market portfolio, the CAPM might not be empirically testable. This was presented in greater depth in a paper by Richard Roll in 1977, and is generally referred to as Roll's critique.
- The model assumes economic agents optimise over a short-term horizon, and in fact investors with longer-term outlooks would optimally choose long-term inflation-linked bonds instead of short-term rates as this would be more risk-free asset to such an agent.
- The model assumes just two dates, so that there is no opportunity to consume and rebalance portfolios repeatedly over time. The basic insights of the model are extended and generalized in the intertemporal CAPM (ICAPM) of Robert Merton, and the consumption CAPM (CCAPM) of Douglas Breeden and Mark Rubinstein.
- CAPM assumes that all active and potential shareholders will consider all of their assets and optimize one portfolio. This is in sharp contradiction with portfolios that are held by individual shareholders: humans tend to have fragmented portfolios or, rather, multiple portfolios: for each goal one portfolio.
- Empirical tests show market anomalies like the size and value effect that cannot be explained by the CAPM.

Fed Model

The "Fed model" is a theory of equity valuation that has found broad application in the investment community. The model compares the stock market's earnings yield (E/P) to the yield on long-term government bonds. In its strongest form the Fed model states that bond and stock market are in equilibrium, and fairly valued, when the one year forward looking earnings yield equals the 10-year Treasury note yield (Y_{10}):

$$\frac{E}{P} = Y_{10}$$

The model is often used as a simple tool to measure attractiveness of equity, and to help allocating funds between equity and bonds. When for example the equity earnings yield is above the government bond yield, investors should shift funds from bonds into equity. The Fed model was so named by Ed Yardeni, at Deutsche Morgan Grenfell, based on a statement made in the Humphrey-Hawkins report of July 22, 1997 [1] issued by the Federal Reserve that warned:

"...changes in this ratio [P/E of the S&P 500 index] have often been inversely related to changes in the long-term Treasury yields, but this year's stock price gains were not matched by a significant net decline in interest rates. As a result, the yield on ten-year Treasury notes now exceeds the ratio of twelve-month-ahead earnings to prices by the largest amount since 1991, when earnings were depressed by the economic slowdown."

The Fed model was never officially endorsed by the Fed, but former Fed chairman Alan Greenspan seemed to make reference to it in his memoirs: "The decline of real (inflation adjusted) long-term interest rates that has occurred in the last two decades has been associated with rising price-to-earnings ratios for stocks, real estate, and in fact all income-earnings assets." A bond yield versus equity yield comparison has been used in practice long before the Fed published the graph and Yardeni gave it a name. A variant of this, first the expected AAA bond yield from the Blue Chip survey verusus the forward-earnings yield on the S&P 500, and then later versus the 10-year Treasury was developed by Dirk van Dijk at I/B/E/S in the mid-1980s.

Support for the Fed Model

While not unanimous, there is broad consensus in the non-academic investing community that the basic comparison underlying the Fed model is valid. A number of arguments are listed by different authors in favour of the Fed model:

Competing Assets Argument

Stocks and bonds are competing asset classes for investors. When stocks yield more than bonds, investors are better off investing in stocks. When funds flow from bonds into stocks on a large scale, the yield on bonds should increase and the yield on stocks decrease, until the Fed model equilibrium is reached.

Present Value

Another argument often mentioned in favour of the Fed model is the present value of stocks should be equal to the sum of its discounted future cash flows. The government bond rate can be seen as a proxy for the risk-free rate. When the government bond rate falls, the discount rate falls, and the present value rises. And this implies that when interest rates fall, E/P also falls.

Historical Data

One of the most compelling arguments in favour of the Fed model is the almost 30 year of data from the S&P 500 index showing a high correlation between the two parameters. For example Salomons shows a correlation of 75% over the 1995-2002 period (and only 19% over 1881-2002). [This needs clarification, this point is actually against the fed model]

Users

MoneyWeek (April 28, 2010) argued that

"The Fed model matters because important people use it. Analysts across the board, from JP Morgan, to ING, to Prudential – I could go on and on – use the Fed model in their calculations. [...] The fact is, influential market players embrace the Fed model. Whether they truly believe in it or not is immaterial. The net result is that the Fed model is a significant valuation tool which prominent investors use to check whether they should be buying stocks or bonds. And when those inflection points come about, markets move. Because when the advocates say it's time to buy, a wave of trading orders are placed."

Inflation and Money Illusion

Clifford Asness argues that investors actually set stock market P/Es based on nominal interest rates but that they do so in error. By confusing real and nominal investors suffer from 'money illusion'. Asness 'fights the Fed model' as a normative model but acknowledges that the model has certain descriptive validity and as a positive model cannot simply be dismissed. Other authors see inflation as the driver behind the Fed model but hypothesize it is not investor stupidity but accounting rules or investor risk aversion during times of inflation that causes the Fed model equilibrium.

Criticism

Criticism on the Fed model has been harsh, and a number of papers with creative titles were published by academia such as *"The fed model: The bad, the worse, and the ugly"* and *"Fight the FED model"*. Academics have concluded that the model is inconsistent with rational valuation of the stock market.

Lack of Theoretical Support

The competing asset argument listed above argues that only when stocks have the same yield as government bonds, both asset classes are equally attractive to investors. But the earnings yield (E/P) of a stock does not describe what an investor actually receives as not all earnings are paid out to the investor. And how do corporate bonds (with a yield above the government bond yield) fit into this picture? A number of assumptions need to be made to go from the constant growth dividend discount model to the Fed model. Estrada starts with the Gordon growth model.

$$P = \frac{D(1+G)}{R_f + RP - G}$$

where P is the current price and D the current dividend, G the expected long term growth rate, R_f the risk free rate (10-year treasury notes) and RP the equity risk premium. If one now assumes that 100% of the earnings are paid as dividend (D=E), the growth rate is equal to zero, and the equity risk premium is also equal to zero, one gets the Fed model: E/P= R_f . The three assumptions seem unrealistic at best. It is also pointed out that the Fed model compares a real magnitude (E/P) with a nominal interest rate. Inflation should affect the bond yield, but not the earnings yield.

Data Selection and International Markets

The Fed model equilibrium was only observed in one market, and for a limited time window. More specifically, the relationship is observed for the S&P 500 index between ~1980 and ~2005 but data outside of this time window, or in different international markets do not show the same pattern. The correlation between earnings yield and government bond yields was only 19% over the 1881-2002 period. Over the period from 1999 to 2010 was reported to be –0.80 with statistical significance [2]. The Fed model equilibrium specifically seemed to break down during the height of the financial crisis in 2008, when the yield on 10-year Treasuries reached an all-time low at 2.4% whereas the S&P 500 earnings yield reached a 20-year high at more than 8%, a gap of 6 percentage points. And a study of international data showed that the Fed model equilibrium only shows up in 2 out of 20 evaluated international markets. It seems that the empirical support for the Fed model is then based on carefully chosen and limited evidence.

Lack of Predictive Power

If the Fed model is indeed an equity valuation theory with descriptive validity, it should be able to identify over-valued and under-valued assets. But it turns out that the Fed model has no power to forecast long term stock returns. Traditional value investing methods using the only the market's P/E have significantly more efficacy than the Fed model.

As an example Tom Lauricella applied the Fed model to S&P500 index on January 19, 2008. He writes:

With the past week's downturn, stocks in the Standard and Poor's 500-stock index are trading at 13 times their expected earnings for 2008. Last June, when the S&P index was 12% higher than it is now, stocks were priced at 14.2 times this year's earnings. Meanwhile, with a U.S. recession now widely expected and the Federal Reserve thought likely to cut short-term rates further, U.S. Treasury yields have fallen sharply. The 10-year Treasury note is yielding 3.64%, its lowest level since July 2003, and down from 3.81% a week ago.

Thus S&P500 forward earning yield (1/13=7.69%) is higher than 10-year Treasury note yield (3.64%), suggesting S&P500 is significantly undervalued. However, over the next twelve months, the S&P500 index fell from 1,325.19 (January 18, 2008) to 805.22 points (January 20, 2009), a drop of more than 39%.

Is the Fed Model Mis-Specified?

The Fed model equilibrium remains an enigma. On one hand 30 years of data is available that shows how S&P earnings yield and 10-year government bond yield move in tandem. On the other hand there is no theoretical foundation to explain the relationship, and the best explanation academics came up with is that investors collectively suffer from 'money illusion'. A number of questions remain unanswered. Why was the relationship observed in the US and not in most other international markets? Do investors in the US (the world's largest equity market) suffer more from 'illusions' than investors in for example Austria and Finland? Why did the relationship not exist in the US before 1980 (or 1965) and why did the equilibrium break down during the 2008 crisis? And if government bonds and stocks are competing assets, what is the role of corporate bonds?

The recently proposed capital structure substitution theory argues that the Fed model indeed needs to be re-specified. It suggests that supply (company management), rather than demand (investors) drives the relationship between E/P and interest rates. Stock market earnings yield tends to equilibrium not with the government bond yield but with the average after-tax corporate bond yield as companies adjust capital structure (mix of equity and bonds) to maximize earnings per share. If managements consistently optimize capital structure by substituting stocks (repurchasing shares) for bonds or vice versa, equilibrium is reached when:

$$\frac{E_X}{P_X} = R_X\,[1-T]$$

where E is the earnings-per-share of company x, P is the share price, R is the nominal interest rate on corporate bonds and T is the corporate tax rate. For a long time the after-tax interest rate on corporate bonds was roughly equal to the 10-year Treasury rate.

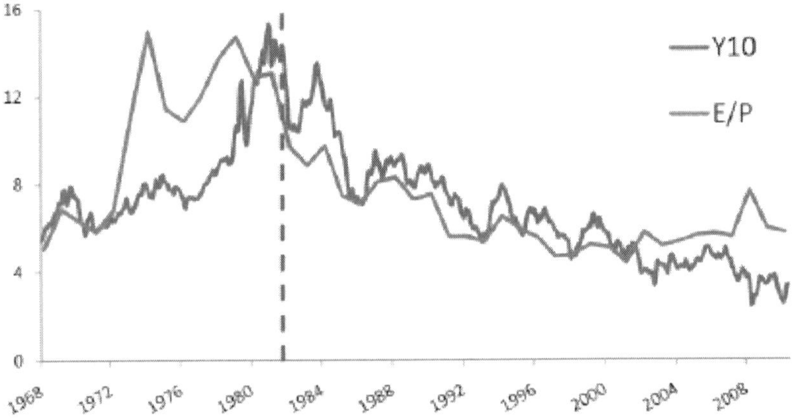

Figure: *Fed model equilibrium comparing S&P 500 earnings yield and 10-year Treasury yield. The descriptive validity of the model is limited before 1982 and after 2007.*

But during the 2008 financial crisis this relationship broke down, as Baa rated corporate bonds peaked at over 9%, and 10-year treasuries bottomed under 2.5%. In the US, SEC Rule 10b-18 (explicitly allowing share repurchases) enabled fine adjustment toward equilibrium as of 1982, explaining why the equilibrium emerged around that time and not before. And in many other countries share repurchases were prohibited until 1998 or are still considered illegal, explaining why the Fed model equilibrium was observed in the US but not in many other international markets.

Figure: *Re-specified Fed model comparing S&P 500 earnings yield with after-tax corporate bond yield (average rating=Baa). Before 1982 the equilibrium could not be reached due to legal limitations in repurchasing shares (SEC Rule 10b-18).*

Is the Fed model miss-specified? Thirty years of investor money illusion (left) or deliberate company policy (right)?

The Determinants of Capital Structure

Determinants of a Company's Capital Structure

Financing and investment are two major decision areas in a firm. In the financing decision the manager is concerned with determining the best financing mix or capital structure for his firm. Capital structure could have two effects. First, firms of the same risk class could possibly have higher cost of capital with higher leverage. Second, capital structure may affect the valuation of the firm, with more leveraged firms, being riskier, being valued lower than less leveraged firms. If we consider that the manager of a firm has the shareholders' wealth maximisation as his objective, then capital structure is an important decision, for it could lead to an optimal financing mix which maximises the market price per share of the firm.

Capital structure has been a major issue in financial economics ever since Modigliani and Miller (henceforth referred to as MM) showed in 1958 that given frictionless markets, homogeneous expectations, etc., the capital structure decision of the firm is irrelevant. This conclusion depends entirely on the assumptions made. By relaxing the assumptions and analysing their effects, theory seeks to determine whether an optimal capital structure exists or not, and if so what could possibly be its determinants. If capital structure is not irrelevant, then there is also another thing to consider: the interaction between financing and investment. But in order to try to distinguish the effects of various determinants on capital structure, it is assumed in this paper that the investment decision is held constant.

Traditional View of Capital Structure

In 1959, Durand listed the alternative approaches to valuation (Van Horne, 1990:321). Let kd represent the yield on debt, ke the yield on equity, and ko the WACC (weighted average cost of capital). Let kd be less than ke. Then, according to the *traditional approach*, ke constantly increases with leverage, and kd increase beyond a point with leverage. Therefore there is a minimum ko at some point. According to the *NI or Net Income approach*, kd and ke remain constant with leverage, and therefore, from the WACC formula, it can be seen that ko declines as debt is increased. Finally, according to the *NOI, or Net Operating Income approach*, ko remains constant irrespective of the debt content.If kd is assumed to be constant, then ke increases with leverage.

Though the entire range of possibilities is covered here, the basic weakness with these approaches is their lack of rigour, and their making direct assumptions about the nature of the costs of debt/equity, without a theoretical basis for these assumptions. Hence not much can be made out about the determinants of capital structure from the traditional view.

Irrelevance of Financing: The Benchmark

The first successful attempt to put the financing decision under a theoretical framework was made by Modigliani and Miller in 1958.

MM's Proposition 1:

with risk-free debt:

In 1958, Modigliani and Miller demonstrated that the firm's choice of financing is irrelevant to the determination of its value. They assumed that capital markets are frictionless, individuals can borrow and lend at the risk-free rate, there are no bankruptcy costs, firms issue only two types of claims: risk-free debt and risky equity, all firms are in the same risk class, there is no growth, expectations are homogeneous (or, there is information symmetry), and agency costs are absent. The *value version* of their *Proposition 1* is that the value of a firm is given by its real assets. Therefore VL = VU where VL is the value of the levered firm, and VU that of the unlevered firm. A firm cannot change the total value of its securities merely by splitting its cash flows into different streams. In this form, the MM Proposition I is the principle of value additivity in reverse, and is known as the law of conservation of value: "The value of an asset is preserved regardless of the nature of the claims against it" (Brealey,1988:386). In fact, the MM proposition is a special case of the proposition developed by Coase (1960) that in the absence of contracting costs and wealth effects, the assignment of property rights leaves the use of real resources unaffected (Smith, 1985:9).

The *cost of capital version* of this proposition, as originally stated by MM, is that "the average cost of capital to any firm is completely independent of its capital structure and is equal to the capitalisation of a pure equity stream of its class" (Modigliani, 1958: 358). This is therefore the same view as held by the traditional NOI approach. The difference is that MM gave a rigourous proof of their propositions.

With risky debt:

By varying only the assumption of risk-free debt to take into account risky debt, the same propositions can be shown to hold good. Stiglitz (1969) used the state-preference framework to prove this (Copeland, 1983: 410). Rubinstein, M.E. (1973) proved this in a CAPM framework. His article was of seminal importance in that it integrated the subject of finance, by creating a bridge between investment theory and corporate finance. Given the "pure" MM assumptions, therefore, there can be no optimal capital structure for a firm.

*Evidence:*MM, in a study in 1958, used cross-section equations on data taken from 43 electric utilities during 1947-1948 and 42 oil companies during 1953. They found that there is no gain from leverage, lending support to their theory (Copeland,1988:517). However, this study was criticised by Weston on two technical grounds, and it is difficult to accept the original findings of MM.

MM's Proposition 2:

The original MM Proposition 2 can be slightly rephrased as: The expected rate of return on equity of a levered firm increases in proportion to the debt-equity ratio, expressed in market values (Brealey, 1988: 391). Therefore, ke = r + (r-kd)_B/_S

where ke is the cost of equity, r is the discount rate for an all-equity firm, _B is the change in B, i.e., change in the market value of debt, _S is the change in S, i.e., change in the market value of stock, or stockholders' wealth.

Evidence: Hamada (1972) combined the Modigliani-Miller theory and the CAPM to test this proposition (Copeland, 1988: 518). Ultimately, he was able to derive indirect evidence to confirm that the cost of equity does increase with higher financial leverage.

Significance of the MM propositions: The MM propositions are important to the rest of the discussion for two reasons. First, the MM theory is a benchmark against which other models are evaluated, since this is a "pure" theory, without most of the "real-life" assumptions. Second, it enables the complete separation of investment and financing decisions (of course, only when the MM assumptions hold), and allows a firm to use capital budgeting procedures without being concerned about the source of funds.

Relevance of Financing Decision in Practice

In real life, evidence is that the capital structure decision does seem to matter.

Aggregate financing patterns in firms in the USA: Taggart (1984) examined the financing patterns of U.S. corporations over the period 1901 to 1979 and found that debt financing saw a major increase over the post-World War II period and reached a maximum in the 1960s and 1970s. Since then, this has tapered off, to become comparable with the pre-war period. Second, short-term liabilities are being increasingly used; also, the number of new issues of equity has declined (Martin, 1988: 370). It is interesting to note the break-up of the aggregate financing pattern for the period 1980-1984: total debt was 36% of total finance, new stock issues, -2%, and gross internal funds, 66%. Out of the debt, long term debt was only 10% of total finance, and short-term liabilities were 26% comprising chiefly of short-term credit market debt at 15% of the total. The MM theory cannot explain this breakup and the trends in debt financing found by Taggart.

Further, Copeland (1988:497) notes that there are cross-sectional regularities in the observed capital structures of U.S. firms. "For example, the electric utility and steel industries have high financial leverage, whereas service industries like accounting firms or brokerage houses have almost no long-term debt." The MM theory predicts randomness in the capital structure and cannot account for these cross-sectional regularities. Belief of executives in optimal capital structure:Scott and Johnson (1982), found that over 90 percent of the executives who responded to a questionnaire believed that an optimal capital structure exists at which the cost of capital is minimised (Clarke, 1988: 167). This belief contradicts the MM theory, and there must be some better explanation than that these executives were irrational.

Target debt ratio: The above study by Scott and Johnson also found that the largest U.S. companies used a particular *target* debt or leverage ratio to make financing decisions. This targeted leverage varied between 26 and 40 percent for different companies. However, there was no consensus on the target ratio and each company uses its own (Clarke,1988: 167). It is seen that firms use a variety of methods to determine a target debt ratio. First, they use external analysis, by comparing their capital structure to other companies operating in the same or similar industries.

They assume that companies in the same industry have similar assets, face similar operating risks, are of similar size, and consequently, require a similar level of debt. But this method has been criticised as leading to costly misjudgements. "The financial difficulties recently experienced by companies such as International Harvester and Caterpillar suggest that ratios based on comparison to other companies may not be suitable " (Clarke, 1988: 175).

Second, and more important, as the study by Scott and Johnson cited above found, managers more commonly take recourse to internal analysis (Clarke,1988:167). This can include EBIT-EPS analysis, cash flow and capability to service debt, probability of insolvency analysis, determination of effect of capital structure on share prices through regression analysis, and survey of analysts and investors (Van Horne, 1990: pp.359-375).

We see therefore, that the financing decision is not irrelevant in practice. There must be important aspects determining capital structure which have not been taken into account in the MM analysis. In the next section we take a broad overview of these elements.

Determinants of Capital Structure

Theorists of finance have postulated a large number of possible determinants of capital structure. The difficulty lies in testing their impact, since it is difficult to find suitable proxies for them and even more difficult to isolate the effect of one from that of others. However, empirical work on the determinants of capital structure has been going on for some time. It is not always based on theory, and therefore can be classified into two types.

Empirical studies without rigourous theory: "Beginning with Hurdle (1974), a number of researchers have sought to utilise variables that are hypothesized to proxy the fundamental forces guiding the design of a firm's capital structure" (Martin,1988:374). These variables include growth, profitability, firm size, operating leverage, bankruptcy costs, and market power. We take note that leverage has been found to be positively associated with higher growth and firm size, and inversely, to market power, profitability, and bankruptcy costs. Unfortunately, most of these studies were not carried out in a rigourous theoretical framework. It is therefore difficult to treat these proxies as fundamental determinants of capital structure, and we do not dwell on these studies here.

Empirical studies based on rigourous theory: There are essentially two types of modern theories of capital structure. Frictionless theories presume that there are no costs incurred in making transactions in any market. "In particular, there are no information costs, brokerage fees, or other costs associated with the purchase or sale or securities or other assets" (Martin, 1988:334). In the other group of theories, transaction costs come in, to differing degrees. We now consider these theories and the empirical studies based on them. A note on the different methodologies used by most of the empirical studies in this area is given in Appendix I.

Frictionless or Perfect Capital Markets Assumption Framework

The frictionless markets approach has derived from neo-classical economics using general equilibrium analysis. This approach has its own weaknesses, which, for paucity of space, we do not touch upon here (Allen, 1989: 12). Three determinants of capital structure can be derived from this approach.

Determinant 1: Corporate Tax:

MM hypothesized in 1963 that corporate tax determines capital structure. There is a difference in the tax treatment of dividends to common shareholders and interest paid to bondholders, at the corporate level. Because interest expense is deductible from corporate income while dividends are not, bond financing leads to a "tax subsidy" to the firm. The mathematical form of this result is: VL = VU + tcB where tc is the corporate tax rate and B is the market value of debt. The term tcB represents gains from leverage, G, and this is, according to Copeland and Weston, "perhaps the single most important result in the theory of corporation finance obtained in the last 25 years" (1987:387). Some studies have examined the existence of gains from leverage. Thus, the more the debt in the capital structure, the higher the after-tax cash flows, leading to a greater market value of the firm. In fact, if this holds good we should find all firms carrying 99.999% debt.

Evidence: In 1966, Miller and Modigliani found results (based on a sample of 63 electric utility firms in 1954, 1956 and 1957) that were consistent with a gain from leverage (Copeland,1988:517). In 1980, Masulis studied the valuation impact of 113 exchange offers that occurred in the USA during the period 1963 to 1978. His evidence was also consistent with the notion that taxes provide an incentive to use debt financing (Martin, 1988:377).

In other words, evidence supports the tax effect as a determinant of capital structure. However, this cannot possibly the entire story, since no firm keeps (or is allowed by financing institutions to keep) 99.99% debt.

Determinant 2: Personal Tax, In Addition to Corporate Tax:

Under the Classical Tax System: Miller proposed the interaction between the personal tax and corporate tax systems as a determinant of capital structure in his presidential address to the American Finance Association in 1977. He analysed the corporate bond market where the supply of savings is made by different individuals. Thee demand for these funds leads to an equilibrium. Since most of the financial literature is written in the USA, the "classical" tax system was taken into consideration by Miller. In the USA, prior to 1986 Tax Reform Act, capital gains were taxed at a maximum of 20%, whereas dividends and interest had a maximum rate of 50%. Different investors (clients) therefore have different personal tax rates, and prefer different securities, leading to a corporate leverage clientele effect. Individual tax-payers in low tax brackets would benefit from investing in highly levered firms. Therefore, initially, firms will issue more debt to capture the funds from tax-exempt clients. "Companies will stop issuing debt when the marginal personal tax rate of a clientele investing in the instrument equals the corporate tax rate" (Van Horne, 1990:334). Until an equilibrium is achieved, however, capital structure is not irrelevant. Mathematically, it can be shown that:

$$VL = VU + B\left[1 - \frac{(1-tc)(1-tps)}{(1-tpd)}\right]$$

where tps is the effective personal tax rate on income to shareholders, being a weighted average of their personal income tax rate and the capital gains tax rate, tpd is the bondholders' personal tax rate. This analysis implies that the gain from leverage may be much smaller than when only corporate taxes are taken into account. Thus, gains from leverage are partially neutralised by personal tax.

Under the Dividend Imputation Tax System: In Australia the dividend imputation tax system is now in force. In this case the equation for gains from leverage, G, derived on the same pattern as above, is:

$$G = B\left[1 - \frac{\_(1-tpe) + (1-\_)(1-tc)(1-tg)}{(1-tpd)}\right]$$

where _ is the dividend payout ratio, tpe is the personal income tax rate of the shareholders, and tg is the tax rate for capital gains on accrual basis (Peirson, 1990:502). Without going into its details here, it would suffice to say that in this case the dividend policy _ and capital structure go together to determine the gains from leverage. In fact, dividend policy becomes more significant under the imputation system than it was under the classical system. Further, the bias in favour of debt has been removed under this system.

Determinant 3: Tax Shields Other than Interest Payments on Debt:

DeAngelo and Masulis (1980) extended the analysis of tax shields, while maintaining zero bankruptcy and zero agency costs. They noted that not all corporations pay the same effective tax rate, and that corporate tax shields also include non-cash charges such as depreciation allowances, investment tax credits, and oil depletion allowances. One can reasonably expect these to serve as tax shield substitutes for interest expenses. They theorise that firms are likely to select a level of debt negatively related to the level of other tax shield substitutes. As more and more of debt is absorbed, the likelihood of zero or negative earnings increases, thus causing inability to fully utilise the tax shields. Therefore the supply curve for corporate debt would have a downward slope, leading to the existence of optimal debt (Weston,1989:592). If bankruptcy costs are allowed, then they show that "there will be an optimum trade-off between the marginal expected benefit of interest tax shields and the marginal expected cost of bankruptcy" (Copeland, 1983:399).

*Evidence:*Cordes and Shefferin (1983) examined cross-sectional differences in the effective tax rates caused by tax carry-backs and carry-forwards, foreign tax credits, investment tax credits, the alternate tax on capital gains, and the minimum tax. "They found significant differences across industries with the highest effective tax rate for tobacco manufacturing (45%) and the lowest rate (16%) for transportation and agriculture" (Copeland, 1988:518). This supports the above theory. In 1984, Bradley, Jarrell, and Kim took the ratio of depreciation plus investment tax credits to earnings as a proxy for non-debt tax shields. By regressing leverage against this variable, it was found significantly positive, indicating that debt does not act as a tax shield (Copeland,1988:518). Also, Long and Maliz (1985) added several additional variables to those used by Bradley et al. By estimating a similar regression, they found non-debt tax shields to be negatively related to leverage (Copeland, 1988: 519).

Transactions Cost Assumption Framework:

In real life, there are many imperfections in markets, all of which could impact on the capital structure. In 1937, Coase proposed the significance of transaction costs as the cause for the existence of firms. Expanding on this, the financial literature now considers agency costs and financial signalling among the more important imperfections caused due to transactions of different types.

Determinant 4: Information Asymmetry and Signalling/ Pecking Order:

Preference for internal over external financing and preference of debt over equity.

Donaldson noted in 1961:"Management strongly favoured internal generation as a source of new funds even to the exclusion of external funds except for occasional unavoidable 'bulges' in the need for funds." (cited in Martin,1988:351). Explanation for this phenomenon has been attempted in a group of related theories based on information asymmetry. Akerlof demonstrated in 1970 that in the face of information barriers and extreme difficulties in the assessment of the quality of a good offered for sale, potential purchasers may, among various alternatives, prefer not to trade at all.

This arises as a consequence of *information asymmetry*, a condition vitiating perfect capital markets. Asymmetric information refers to the situation where one party has information not possessed by another party. Both Ross (1977) and Leland and Pyle (1977) have used this concept to postulate that manager-insiders have information about their own firms not possessed by outsiders. Therefore investors look for two types of signals from the managers: the amounts of (a) debt and (b) dividends, issued. We note that these theories are based on the relaxation of the homogeneous expectations assumption of the pure MM framework (Brigham: 193).

Signalling:

a) Ross (1977) considered two types of firms: Type A, a firm that is likely to be successful, and Type B, a firm that is likely to be unsuccessful. "With reference to a critical level of debt D*, the market perceives the firm to be Type A if it issues debt greater than this amount and Type B if it issues debt less than this amount. In order for the management of a Type B firm to have the incentive to signal that the firm will be unsuccessful, the payoff from telling the truth must be greater than that produced by telling lies. This is achieved by assessing a substantial penalty against the manager if his firm experiences bankruptcy" (Weston,1989:595).

b) Leland and Pyle showed in 1977 that the value of a firm increases with the proportion of equity held by the original owners. If the owners feel that the firm's shares are undervalued, they will not issue new stock. Therefore the act of issuing stock is viewed by the markets as a signal that the shares are overpriced, and accordingly, the markets adjust the prices downwards. If debt is issued, the reverse is signalled, and stock prices are adjusted upwards. Leland and Pyle also explain the existence of financial intermediation institutions which specialise in reducing the information barrier between the owners and the public.

Both these theories offer an explanation for the preference of use of internal funds over external funds.

Evidence: Masulis (1980), in his cross-sectional study of the announcement returns of 133 exchange offers, found evidence to support the conclusion that stock prices are positively related to leverage changes because of a positive signalling effect (Copeland, 1988: 520). Pinegar and Lease (1986) In another study of exchange offers, the above result of Masulis was confirmed (Copeland, 1988:520). Lee (1987) found that insiders typically do not sell their shares during leverage-increasing exchange offers. Instead, they buy stock and increase their ownership. This is because they value the shares at prices higher than their market price and are taking advantage of their better knowledge about the future prospects of the firm (Copeland, 1988: 520).

Therefore, the signalling hypothesis has been shown to exert an influence on capital structure.

Pecking Order

In his Presidential Address to the American Finance Association in 1984, "The Capital Structure Puzzle", Myers expanded upon the observation of Gordon Donaldson cited above. He proposed that a "pecking order" holds, with internal financing being preferred to debt, and debt being preferred to equity.

Myers and Majluf (1984) used the concept of asymmetric information to explain a "pecking-order" in the firms. They refined the propositions of Leland and Pyle discussed above, and showed that the action of the original owners or "old" shareholders to issue equity does not fool the market, and by adjusting the share prices downwards, the market immediately adjusts for the bad news, reducing the total payoff to the old shareholders. Therefore the original shareholders cannot take advantage of their superior information, and remain indifferent between doing nothing and issuing new equity. The conclusion of Myers and Majluf is that the market will therefore attach no significance to the issue of new equity.

They also showed that in the presence of asymmetric information, the firm may sometimes pass up a positive NPV project as the market does not value the project as the owners do, and is unwilling to make capital available at its true risk-adjusted cost to the firm. This restriction is therefore circumvented by the owners by taking recourse to internal financing. This shows that "old" shareholders will prefer to use available liquid assets to finance positive NPV projects rather than going in for equity. Further, in a situation where external financing is essential, debt is perceived by the firm to be safer than equity, since its market value does not change much over time.

Evidence: The Titman and Wessels (1985) study shows that more profitable firms will tend to use less external financing and provides support for the pecking order theory (Copeland, 1988: 519). Event studies show that issue of equity is interpreted as bad news by the market, with significantly negative announcement date effects on equity prices [Masulis and Korwar (1986), Asquith and Mullins (1986), Kolodny and Suhler (1985) and Mikkelson and Partch (1986)].

This is consistent with the "pecking order" theory. Therefore firms will resort to equity issues only as a last resort (Copeland, 1988: 522).

We conclude that evidence supports the pecking order theory.

Determinant 5: Bankruptcy Costs

Explanation for the Use of Equity.

Whereas Determinant 4 explains the preference of debt over equity, and of internal financing over external, yet firms do issue equity too. This is explained by the existence of direct bankruptcy costs, which include legal, accounting, and other administrative costs attributable to financial readjustments and legal proceedings at bankruptcy. Some indirect costs also arise before the actual legal proceedings take place. Higher levels of debt lead to higher fixed charges and lower coverage of debt.

Therefore there is a limit to the amount of debt that a firm can take. Theories considering various aspects of bankruptcy have been in the literature for some time, and were classified into three types by Myers and Pogue in 1974. These theories are known as the "poultry" theories (Martin,1988:355).

i) *management chickens out first*: In this, management does not wish to increase leverage because of the risk of failure of the firm, which will reduce their own market value and future prospects.

ii) *owners chicken out first*: In this case, it is the owners who first chicken out due to the risk of financial distress with greater leverage.

iii) *creditors chicken out first*: In this case, creditors may place the firm under a capital ration due to their fear of excessive leverage, to prevent their money from being put to risky uses (as we shall see in the application of agency costs, it is likely that both management and stockholders may have a fling with risky projects under such a situation).

Evidence:

Warner (1977) first studied the explicit (direct) costs of bankruptcy for a sample of 11 railroads where bankruptcy occurred between 1933 and 1955. He found that the direct costs of bankruptcy are trivial and cannot explain the use of equity in place of debt. In another study, he examined the effects of bankruptcy on the market returns of 73 defaulted bonds of 20 separate railroads. He found a significant negative return to bondholders on the date of the bankruptcy petition, leading to the conclusion that bankruptcy costs are non-trivial (Copeland, 1988: 500).

Altman (1984) also found that the direct costs of bankruptcy are small but significant. But when indirect costs are also taken into account, bankruptcy costs could be as much as 20 percent of the value of the firm (Weston, 1989: 598). Bradley, Jarrell, and Kim, 1984:They considered earnings volatility as a proxy for bankruptcy costs and found it to be significantly negative when regressed against leverage, supporting the importance of bankruptcy costs.

Evidence on bankruptcy costs as a determinant of capital structure is therefore significant, and if the indirect costs are considered, does put a brake on the limitless issue of debt.

Determinant 6: Bondholder Wealth Expropriation Hypothesis: or, Equity As An Option:

Black and Scholes (1973) recognised that equity ownership in a firm with outstanding debt can be regarded as a call option. By selling bonds, equity holders receive cash as well as a call option. Mathematically, the equity's value E, is given by max[0,V-B]. The five variables under the Black and Scholes formula would be:

E = E(V,B,Ív¨,rf,T)

where Ív¨ is the variance of V, rf is the risk-free rate, and T is the time maturity of the debt (Bishop, 1988:243).

If, on the maturation of the debt, the value of the firm exceeds the face value of the bonds, then the equity holders will exercise the call option by paying off the bondholders the face value of the debt. On the other hand, if the value of the firm is less than the face value of the debt, the equity holders will simply "walk away from the mess" (Allen, 1993), and the bondholders will receive merely the value of the firm. Thus, the equity holders expropriate bondholders' wealth.

When new debt is issued to retire equity and the assets of the firm remains unchanged, there is an implication for "old" bondholders.

The new bondholders have an equal claim on the assets with the original bondholders. The old bondholders would therefore have a smaller proportionate claim to the same assets of the firm than they had before the new debt was issued. The old bondholders are therefore placed in a riskier position. It is to avoid this that the issue of new debt is often pre-empted through their contract with the firm (Weston,1989:592).

In both these cases, the bondholders wealth is expropriated, either by existing equityholders, or by new bondholders. Hence the name "bondholder wealth expropriation hypothesis."

*Evidence:*Masulis (1980) found that the expropriation hypothesis is weakly supported by their study which used exchange-offers (Copeland, 1988: 520). Pinegar and Lease (1986) also studied exchange offers and found the evidence consistent with the bondholder wealth expropriation hypothesis (Copeland, 1988:520).

Thus there does seem to be some evidence of the use of equity as an option.

Determinant 7: Agency Costs:

Jensen and Meckling (1976) examined the relationship between a principal, e.g., a shareholder, and an agent of the principal, e.g., the company's manager. The principal incurs three agency costs. Monitoring costs are incurred in the monitoring of expenditures made by the agents. Bonding costs are incurred in drawing up contracts and agreements by the principal with the agent. This procedure obviously leaves the agents with lesser freedom to operate and has its own opportunity costs, in terms of a residual loss to the firm.

Agency problems are sometimes associated with the use of outside equity. An owner-manager, on selling part of his equity, can begin to indulge in lavish perquisites for himself. In such a case he bears only a portion of their cost, and the rest is paid for by the new equity holders. Thus the new shareholders have to incur monitoring costs to ensure that the original owner-manager acts in their interest.

In another instance, it is possible for equityholders to cause the position of bondholders to be affected adversely by shifting to more risky investment programs. If the company has two projects, each with the same expected value, but with different standard deviations, then it is often in the interest of the equity holders to go in for a project with higher risk, since they are likely to get a higher return if the project succeeds, whereas if it fails then the bondholders loose. Hence, agency costs are incurred by bondholders to restrain the equity holders from going in for a more risky project, and these costs increase as the debt increases.

Similarly, companies which manufacture durable products requiring long-term service contracts find that the consumer demand for their product diminishes when they take on greater debt, as consumers face a greater risk that the company shall not be able to service the sales.

This applies to workers too as they will not prefer to work in a firm where, in the event of bankruptcy, their skills are not of any use elsewhere. Firms using highly specialised labour therefore have to avoid the possibility of bankruptcy by keeping debt at low levels. Titman (1984) accordingly stated that firms with unique assets have necessarily to carry less debt, due to agency costs (Copeland, 1983:446).

Therefore agency costs can come into play in different ways and restrict the issue of equity/ debt, depending on the situation. Capital structure is therefore influenced by these costs.

Evidence: Titman and Wessels (1985) found that asset uniqueness is significantly negatively related to leverage, which confirms the existence of agency costs (Copeland, 1988: 519). Smith and Warner (1979) found that as many as 91% of the bond covenants restrict the issuance of additional debt.

There is thus evidence of the existence of agency costs in firms, which go towards determining capital structure.

Determinant 8: Bond Indenture Provisions and Bond Rating Agencies:

Partly arising from the existence of agency costs and partly on account of information asymmetry, this determinant - which has no theoretical rigour, is often found to play an important role in determining capital structure in reality. Empirical evidence shows that bond indenture provisions can, apart from restricting the issue of new debt, also restrict dividend (study by Kalay, 1979). Some covenants restrict mergers also, and many even restrict investment decisions. Obviously, all these restrictions go towards the determination of capital structure.

There is also a possibility that the ratings by bond-ratings influence firm value. However, this has been discounted by evidence from Wakeman (1978) and Weinstein (1978), since capital markets quickly absorb the relevant news months before the bond rating agencies change their ratings.

Conclusion

The models and evidence outlined above go to show the complexity of capital structure determination. Myers entitled his address to the American Finance Association in 1983, "The Capital Structure Puzzle", which aptly describes the prevailing situation. The basic question of whether a firm's financing decisions impact on its value remains unresolved. Evidence on capital structure is difficult to reconcile together. As Copeland and Weston point out, "A great deal of work needs to be done before a consensus about the effect of capital structure on the cost of capital will be reached" (Copeland, 1983:459). "Thus, the present consensus on this issue in the financial literature appears to indicate that the determinants of a firm's capital structure are still subject to debate and require further empirical investigation" (Martin,1988:379).

As seen above, there is by now some evidence that financing decisions do play a role in determining value and an optimal capital structure could theoretically well exist. The difficulty is in determining it. An eclectic approach may be useful to adopt in this matter, by viewing different theories and models as different approaches, and taking these into account in determining a suitable financing mix. But the task has definitely not reached a stage where a practicing manager can apply the knowledge so far gained to his firm in the form of a simple checklist.

However, it is the Brealey and Myer's Third Law which puts the issue in its proper perspective: "You can make a lot more money on the left-hand side of the balance sheet than on the right" (Brealey,1988:450). Therefore, it is more relevant for a company to spend time and energy in its investment decisions than bother too much about its source of funds.

3

Capital Structure and Market Power

Market Power

Market power is the ability of a firm to profitably raise the market price of a good or service over marginal cost. In perfectly competitive markets, market participants have no market power. A firm with total market power can raise prices without losing any customers to competitors. Market participants that have market power are therefore sometimes referred to as "price makers," while those without are sometimes called "price takers." Significant market power is when prices exceed marginal cost and long run average cost, so the firm makes economic profits.

A firm with market power has the ability to individually affect either the total quantity or the prevailing price in the market. Price makers face a downward-sloping demand curve, such that price increases lead to a lower quantity demanded. The decrease in supply as a result of the exercise of market power creates an economic deadweight loss which is often viewed as socially undesirable. As a result, many countries have anti-trust or other legislation intended to limit the ability of firms to accrue market power. Such legislation often regulates mergers and sometimes introduces a judicial power to compel divestiture.

A firm usually has market power by virtue of controlling a large portion of the market. In extreme cases - monopoly and monopsony - the firm controls the entire market. However, market size alone is not the only indicator of market power. Highly concentrated markets may be contestable if there are no barriers to entry or exit, limiting the incumbent firm's ability to raise its price above competitive levels.

Market power gives firms the ability to engage in unilateral anti-competitive behaviour. Some of the behaviours that firms with market power are accused of engaging in include predatory pricing, product tying, and creation of overcapacity or other barriers to entry. If no individual participant in the market has significant market power, then anti-competitive behaviour can take place only through collusion, or the exercise of a group of participants' collective market power.

The Lerner index and Herfindahl index may be used to measure market power.

Oligopoly

When several firms control a significant share of market sales, the resulting market structure is called an oligopoly or oligopsony. An oligopoly may engage in collusion, either tacit or overt, and thereby exercise market power. An explicit agreement in an oligopoly to affect market price or output is called a cartel. The behaviour of firms in perfect competition or monopoly can be treated as a simple optimization, but an oligopoly requires game theoretic analysis.

Monopoly Power

Monopoly power is an example of market failure which occurs when one or more of the participants has the ability to influence the price or other outcomes in some general or specialised market. The most commonly discussed form of market power is that of a monopoly, but other forms such as monopsony, and more moderate versions of these two extremes, exist.

A well-known example of monopolistic market power is Microsoft's market share in PCoperating systems. The *United States v. Microsoft* case dealt with an allegation that Microsoft illegally exercised its market power by bundling its web browser with its operating system. In this respect, the notion of dominance and dominant position in EU Antitrust Law is a strictly related aspect.

Source of Market Power

A monopoly can raise prices and retain customers because the monopoly has no competitors. If a customer has no other place to go to obtain the goods or services, they either pay the increased price or do without. Thus the key to market power is to preclude competition through high barriers of entry. Barriers to entry those are significant sources of market power are control of scarce resources, increasing returns to scale, technological superiority and government created barriers to entry. OPEC is an example of an organisation that has market power due to control over scarce resources - oil. Increasing returns to scale are another important source of market power. Firms experiencing increasing returns to scale are also experiencing decreasing average total costs. Firms in such industries become more profitable with size. Therefore over time the industry is dominated by a few large firms.

This dominance makes it difficult for start up firms to succeed. Firms like power companies, cable television companies and wireless communication companies with large start up costs fall within this category. A company wishing to enter such industries must have the financial ability to spend millions of dollars before starting operations and generating any revenue.

Similarly established firms also have a competitive advantage over new firms. An established firm threatened by a new competitor can lower prices to drive out the competition. Microsoft is a firm that has substantial pricing or market power due to technological superiority in its design and production processes. Finally government created barriers to entry can be a source of market power. A prime example are patents granted to pharmaceutical companies. These patents give the drug companies a virtual monopoly in the protected product for the term of the patent.

Measuring Market Power

Concentration ratios are the most common measures of market power. The four-firm concentration ratio measures the percentage of total industry output attributable to the top four companies. For monopolies the four firm ratio is 100 per cent while the ratio is zero for perfect competition. Another measure of concentration is the Herfindahl-Hirschman Index (HHI) which is calculated by "summing the squares of the percentage market shares of all participants in the market." The HHI index for perfect competition is zero; for monopoly, 10,000. The four firm concentration domestic (U.S) ratios for cigarettes is 93%; for automobiles, 84% and for beer, 85%.

Market Power and Elasticity of Demand

Market power is the ability to raise price above marginal cost and earn a positive profit. The degree to which a firm can raise price above marginal cost depends on the shape of the demand curve at the profit maximizing output. That is, elasticity is the critical factor in determining market power. The relationship between market power and the price elasticity of demand (PED) can be summarized by the equation:

$$\frac{P}{MC} = \frac{PED}{1 + PED}.$$

Note that PED will be negative, so the ratio is always greater than one. The higher the P/MC ratio, the more market power the firm possesses. As PED increases in magnitude, the P/MC ratio approaches one, and market power approaches zero. The equation is derived from the monopolist pricing rule:

$$\frac{(P - MC)}{P} = -\frac{1}{PED}.$$

Security (Finance)

A security is a tradable asset of any kind. Securities are broadly categorized into:

- debt securities (such as banknotes, bonds and debentures),
- equity securities, e.g., common stocks; and,
- derivative contracts, such as forwards, futures, options and swaps.

The company or other entity issuing the security is called the issuer. A country's regulatory structure determines what qualifies as a security. For example, private investment pools may have some features of securities, but they may not be registered or regulated as such if they meet various restrictions.

Securities may be represented by a certificate or, more typically, "non-certificated", that is in electronic or "book entry" only form. Certificates may be *bearer*, meaning they entitle the holder to rights under the security merely by holding the security, or *registered*, meaning they entitle the holder to rights only if he or she appears on a security register maintained by the issuer or an intermediary. They include shares of corporate stock or mutual funds, bonds issued by corporations or governmental agencies, stock options or other options, limited partnership units, and various other formal investment instruments that are negotiable and fungible.

Debt

A debt is an obligation owed by one party (the debtor) to a second party, the creditor; usually this refers to assets granted by the creditor to the debtor, but the term can also be used metaphorically to cover moral obligations and other interactions not based on economic value.

A debt is created when a creditor agrees to lend a sum of assets to a debtor. Debt is usually granted with expected repayment; in modern society, in most cases, this includes repayment of the original sum, plus interest. In finance, debt is a means of using anticipated income and future purchasing power in the present before it has actually been earned. Some companies and corporations use debt as a part of their overall corporate finance strategy.

Terms

Interest: Interest is the fee charged by the creditor to the debtor. Interest is generally calculated as a percentage of the principal sum per year, and is generally paid periodically at intervals, such as monthly or semi-annually.

Interest rates may be fixed or floating. In floating-rate structures, the rate of interest that the borrower pays during each time period is tied to a pre-established benchmark such as LIBOR or, in the case of inflation-indexed bonds, inflation.

Repayment

Loans may be structured so that the entire principal balance is due at the maturity of the loan; so that the entire principal balance is paid slowly or amortized over the term of the loan; or so that the loan partially amortizes during the term of the loan and a larger "balloon payment" is due at maturity. Amortization structures are common in mortgages and credit cards.

Collateral and Recourse

A debt obligation is considered secured if creditors have recourse to specific collateral. Collateral may include claims on tax receipts (in the case of a government), specific assets (in the case of a company) or a home (in the case of a consumer). Unsecured debt comprises financial obligations for which creditors do not have recourse to the assets of the borrower to satisfy their claims.

Issuers of Debt

Governments: Governments issue debt to pay for ongoing expenses as well as major capital projects. Government debt may be issued by sovereign states as well as by local governments.

The overall level of indebtedness by a government is typically shown as a ratio of debt / GDP. This ratio helps to assess the speed of changes in government indebtedness and the size of the debt due.

Businesses

A company may use various kinds of debt to finance its operations. The various types of debt can generally be categorized into: 1) secured and unsecured debt, 2) private and public debt, 3) syndicated and bilateral debt, and 4) other types of debt that display one or more of the characteristics noted above.

Private debt comprises bank-loan type obligations, whether senior or mezzanine. Public debt is a general definition covering all financial instruments that are freely tradeable on a public exchange or over the counter, with few if any restrictions.

A basic loan or "term loan" is the simplest form of debt. It consists of an agreement to lend a fixed amount of money, called the principal sum or principal, for a fixed period of time, with this amount to be repaid by a certain date. In commercial loans interest, calculated as a percentage of the principal sum per year, will also have to be paid by that date, or may be paid periodically in the interval, such as annually or monthly. Such loans are also colloquially called bullet loans, particularly if there is only a single payment at the end – the "bullet" – without a "stream" of interest payments during the life of the loan. There are many conventions on how interest is calculated – while a standard convention is the annual percentage rate (APR), widely used and required by regulation in the United States and United Kingdom, though there are different forms of APR.

In some loans, the amount actually loaned to the debtor is less than the principal sum to be repaid; the additional principal has the same economic effect as a higher interest rate, and is sometimes referred to as a banker's dozen, a play on "baker's dozen" – owe twelve (a dozen), receive a loan of eleven (a banker's dozen). Note that the effective interest rate is not equal to the discount: if one borrows $10 and must repay $11, then this is ($11–$10)/$10 = 10% interest; however, if one borrows $9 and must repay $10, then this is ($10–$9)/$9 = 11 1/9% interest.

A syndicated loan is a loan that is granted to companies that wish to borrow more money than any single lender is prepared to risk in a single loan. A syndicated loan is provided by a group of lenders and is structured, arranged, and administered by one or several commercial banks or investment banks known as arrangers. Loan syndication is a risk management tool that allows the lead banks underwriting the debt to reduce their risk and free up lending capacity.

A bond is a debt security issued by certain institutions such as companies and governments. A bond entitles the holder to repayment of the principal sum, plus interest. Bonds are issued to investors in a marketplace when an institution wishes to borrow money. Bonds have a fixed lifetime, usually a number of years; with long-term bonds, lasting over 30 years, being less common. At the end of the bond's life the money should be repaid in full. Interest may be added to the end payment, or can be paid in regular installments (known as coupons) during the life of the bond. Bonds may be traded in the bond markets, and are widely used as relatively safe investments in comparison to equity.

A letter of credit or LC can also be the source of payment for a transaction, meaning that redeeming the letter of credit will pay an exporter. Letters of credit are used primarily in international trade transactions of significant value, for deals between a supplier in one country and a customer in another. They are also used in the land development process to ensure that approved public facilities (streets, sidewalks, stormwater ponds, etc.) will be built. The parties to a letter of credit are usually a beneficiary who is to receive the money, the issuing bank of whom the applicant is a client, and the advising bank of whom the beneficiary is a client. Almost all letters of credit are irrevocable, i.e., cannot be amended or canceled without prior agreement of the beneficiary, the issuing bank and the confirming bank, if any. In executing a transaction, letters of credit incorporate functions common to giros and Traveler's cheques. Typically, the documents a beneficiary has to present in order to receive payment include a commercial invoice, bill of lading, and a document proving the shipment was insured against loss or damage in transit. However, the list and form of documents is open to imagination and negotiation and might contain requirements to present documents issued by a neutral third party evidencing the quality of the goods shipped, or their place of origin.

Consumers

Common types of debt owed by consumers include mortgage loans, car loans, and credit card debt.

Private Households

Besides these more formal debts, private households also lend informally to other people, mostly relatives or friends. One reason for such informal debts is that many people, in particular those who are poor, have no access to affordable credit. Such debts can cause problems when they are not paid back according to expectations of the lending household. In 2011, 8% of people in the 28 European Union countries reported their households has been in arrears, that is, unable to pay as scheduled 'payments related to informal loans from friends or relatives not living in your household'.

Debt Markets

Market Interest Rates

Role of Central Banks: Central banks, such as the US Federal Reserve System, play a key role in the debt markets. Debt is normally denominated in a particular currency, and so changes in the valuation of that currency can change the effective size of the debt. This can happen due to inflation or deflation, so it can happen even though the borrower and the lender are using the same currency.

Role of Rating Agencies

Specific bond debts owed by both governments and private corporations are rated by rating agencies, such as Moody's, Standard & Poor's, Fitch Ratings, and A. M. Best. The government or company itself will also be given its own separate rating. These agencies assess the ability of the debtor to honour his obligations and accordingly give him or her a credit rating. Moody's uses the letters *AaaAa A Baa Ba B CaaCa C*, where ratings *Aa-Caa* are qualified by numbers 1-3. S&P and other rating agencies have slightly different systems using capital letters and +/- qualifiers.

A change in ratings can strongly affect a company, since its cost of refinancing depends on its creditworthiness. Bonds below Baa/BBB (Moody's/S&P) are considered junk- or high risk bonds. Their high risk of default (approximately 1.6% for Ba) is compensated by higher interest payments. Bad Debt is a loan that can not (partially or fully) be repaid by the debtor. The debtor is said to default on his debt. These types of debt are frequently repackaged and sold below face value. Buying junk bonds is seen as a risky but potentially profitable form of investment.

Securitization Markets

Securitization occurs when a company groups together assets or receivables and sells them in units to the market through a trust. Any asset with a cashflow can be securitized. The cash flows from these receivables are used to pay the holders of these units. Companies often do this in order to remove these assets from their balance sheets and monetize an asset. Although these assets are "removed" from the balance sheet and are supposed to be the responsibility of the trust, that does not end the company's involvement. Often the company maintains a special interest in the trust which is called an "interest only strip" or "first loss piece". Any payments from the trust must be made to regular investors in precedence to this interest. This protects investors from a degree of risk, making the securitization more attractive. The aforementioned brings into question whether the assets are truly off-balance-sheet given the company's exposure to losses on this interest.

Metrics and Functions

Risk Free Interest Rates: Lendings to stable financial entities such as large companies or governments are often termed "risk free" or "low risk" and made at a so-called "risk-free interest rate". This is because the debt and interest are highly unlikely to be defaulted. A good example of such risk-free interest is a US Treasury security – it yields the minimum return available in economics, but investors have the comfort of the (almost) certain expectation that the US Treasury will not default on its debt instruments. A risk-free rate is also commonly used in setting floating interest rates, which are usually calculated as the risk-free interest rate plus a bonus to the creditor based on the creditworthiness of the debtor (in other words, the risk of him or her defaulting and the creditor losing the debt). In reality, no lending is truly risk free, but borrowers at the "risk free" rate are considered the least likely to default.

However, if the real value of a currency changes during the term of the debt, the purchasing power of the money repaid may vary considerably from that which was expected at the commencement of the loan. So from a practical investment point of view, there is still considerable risk attached to "risk free" or "low risk" lendings. The real value of the money may have changed due to inflation, or, in the case of a foreign investment, due to exchange rate fluctuations.

The Bank for International Settlements is an organisation of central banks that sets rules to define how much capital banks have to hold against the loans they give out.

Debt Consolidation

Debt consolidation entails taking out one loan to pay off many others. This is often done to secure a lower interest rate, secure a fixed interest rate or for the convenience of servicing only one loan.

Debt consolidation can simply be from a number of unsecured loans into another unsecured loan, but more often it involves a secured loan against an asset that serves as collateral, most commonly a house. In this case, a mortgage is secured against the house. The collateralization of the loan allows a lower interest rate than without it, because by collateralizing, the asset owner agrees to allow the forced sale (foreclosure) of the asset to pay back the loan. The risk to the lender is reduced so the interest rate offered is lower.

Sometimes, debt consolidation companies can discount the amount of the loan. When the debtor is in danger of bankruptcy, the debt consolidator will buy the loan at a discount. A prudent debtor can shop around for consolidators who will pass along some of the savings. Consolidation can affect the ability of the debtor to discharge debts in bankruptcy, so the decision to consolidate must be weighed carefully.

Debt consolidation is often advisable in theory when someone is paying credit card debt. Credit cards can carry a much larger interest rate than even an unsecured loan from a bank. Debtors with property such as a home or car may get a lower rate through a secured loan using their property as collateral. Then the total interest and the total cash flow paid towards the debt is lower allowing the debt to be paid off sooner, incurring less interest.

Student Loan Consolidation

In the United States, federal student loans are consolidated somewhat differently than in the UK, as federal student loans are guaranteed by the U.S. government.

United States

In a federal student loan consolidation, existing loans are purchased by the Department of Education. Upon consolidation, a fixed interest rate is set based on the then-current interest rate. Reconsolidating does not change that rate. If the student combines loans of different types and rates into one new consolidation loan, a weighted average calculation will establish the appropriate rate based on the then-current interest rates of the different loans being consolidated together.

Federal student loan consolidation is often referred to as refinancing, which is incorrect because the loan rates are not changed, merely locked in. Unlike private sector debt consolidation, student loan consolidation does not incur any fees for the borrower; private companies make money on student loan consolidation by reaping subsidies from the federal government.

United Kingdom

In the UK student loan entitlements are guaranteed, and are recovered using a means-tested system from the students future income. Student Loans in the UK can not be included in Bankruptcy, but do not affect a persons credit rating because the repayments are recovered from the students future salary at source by the employer before any income is paid, similar to Income Tax and National Insurance contributions. Many students however, are struggling with debt well after their courses have finished

As of June 2011, total personal debt in the UK stood at £1,451bn. The annual growth rate remained at 0.8%.

Concerns

In recent years, reports in the media have raised concerns about the use of consolidation loans. The worry is that many people are tempted to consolidate unsecured debt into secured debt, usually secured against their home. Although the monthly payments can often be lower, the total amount repaid is often significantly higher due to the long period of the loan. Debt consolidation sometimes only treats the symptoms of debt and does not address the root problem. In some circumstances, snowballing debt may be a better solution. In other cases, consolidation loans may make it much longer to get rid of the debts that you have.

Alternatives

Other options available to overburdened debtors include credit counselling, debt settlement and personal bankruptcy. Some consolidation lenders will renegotiate with the creditors on the debtor's behalf, as a credit counsellor does.

Cancellation

Short of bankruptcy, it is rare that debts are wholly or partially relinquished. Traditions in some cultures demand that this be done on a regular (often annual) basis, in order to prevent systemic inequities between groups in society, or anyone becoming a specialist in holding debt and coercing repayment. An example is the Biblical Jubilee year, described in the Book of Leviticus.

Under English law, when the creditor is deceived into relinquishing the debt, this is a crime under the Theft Act 1978.

International Third World debt has reached the scale that many economists are convinced that debt cancellation is the only way to restore global equity in relations with the developing nations.

Effects of Debt

Debt allows people and organisations to do things that they would otherwise not be able, or allowed, to do. Commonly, people in industrialised nations use it to purchase houses, cars and many other things too expensive to buy with cash on hand. Companies also use debt in many ways to leverage the investment made in their assets, "leveraging" the return on their equity. This leverage, the proportion of debt to equity, is considered important in determining the riskiness of an investment; the more debt per equity, the riskier. For both companies and individuals, this increased risk can lead to poor results, as the cost of servicing the debt can grow beyond the ability to pay due to either external events (income loss) or internal difficulties (poor management of resources).

Excesses in debt accumulation have been blamed for exacerbating economic problems. For example, prior to the beginning of the Great Depression debt/GDP ratio was very high. Economic agents were heavily indebted. This excess of debt, equivalent to excessive expectations on future returns, accompanied asset bubbles on the stock markets. When expectations corrected, deflation and a credit crunch followed. Deflation effectively made debt more expensive and, as Fisher explained, this reinforced deflation again, because, in order to reduce their debt level, economic agents reduced their consumption and investment. The reduction in demand reduced business activity and caused further unemployment. In a more direct sense, more bankruptcies also occurred due both to increased debt cost caused by deflation and the reduced demand.

It is possible for some organisations to enter into alternative types of borrowing and repayment arrangements which will not result in bankruptcy. For example, companies can sometimes convert debt that they owe into equity in themselves. In this case, the creditor hopes to regain something equivalent to the debt and interest in the form of dividends and capital gains of the borrower. The "repayments" are therefore proportional to what the borrower earns and so can not in themselves cause bankruptcy. Once debt is converted in this way, it is no longer known as debt.

Etymology

The word comes from the French *dette* and ultimately Latin *debere* (to owe), from *de habere* (to have). The letter *b* in the word *debt* was reintroduced in the 18th century, possibly by Samuel Johnson in his Dictionary of 1755 – several other words that had existed without a *b* had them reinserted at around that time.

History of Debt

The anthropologist David Graeber argues in *Debt: The First 5000 Years* that trade starts with some sort of credit namely the promise to pay later for already handed over goods. Therefore credit and debt existed even before coins.

Criticisms

Some argue against debt as an instrument and institution, on a personal, family, social, corporate and governmental level. Islamforbids lending with interest even today.

Debt will increase through time if it is not repaid faster than it grows through interest. This effect may be termed usury, while the term "usury" in other contexts refers only to an excessive rate of interest, in excess of a reasonable profit for the risk accepted.

In international legal thought, Odious debt is debt that is incurred by a regime for purposes that do not serve the interest of the state. Such debts are thus considered by this doctrine to be personal debts of the regime that incurred them and not debts of the state.

In an economy with high interest rates, debt will be more costly to a business than more flexible dividends on equity investment. It may be easier for a struggling business to be financed through equity investment as it may be possible to avoid paying a dividend if times are hard.

At the household level, debts can also have detrimental effects. In particular when households make spending decisions assuming income to increase, or remain stable, for the years to come. When households take on credit based on this assumption, life events can easily change indebtedness into over-indebtedness. Such life events include unexpected unemployment, relationship break-up, leaving the parental home, business failure, illness, or home repairs. Over-indebtedness has severe social consequences, such as financial hardship, poor physical and mental health, family stress, stigma, difficulty obtaining employment, exclusion from basic financial services (European Commission, 2009), work accidents and industrial disease, a strain on social relations (Carpentier and Van den Bosch, 2008), absenteeism at work and lack of organisational commitment (Kim *et al.*, 2003), feeling of insecurity, and relational tensions.

Stock

The stock (also capital stock) of a corporation constitutes the equity stake of its owners. It represents the residual assets of the company that would be due to stockholders after discharge of all senior claims such as secured and unsecured debt. Stockholders' equity cannot be withdrawn from the company in a way that is intended to be detrimental to the company's creditors. The stock of a corporation is partitioned into shares, the total of which are stated at the time of business formation. Additional shares may subsequently be authorized by the existing shareholders and issued by the company. In some jurisdictions, each share of stock has a certain declared par value, which is a nominal accounting value used to represent the equity on the balance sheet of the corporation. In other jurisdictions, however, shares of stock may be issued without associated par value.

Shares represent a fraction of ownership in a business. A business may declare different types (*classes*) of shares, each having distinctive ownership rules, privileges, or share values. Ownership of shares may be documented by issuance of a stock certificate. A stock certificate is a legal document that specifies the amount of shares owned by the shareholder, and other specifics of the shares, such as the par value, if any, or the class of the shares.

In the United Kingdom, Republic of Ireland, South Africa, and Australia, *stock* can also refer to completely different financial instruments such as government bonds or, less commonly, to all kinds of marketable securities.

Types of Stock

Stock typically takes the form of shares of either common stock or preferred stock. As a unit of ownership, common stock typically carries voting rights that can be exercised in corporate decisions. Preferred stock differs from common stock in that it typically does not carry voting rights but is legally entitled to receive a certain level of dividend payments before any dividends can be issued to other shareholders. Convertible preferred stock is preferred stock that includes an option for the holder to convert the preferred shares into a fixed number of common shares, usually any time after a predetermined date. Shares of such stock are called "convertible preferred shares" (or "convertible preference shares" in the UK).

New equity issue may have specific legal clauses attached that differentiate them from previous issues of the issuer. Some shares of common stock may be issued without the typical voting rights, for instance, or some shares may have special rights unique to them and issued only to certain parties. Often, new issues that have not been registered with a securities governing body may be restricted from resale for certain periods of time.

Preferred stock may be hybrid by having the qualities of bonds of fixed returns and common stock voting rights. They also have preference in the payment of dividends over common stock and also have been given preference at the time of liquidation over common stock. They have other features of accumulation in dividend. In addition, preferred stock usually comes with a letter designation at the end of the security; for example, Berkshire-Hathaway Class "B" shares sell under stock ticker BRK.B, whereas Class "A" shares of ORION DHC, Inc will sell under ticker OODHA until the company drops the "A" creating ticker OODH for its "Common" shares only designation. This extra letter does not mean that any exclusive rights exist for the shareholders but it does let investors know that the shares are considered for such, however, these rights or privileges may change based on the decisions made by the underlying company.

Rule 144 Stock

"Rule 144 Stock" is a common name given to shares of stock subject SEC Rule 144: Selling Restricted and Control Securities. Under Rule 144, restricted and controlled securities are acquired in unregistered form. Investors either purchase or take ownership of these securities through private sales (or other means such as via ESOPs or in exchange for seed money) from the issuing company (as in the case with Restricted Securities) or from an affiliate of the issuer (as in the case with Control Securities). Investors wishing to sell these securities are subject to different rules than those selling traditional common or preferred stock. These individuals will only be allowed to liquidate their securities after meeting the specific conditions set forth by SEC Rule 144.

Stock Derivatives

A stock derivative is any financial instrument which has a value that is dependent on the price of the underlying stock. Futures and options are the main types of derivatives on stocks. The underlying security may be a stock index or an individual firm's stock, e.g. single-stock futures.

Stock futures are contracts where the buyer is long, i.e., takes on the obligation to buy on the contract maturity date, and the seller is short, i.e., takes on the obligation to sell. Stock index futures are generally not delivered in the usual manner, but by cash settlement.

A stock option is a class of option. Specifically, a call option is the right (*not* obligation) to buy stock in the future at a fixed price and a put option is the right (*not* obligation) to sell stock in the future at a fixed price. Thus, the value of a stock option changes in reaction to the underlying stock of which it is a derivative. The most popular method of valuing stock options is the Black Scholes model. Apart from call options granted to employees, most stock options are transferable.

History

During the Roman Republic, the state contracted (leased) out many of its services to private companies. These government contractors were called *publicani*, or *societaspublicanorum* as individual company. These companies were similar to modern corporations, or joint- stock companies more specifically, in couple of aspects. They issued shares called *partes* (for large cooperatives) and *particulae* which were small shares that acted like today's over-the-counter shares. Polybius mentions that "almost every citizen" participated in the government leases. There is also an evidence that the price of stocks fluctuated. The great Roman orator Cicero speaks of *partesillo tempore carissimae*, which means "share that had a very high price at that time." This implies a fluctuation of price and stock market behaviour in Rome.

Around 1250 in France at Toulouse, 96 shares of the *Société des Moulins du Bazacle*, or Bazacle Milling Company were traded at a value that depended on the profitability of the mills the society owned. As early as 1288, the Swedish mining and forestry products company Stora has documented a stock transfer, in which that the Bishop of Västerås acquired a 12.5% interest in the mine (or more specifically, the mountain in which the copper resource was available, Great Copper Mountain) in exchange for an estate.

Figure: *The East India Company's flag initially had the flag of England, St. George's Cross, in the corner.*

The earliest recognised joint-stock company in modern times was the English (later British) East India Company, one of the most famous joint-stock companies. It was granted an English Royal Charter by Elizabeth I on December 31, 1600, with the intention of favouring trade privileges in India. The Royal Charter effectively gave the newly created *Honourable East India Company* (HEIC) a 15-year monopoly on all trade in the East Indies. The Company transformed from a commercial trading venture to one that virtually ruled India as it acquired auxiliary governmental and military functions, until its dissolution.

Soon afterwards, in 1602, the Dutch East India Company issued the first shares that were made tradeable on the Amsterdam Stock Exchange, an invention that enhanced the ability of joint-stock companies to attract capital from investors as they now easily could dispose of their shares. The Dutch East India Company became the first multinational corporation and the first megacorporation. Between 1602 and 1796 it had traded 2.5 million tons of cargo with Asia on 4,785 ships and had sent a million Europeans to work in Asia, surpassing all other rivals.

The innovation of joint ownership made a great deal of Europe's economic growth possible following the Middle Ages. The technique of pooling capital to finance the building of ships, for example, made the Netherlands a maritime superpower. Before adoption of the joint-stock corporation, an expensive venture such as the building of a merchant ship could be undertaken only by governments or by very wealthy individuals or families. Economic historians find the Dutch stock market of the 17th century particularly interesting: there is clear documentation of the use of stock futures, stock options, short selling, the use of credit to purchase shares, a speculative bubble that crashed in 1695, and a change in fashion that unfolded and reverted in time with the market (in this case it was headdresses instead of hemlines). Dr.Edward Stringham also noted that the uses of practices such as short selling continued to occur during this time despite the government passing laws against it. This is unusual because it shows individual parties fulfilling contracts that were not legally enforceable and where the parties involved could incur a loss. Stringham argues that this shows that contracts can be created and enforced without state sanction or, in this case, in spite of laws to the contrary.

Shareholder

A shareholder (or *stockholder*) is an individual or company (including a corporation) that legally owns one or more shares of stock in a joint stock company. Both private and public traded companies have shareholders. Companies listed at the stock market are expected to strive to enhance shareholder value.

Shareholders are granted special privileges depending on the class of stock, including the right to vote on matters such as elections to the board of directors, the right to share in distributions of the company's income, the right to purchase new shares issued by the company, and the right to a company's assets during a liquidation of the company. However, shareholder's rights to a company's assets are subordinate to the rights of the company's creditors.

Shareholders are considered by some to be a partial subset of stakeholders, which may include anyone who has a direct or indirect equity interest in the business entity or someone with even a non-pecuniary interest in a non-profit organisation. Thus it might be common to call volunteer contributors to an association stakeholders, even though they are not shareholders.

Although directors and officers of a company are bound by fiduciary duties to act in the best interest of the shareholders, the shareholders themselves normally do not have such duties towards each other.

However, in a few unusual cases, some courts have been willing to imply such a duty between shareholders. For example, in California, USA, majority shareholders of closely held corporations have a duty to not destroy the value of the shares held by minority shareholders.

The largest shareholders (in terms of percentages of companies owned) are often mutual funds, and, especially, passively managed exchange-traded funds.

Application

The owners of a private company may want additional capital to invest in new projects within the company. They may also simply wish to reduce their holding, freeing up capital for their own private use. They can achieve these goals by selling shares in the company to the general public, through a sale on a stock exchange. This process is called an initial public offering, or IPO.

By selling shares they can sell part or all of the company to many part-owners. The purchase of one share entitles the owner of that share to literally share in the ownership of the company, a fraction of the decision-making power, and potentially a fraction of the profits, which the company may issue as dividends.

In the common case of a publicly traded corporation, where there may be thousands of shareholders, it is impractical to have all of them making the daily decisions required to run a company. Thus, the shareholders will use their shares as votes in the election of members of the board of directors of the company. In a typical case, each share constitutes one vote. Corporations may, however, issue different classes of shares, which may have different voting rights. Owning the majority of the shares allows other shareholders to be out-voted – effective control rests with the majority shareholder (or shareholders acting in concert). In this way the original owners of the company often still have control of the company.

Shareholder Rights

Although ownership of 50% of shares does result in 50% ownership of a company, it does not give the shareholder the right to use a company's building, equipment, materials, or other property. This is because the company is considered a legal person, thus it owns all its assets itself. This is important in areas such as insurance, which must be in the name of the company and not the main shareholder.

In most countries, boards of directors and company managers have a fiduciary responsibility to run the company in the interests of its stockholders. Nonetheless, as Martin Whitman writes:

...it can safely be stated that there does not exist any publicly traded company where management works exclusively in the best interests of OPMI [Outside Passive Minority Investor] stockholders. Instead, there are both "communities of interest" and "conflicts of interest" between stockholders (principal) and management (agent). This conflict is referred to as the principal/agent problem. It would be naive to think that any management would forego management compensation, and management entrenchment, just because some of these management privileges might be perceived as giving rise to a conflict of interest with OPMIs.

Even though the board of directors runs the company, the shareholder has some impact on the company's policy, as the shareholders elect the board of directors. Each shareholder typically has a percentage of votes equal to the percentage of shares he or she owns.

So as long as the shareholders agree that the management (agent) are performing poorly they can select a new board of directors which can then hire a new management team. In practice, however, genuinely contested board elections are rare. Board candidates are usually nominated by insiders or by the board of the directors themselves, and a considerable amount of stock is held or voted by insiders.

Owning shares does not mean responsibility for liabilities. If a company goes broke and has to default on loans, the shareholders are not liable in any way. However, all money obtained by converting assets into cash will be used to repay loans and other debts first, so that shareholders cannot receive any money unless and until creditors have been paid (often the shareholders end up with nothing).

Means of Financing

Financing a company through the sale of stock in a company is known as equity financing. Alternatively, debt financing (for example issuing bonds) can be done to avoid giving up shares of ownership of the company. Unofficial financing known as trade financing usually provides the major part of a company's working capital (day-to-day operational needs).

Trading

In general, the shares of a company may be transferred from shareholders to other parties by sale or other mechanisms, unless prohibited. Most jurisdictions have established laws and regulations governing such transfers, particularly if the issuer is a publicly traded entity.

The desire of stockholders to trade their shares has led to the establishment of stock exchanges, organisations which provide marketplaces for trading shares and other derivatives and financial products. Today, stock traders are usually represented by a stockbroker who buys and sells shares of a wide range of companies on such exchanges. A company may list its shares on an exchange by meeting and maintaining the listing requirements of a particular stock exchange. In the United States, through the intermarket trading system, stocks listed on one exchange can often also be traded on other participating exchanges, including electronic communication networks (ECNs), such as Archipelago or Instinet.

Many large non-U.S companies choose to list on a U.S. exchange as well as an exchange in their home country in order to broaden their investor base. These companies must maintain a block of shares at a bank in the US, typically a certain percentage of their capital. On this basis, the holding bank establishes American depositary shares and issues an American depositary receipt (ADR) for each share a trader acquires. Likewise, many large U.S. companies list their shares at foreign exchanges to raise capital abroad.

Small companies that do not qualify and cannot meet the listing requirements of the major exchanges may be traded over-the-counter (OTC) by an off-exchange mechanism in which trading occurs directly between parties. The major OTC markets in the United States are the electronic quotation systems OTC Bulletin Board (OTCBB) and OTC Markets Group (formerly known as Pink OTC Markets Inc.)where individual retail investors are also represented by a brokerage firm and the quotation service's requirements for a company to be listed are minimal. Shares of companies in bankruptcy proceeding are usually listed by these quotation services after the stock is delisted from an exchange.

Buying

There are various methods of buying and financing stocks, the most common being through a stockbroker. Brokerage firms, whether they are a full-service or discount broker, arrange the transfer of stock from a seller to a buyer. Most trades are actually done through brokers listed with a stock exchange.

There are many different brokerage firms from which to choose, such as full service brokers or discount brokers. The full service brokers usually charge more per trade, but give investment advice or more personal service; the discount brokers offer little or no investment advice but charge less for trades. Another type of broker would be a bank or credit union that may have a deal set up with either a full-service or discount broker.

There are other ways of buying stock besides through a broker. One way is directly from the company itself. If at least one share is owned, most companies will allow the purchase of shares directly from the company through their investor relations departments. However, the initial share of stock in the company will have to be obtained through a regular stock broker. Another way to buy stock in companies is through Direct Public Offerings which are usually sold by the company itself. A direct public offering is an initial public offering in which the stock is purchased directly from the company, usually without the aid of brokers.

When it comes to financing a purchase of stocks there are two ways: purchasing stock with money that is currently in the buyer's ownership, or by buying stock on margin. Buying stock on margin means buying stock with money borrowed against the value of stocks in the same account. These stocks, or collateral, guarantee that the buyer can repay the loan; otherwise, the stockbroker has the right to sell the stock (collateral) to repay the borrowed money. He can sell if the share price drops below the margin requirement, at least 50% of the value of the stocks in the account. Buying on margin works the same way as borrowing money to buy a car or a house, using a car or house as collateral. Moreover, borrowing is not free; the broker usually charges 8–10% interest.

Selling

Selling stock is procedurally similar to buying stock. Generally, the investor wants to buy low and sell high, if not in that order (short selling); although a number of reasons may induce an investor to sell at a loss, e.g., to avoid further loss.

As with buying a stock, there is a transaction fee for the broker's efforts in arranging the transfer of stock from a seller to a buyer. This fee can be high or low depending on which type of brokerage, full service or discount, handles the transaction.

After the transaction has been made, the seller is then entitled to all of the money. An important part of selling is keeping track of the earnings. Importantly, on selling the stock, in jurisdictions that have them, capital gains taxes will have to be paid on the additional proceeds, if any, that are in excess of the cost basis.

Stock Price Fluctuations

The price of a stock fluctuates fundamentally due to the theory of supply and demand. Like all commodities in the market, the price of a stock is sensitive to demand. However, there are many factors that influence the demand for a particular stock. The fields of fundamental analysis and technical analysis attempt to understand market conditions that lead to price changes, or even predict future price levels. A recent study shows that customer satisfaction, as measured by the American Customer Satisfaction Index (ACSI), is significantly correlated to the market value of a stock. Stock price may be influenced by analysts' business forecast for the company and outlooks for the company's general market segment. Stocks can also fluctuate greatly due to pump and dump scams.

Share Price Determination

At any given moment, an equity's price is strictly a result of supply and demand. The supply, commonly referred to as the *float*, is the number of shares offered for sale at any one moment. The demand is the number of shares investors wish to buy at exactly that same time. The price of the stock moves in order to achieve and maintain equilibrium. The product of this instantaneous price and the float at any one time is the market capitalization of the entity offering the equity at that point in time.

When prospective buyers outnumber sellers, the price rises. Eventually, sellers attracted to the high selling price enter the market and/or buyers leave, achieving equilibrium between buyers and sellers.

When sellers outnumber buyers, the price falls. Eventually buyers enter and/or sellers leave, again achieving equilibrium.

Thus, the value of a share of a company at any given moment is determined by all investors voting with their money. If more investors want a stock and are willing to pay more, the price will go up. If more investors are selling a stock and there aren't enough buyers, the price will go down.

- Note: "For Nasdaq-listed stocks, the price quote includes information on the bid and ask prices for the stock."

Of course, that does not explain how people decide the maximum price at which they are willing to buy or the minimum at which they are willing to sell. In professional investment circles the efficient market hypothesis (EMH) continues to be popular, although this theory is widely discredited in academic and professional circles. Briefly, EMH says that investing is overall (weighted by the standard deviation) rational; that the price of a stock at any given moment represents a rational evaluation of the known information that might bear on the future value of the company; and that share prices of equities are priced *efficiently*, which is to say that they represent accurately the expected value of the stock, as best it can be known at a given moment. In other words, prices are the result of discounting expected future cash flows.

The EMH model, if true, has at least two interesting consequences. First, because financial risk is presumed to require at least a small premium on expected value, the return on equity can be expected to be slightly greater than that available from non-equity investments: if not, the same rational calculations would lead equity investors to shift to these safer non-equity investments that could be expected to give the same or better return at lower risk. Second, because the price of a share at every given moment is an "efficient" reflection of expected value, then—relative to the curve of expected return—prices will tend to follow a random walk, determined by the emergence of information (randomly) over time. Professional equity investors therefore immerse themselves in the flow of fundamental information, seeking to gain an advantage over their competitors (mainly other professional investors) by more intelligently interpreting the emerging flow of information (news).

The EMH model does not seem to give a complete description of the process of equity price determination. For example, stock markets are more volatile than EMH would imply. In recent years it has come to be accepted that the share markets are not perfectly efficient, perhaps especially in emerging markets or other markets that are not dominated by well-informed professional investors.

Another theory of share price determination comes from the field of Behavioural Finance. According to Behavioural Finance, humans often make irrational decisions—particularly, related to the buying and selling of securities—based upon fears and misperceptions of outcomes. The irrational trading of securities can often create securities prices which vary from rational, fundamental price valuations. For instance, during the technology bubble of the late 1990s (which was followed by the dot-com bust of 2000–2002), technology companies were often bid beyond any rational fundamental value because of what is commonly known as the "greater fool theory". The "greater fool theory" holds that, because the predominant method of realising returns in equity is from the sale to another investor, one should select securities that they believe that someone else will value at a higher level at some point in the future, without regard to the basis for that other party's willingness to pay a higher price. Thus, even a rational investor may bank on others' irrationality.

Arbitrage Trading

When companies raise capital by offering stock on more than one exchange, the potential exists for discrepancies in the valuation of shares on different exchanges. A keen investor with access to information about such discrepancies may invest in expectation of their eventual convergence, known as arbitrage trading. Electronic trading has resulted in extensive price transparency (efficient-market hypothesis) and these discrepancies, if they exist, are short-lived and quickly equilibrated.

Derivative (Finance)

A derivative is a financial contract which *derives* its value from the performance of another entity such as an asset, index, or interest rate, called the "underlying". Derivatives are one of the three main categories of financial instruments, the other two being equities (i.e. stocks) and debt (i.e. bonds and mortgages). Derivatives include a variety of financial contracts, including futures, forwards, swaps, options, and variations of these such as caps, floors, collars, and credit default swaps. Most derivatives are traded over-the-counter (off-exchange) or on an exchange such as the Chicago Mercantile Exchange, while most insurance contracts have developed into a separate industry.

Many money managers use derivatives for a variety of purposes, such as hedging—by taking a position in a derivative, losses on portfolio holdings may be minimized or offset by profits on the derivative. Likewise, derivatives can be used to gain quicker and more efficient access to markets; for example, it may be easier and quicker to purchase an S & P 500 futures contract than to invest in the underlying securities.

Basics

Derivatives are a contract between two parties that specify conditions (especially the dates, resulting values and definitions of the underlying variables, the parties' contractual obligations, and the notional amount) under which payments are to be made between the parties. The most common underlying assets include commodities, stocks, bonds, interest rates and currencies, but they can also be other derivatives, which adds another layer of complexity to proper valuation. The components of a firm's capital structure, e.g. bonds and stock, can also be considered derivatives, more precisely options, with the underlying being the firm's assets, but this is unusual outside of technical contexts.

There are two groups of derivative contracts: the privately traded over-the-counter (OTC) derivatives such as swaps that do not go through an exchange or other intermediary, and exchange-traded derivatives (ETD) that are traded through specialised derivatives exchanges or other exchanges.

Derivatives are more common in the modern era, but their origins trace back several centuries. One of the oldest derivatives is rice futures, which have been traded on the Dojima Rice Exchange since the eighteenth century. Derivatives are broadly categorized by the relationship between the underlying asset and the derivative (such as forward, option, swap); the type of underlying asset (such as equity derivatives, foreign exchange derivatives, interest rate derivatives, commodity derivatives, or credit derivatives); the market in which they trade (such as exchange-traded or over-the-counter); and their pay-off profile.

Derivatives may broadly be categorized as "lock" or "option" products. Lock products (such as swaps, futures, or forwards) obligate the contractual parties to the terms over the life of the contract. Option products (such as interest rate caps) provide the buyer the right, but not the obligation to enter the contract under the terms specified.

Derivatives can be used either for risk management (i.e. to "hedge" by providing offsetting compensation in case of an undesired event, a kind of "insurance") or for speculation (i.e. making a financial "bet"). This distinction is important because the former is a prudent aspect of operations and financial management for many firms across many industries; the latter offers managers and investors a risky opportunity to increase profit, which may not be properly disclosed to stakeholders.

Along with many other financial products and services, derivatives reform is an element of the Dodd–Frank Wall Street Reform and Consumer Protection Act of 2010. The Act delegated many rule-making details of regulatory oversight to the Commodity Futures Trading Commission and those details are not finalized nor fully implemented as of late 2012.

Size of Market

To give an idea of the size of the derivative market, *The Economist* magazine has reported that as of June 2011, the over-the-counter (OTC) derivatives market amounted to approximately $700 trillion, and the size of the market traded on exchanges totaled an additional $83 trillion. However, these are "notional" values, and some economists say that this value greatly exaggerates the market value and the true credit risk faced by the parties involved. For example, in 2010, while the aggregate of OTC derivatives exceeded $600 trillion, the value of the market was estimated much lower, at $21 trillion. The credit risk equivalent of the derivative contracts was estimated at $3.3 trillion.

Still, even these scaled down figures represent huge amounts of money. For perspective, the budget for total expenditure of the United States Government during 2012 was $3.5 trillion, and the total current value of the US stock market is an estimated $23 trillion. The world annual Gross Domestic Product is about $65 trillion.

And for one type of derivative at least, Credit Default Swaps (CDS), for which the inherent risk is considered high, the higher, nominal value, remains relevant. It was this type of derivative that investment magnate Warren Buffet referred to in his famous 2002 speech in which he warned against "weapons of financial mass destruction." CDS notional value in early 2012 amounted to $25.5 trillion, down from $55 trillion in 2008.

Usage

Derivatives are used for the following:

- Hedge or mitigate risk in the underlying, by entering into a derivative contract whose value moves in the opposite direction to their underlying position and cancels part or all of it out

- Create option ability where the value of the derivative is linked to a specific condition or event (e.g. the underlying reaching a specific price level)
- Obtain exposure to the underlying where it is not possible to trade in the underlying (e.g. weather derivatives)
- Provide leverage (or gearing), such that a small movement in the underlying value can cause a large difference in the value of the derivative
- Speculate and make a profit if the value of the underlying asset moves the way they expect (e.g. moves in a given direction, stays in or out of a specified range, reaches a certain level)
- Switch asset allocations between different asset classes without disturbing the underlying assets, as part of transition management
- Avoid paying taxes. For example, an equity swap allows an investor to receive steady payments, e.g. based on LIBOR rate, while avoiding paying capital gains tax and keeping the stock.

Mechanics and Valuation Basics

Lock products are theoretically valued at zero at the time of execution and thus do not typically require an up-front exchange between the parties. Based upon movements in the underlying asset over time, however, the value of the contract will fluctuate, and the derivative may be either an asset (i.e. "in the money") or a liability (i.e. "out of the money") at different points throughout its life. Importantly, either party is therefore exposed to the credit quality of its counterparty and is interested in protecting itself in an event of default.

Option products have immediate value at the outset because they provide specified protection (intrinsic value) over a given time period (time value). One common form of option product familiar to many consumers is insurance for homes and automobiles. The insured would pay more for a policy with greater liability protections (intrinsic value) and one that extends for a year rather than six months (time value). Because of the immediate option value, the option purchaser typically pays an up front premium. Just like for lock products, movements in the underlying asset will cause the option's intrinsic value to change over time while its time value deteriorates steadily until the contract expires. An important difference between a lock product is that, after the initial exchange, the option purchaser has no further liability to its counterparty; upon maturity, the purchaser will execute the option if it has positive value (i.e. if it is "in the money") or expire at no cost (other than to the initial premium) (i.e. if the option is "out of the money").

Hedging

Derivatives allow risk related to the price of the underlying asset to be transferred from one party to another. For example, a wheat farmer and a miller could sign a futures contract to exchange a specified amount of cash for a specified amount of wheat in the future. Both parties have reduced a future risk: for the wheat farmer, the uncertainty of the price, and for the miller, the availability of wheat. However, there is still the risk that no wheat will be available because of events unspecified by the contract, such as the weather, or that one party will renege on the contract. Although a third party, called a clearing house, insures a futures contract, not all derivatives are insured against counter-party risk.

From another perspective, the farmer and the miller both reduce a risk and acquire a risk when they sign the futures contract: the farmer reduces the risk that the price of wheat will fall below the price specified in the contract and acquires the risk that the price of wheat will rise above the price specified in the contract (thereby losing additional income that he could have earned). The miller, on the other hand, acquires the risk that the price of wheat will fall below the price specified in the contract (thereby paying more in the future than he otherwise would have) and reduces the risk that the price of wheat will rise above the price specified in the contract. In this sense, one party is the insurer (risk taker) for one type of risk, and the counter-party is the insurer (risk taker) for another type of risk.

Hedging also occurs when an individual or institution buys an asset (such as a commodity, a bond that has coupon payments, a stock that pays dividends, and so on) and sells it using a futures contract. The individual or institution has access to the asset for a specified amount of time, and can then sell it in the future at a specified price according to the futures contract. Of course, this allows the individual or institution the benefit of holding the asset, while reducing the risk that the future selling price will deviate unexpectedly from the market's current assessment of the future value of the asset.

Derivatives trading of this kind may serve the financial interests of certain particular businesses. For example, a corporation borrows a large sum of money at a specific interest rate. The interest rate on the loan reprices every six months. The corporation is concerned that the rate of interest may be much higher in six months. The corporation could buy a forward rate agreement (FRA), which is a contract to pay a fixed rate of interest six months after purchases on a notional amount of money. If the interest rate after six months is above the contract rate, the seller will pay the difference to the corporation, or FRA buyer. If the rate is lower, the corporation will pay the difference to the seller. The purchase of the FRA serves to reduce the uncertainty concerning the rate increase and stabilize earnings.

Speculation and Arbitrage

Derivatives can be used to acquire risk, rather than to hedge against risk. Thus, some individuals and institutions will enter into a derivative contract to speculate right derivative on the value of the underlying asset, betting that the party seeking insurance will be wrong about the future value of the underlying asset. Speculators look to buy an asset in the future at a low price according to a derivative contract when the future market price is high, or to sell an asset in the future at a high price according to a derivative contract when the future market price is less.

Individuals and institutions may also look for arbitrage opportunities, as when the current buying price of an asset falls below the price specified in a futures contract to sell the asset.

Speculative trading in derivatives gained a great deal of notoriety in 1995 when Nick Leeson, a trader at Barings Bank, made poor and unauthorized investments in futures contracts. Through a combination of poor judgment, lack of oversight by the bank's management and regulators, and unfortunate events like the Kobe earthquake, Leeson incurred a US$1.3 billion loss that bankrupted the centuries-old institution.

Proportion Used for Hedging and Speculation

Unfortunately, the true proportion of derivatives contracts used for legitimate hedging purposes is unknown (and perhaps unknowable), but it appears to be relatively small. Also, derivatives contracts account for only 3–6% of the median firms' total currency and interest rate exposure. Nonetheless, we know that many firms' derivatives activities have at least some speculative component for a variety of reasons.

Types

OTC and Exchange-Traded: In broad terms, there are two groups of derivative contracts, which are distinguished by the way they are traded in the market:

- Over-the-counter (OTC) derivatives are contracts that are traded (and privately negotiated) directly between two parties, without going through an exchange or other intermediary. Products such as swaps, forward rate agreements, exotic options – and other exotic derivatives – are almost always traded in this way. The OTC derivative market is the largest market for derivatives, and is largely unregulated with respect to disclosure of information between the parties, since the OTC market is made up of banks and other highly sophisticated parties, such as hedge funds. Reporting of OTC amounts is difficult because trades can occur in private, without activity being visible on any exchange.

According to the Bank for International Settlements, who first surveyed OTC derivatives in 1995, reported that the "gross market value, which represent the cost of replacing all open contracts at the prevailing market prices, ... increased by 74% since 2004, to $11 trillion at the end of June 2007 (BIS 2007:24)." Positions in the OTC derivatives market increased to $516 trillion at the end of June 2007, 135% higher than the level recorded in 2004. The total outstanding notional amount is US$708 trillion (as of June 2011). Of this total notional amount, 67% are interest rate contracts, 8% are credit default swaps (CDS), 9% are foreign exchange contracts, 2% are commodity contracts, 1% are equity contracts, and 12% are other. Because OTC derivatives are not traded on an exchange, there is no central counter-party. Therefore, they are subject to counterparty risk, like an ordinary contract, since each counter-party relies on the other to perform.

- Exchange-traded derivatives (ETD) are those derivatives instruments that are traded via specialised derivatives exchanges or other exchanges. A derivatives exchange is a market where individuals trade standardized contracts that have been defined by the exchange. A derivatives exchange acts as an intermediary to all related transactions, and takes initial margin from both sides of the trade to act as a guarantee. The world's largest derivatives exchanges (by number of transactions) are the Korea Exchange (which lists KOSPI Index Futures & Options), Eurex (which lists a wide range of European products such as interest rate & index products), and CME Group (made up of the 2007 merger of the Chicago Mercantile Exchange and the Chicago Board of Trade and the 2008 acquisition of the New York Mercantile Exchange). According to BIS, the combined turnover in the world's derivatives exchanges totaled USD 344 trillion during Q4 2005. By December 2007 the Bank for International Settlements reported that "derivatives traded on exchanges surged 27% to a record $681 trillion."

Common Derivative Contract Types

Some of the common variants of derivative contracts are as follows:

1. *Forwards:* A tailored contract between two parties, where payment takes place at a specific time in the future at today's pre-determined price.
2. *Futures:* are contracts to buy or sell an asset on or before a future date at a price specified today. A futures contract differs from a forward contract in that the futures contract is a standardized contract written by a clearing house that operates an exchange where the contract can be bought and sold; the forward contract is a non-standardized contract written by the parties themselves.
3. Options are contracts that give the owner the right, but not the obligation, to buy (in the case of a call option) or sell (in the case of a put option) an asset. The price at which the sale takes place is known as the strike price, and is specified at the time the parties enter into the option. The option contract also specifies a maturity date. In the case of a European option, the owner has the right to require the sale to take place on (but not before) the maturity date; in the case of an American option, the owner can require the sale to take place at any time up to the maturity date. If the owner of the contract exercises this right, the counter-party has the obligation to carry out the transaction. Options are of two types: call option and put option. The buyer of a Call option has a right to buy a certain quantity of the underlying asset, at a specified price on or before a given date in the future, he however has no obligation whatsoever to carry out this right. Similarly, the buyer of a Put option has the right to sell a certain quantity of an underlying asset, at a specified price on or before a given date in the future, he however has no obligation whatsoever to carry out this right.
4. Binary options are contracts that provide the owner with an all-or-nothing profit profile.
5. Warrants: Apart from the commonly used short-dated options which have a maximum maturity period of 1 year, there exists

certain long-dated options as well, known as Warrant (finance). These are generally traded over-the-counter.

6. Swaps are contracts to exchange cash (flows) on or before a specified future date based on the underlying value of currencies exchange rates, bonds/interest rates, commodities exchange, stocks or other assets. Another term which is commonly associated to Swap is Swaption which is basically an option on the forward Swap. Similar to a Call and Put option, a Swaption is of two kinds: a receiver Swaption and a payer Swaption. While on one hand, in case of a receiver Swaption there is an option wherein you can receive fixed and pay floating, a payer swaption on the other hand is an option to pay fixed and receive floating.

Swaps can basically be categorized into two types:

- *Interest rate swap:* These basically necessitate swapping only interest associated cash flows in the same currency, between two parties.
- *Currency swap:* In this kind of swapping, the cash flow between the two parties includes both principal and interest. Also, the money which is being swapped is in different currency for both parties.

Some common examples of these derivatives are the following:

UNDERLYING	***CONTRACT TYPES***				
	Exchange-traded futures	Exchange-traded options	OTC swap	OTC forward	OTC option
Equity	DJIA Index future Single-stock future	Option on DJIA Index future Single-share option	Equity swap	Back-to-back Repurchase agreement	Stock option Warrant Turbo warrant
Interest rate	Eurodollar future Euribor future	Option on Eurodollar future Option on Euribor future	Interest rate swap	Forward rate agreement	Interest rate cap and floor Swaption Basis swap Bond option
Credit	Bond future	Option on Bond future	Credit default swap Total return swap	Repurchase agreement	Credit default option
Foreign exchange	Currency future	Option on currency future	Currency swap	Currency forward	Currency option
Commodity	WTI crude oil futures	Weather derivative	Commodity swap	Iron ore forward contract	Gold option

Economic Function of the Derivative Market

Some of the salient economic functions of the derivative market include:

1. Prices in a structured derivative market not only replicate the discernment of the market participants about the future but also lead the prices of underlying to the professed future level. On the expiration of the derivative contract, the prices of derivatives congregate with the prices of the underlying. Therefore, derivatives are essential tools to determine both current and future prices.
2. The derivatives market reallocates risk from the people who prefer risk aversion to the people who have an appetite for risk.
3. The intrinsic nature of derivatives market associates them to the underlying Spot market. Due to derivatives there is a considerable increase in trade volumes of the underlying Spot market. The dominant factor behind such an escalation is increased participation by additional players who would not have otherwise participated due to absence of any procedure to transfer risk.
4. As supervision, reconnaissance of the activities of various participants becomes tremendously difficult in assorted markets; the establishment of an organised form of market becomes all the more imperative. Therefore, in the presence of an organised derivatives market, speculation can be controlled, resulting in a more meticulous environment.
5. Third parties can use publicly available derivative prices as educated predictions of uncertain future outcomes, for example, the likelihood that a corporation will default on its debts.

In a nutshell, there is a substantial increase in savings and investment in the long run due to augmented activities by derivative Market participant.

Valuation

Market and Arbitrage-Free Prices

Two common measures of value are:

- Market price, i.e. the price at which traders are willing to buy or sell the contract
- Arbitrage-free price, meaning that no risk-free profits can be made by trading in these contracts

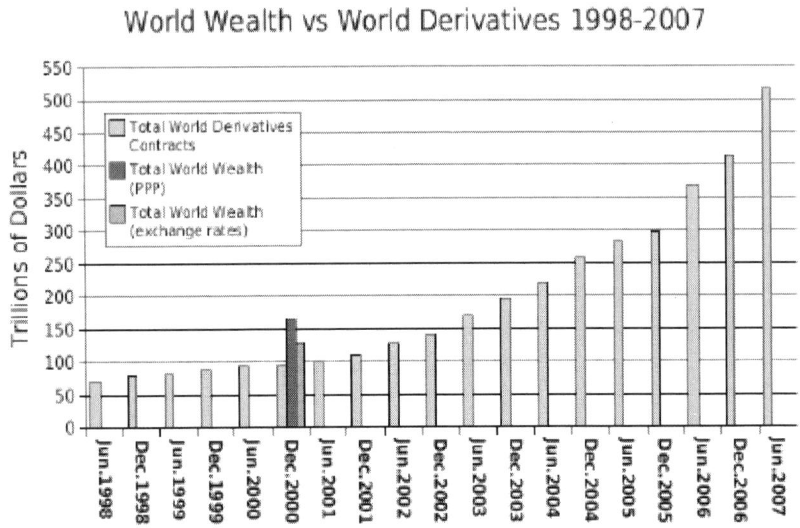

Figure: *Total world derivatives from 1998 to 2007 compared to total world wealth in the year 2000*

Determining the Market Price

For exchange-traded derivatives, market price is usually transparent (often published in real time by the exchange, based on all the current bids and offers placed on that particular contract at any one time). Complications can arise with OTC or floor-traded contracts though, as trading is handled manually, making it difficult to automatically broadcast prices. In particular with OTC contracts, there is no central exchange to collate and disseminate prices.

Determining the Arbitrage-Free Price

The arbitrage-free price for a derivatives contract can be complex, and there are many different variables to consider. Arbitrage-free pricing is a central topic of financial mathematics. For futures/forwards the arbitrage free price is relatively straightforward, involving the price of the underlying together with the cost of carry (income received less interest costs), although there can be complexities.

However, for options and more complex derivatives, pricing involves developing a complex pricing model: understanding the stochastic process of the price of the underlying asset is often crucial. A key equation for the theoretical valuation of options is the Black–Scholes formula, which is based on the assumption that the cash flows from a European stock option can be replicated by a continuous buying and selling strategy using only the stock. A simplified version of this valuation technique is the binomial options model. OTC represents the biggest challenge in using models to price derivatives. Since these contracts are not publicly traded, no market price is available to validate the theoretical valuation. Most of the model's results are input-dependent (meaning the final price depends heavily on how we derive the pricing inputs).

Therefore it is common that OTC derivatives are priced by Independent Agents that both counterparties involved in the deal designate upfront (when signing the contract).

Criticisms

Derivatives are often subject to the following criticisms:

Hidden Tail Risk

According to Raghuram Rajan, a former chief economist of the International Monetary Fund (IMF), "... it may well be that the managers of these firms [investment funds] have figured out the correlations between the various instruments they hold and believe they are hedged. Yet as Chan and others (2005) point out, the lessons of summer 1998 following the default on Russian government debt is that correlations that are zero or negative in normal times can turn overnight to one — a phenomenon they term "phase lock-in." A hedged position can become unhedged at the worst times, inflicting substantial losses on those who mistakenly believe they are protected."

Risks

The use of derivatives can result in large losses because of the use of leverage, or borrowing. Derivatives allow investors to earn large returns from small movements in the underlying asset's price. However, investors could lose large amounts if the price of the underlying moves against them significantly. There have been several instances of massive losses in derivative markets, such as the following:

- American International Group (AIG) lost more than US$18 billion through a subsidiary over the preceding three quarters on credit default swaps (CDSs). The United States Federal Reserve Bank announced the creation of a secured credit facility of up to US$85 billion, to prevent the company's collapse by enabling AIG to meet its obligations to deliver additional collateral to its credit default swap trading partners.
- The loss of US$7.2 Billion by SociétéGénérale in January 2008 through mis-use of futures contracts.

- The loss of US$6.4 billion in the failed fund Amaranth Advisors, which was long natural gas in September 2006 when the price plummeted.
- The loss of US$4.6 billion in the failed fund Long-Term Capital Management in 1998.
- The loss of US$1.3 billion equivalent in oil derivatives in 1993 and 1994 by Metallgesellschaft AG.
- The loss of US$1.2 billion equivalent in equity derivatives in 1995 by Barings Bank.
- UBS AG, Switzerland's biggest bank, suffered a $2 billion loss through unauthorized trading discovered in September 2011.

This comes to a staggering $39.5 billion, the majority in the last decade after the Commodity Futures Modernisation Act of 2000 was passed.

Counter Party Risk

Some derivatives (especially swaps) expose investors to counterparty risk, or risk arising from the other party in a financial transaction. Different types of derivatives have different levels of counter party risk.

For example, standardized stock options by law require the party at risk to have a certain amount deposited with the exchange, showing that they can pay for any losses; banks that help businesses swap variable for fixed rates on loans may do credit checks on both parties. However, in private agreements between two companies, for example, there may not be benchmarks for performing due diligence and risk analysis.

Large Notional Value

Derivatives typically have a large notional value. As such, there is the danger that their use could result in losses for which the investor would be unable to compensate. The possibility that this could lead to a chain reaction ensuing in an economic crisis was pointed out by famed investor Warren Buffett in Berkshire Hathaway's 2002 annual report. Buffett called them 'financial weapons of mass destruction.' A potential problem with derivatives is that they comprise an increasingly larger notional amount of assets which may lead to distortions in the underlying capital and equities markets themselves. Investors begin to look at the derivatives markets to make a decision to buy or sell securities and so what was originally meant to be a market to transfer risk now becomes a leading indicator.

Financial Reform and Government Regulation

Under US law and the laws of most other developed countries, derivatives have special legal exemptions that make them a particularly attractive legal form to extend credit. The strong creditor protections afforded to derivatives counterparties, in combination with their complexity and lack of transparency however, can cause capital markets to underprice credit risk. This can contribute to credit booms, and increase systemic risks. Indeed, the use of derivatives to conceal credit risk from third parties while protecting derivative counterparties contributed to the financial crisis of 2008 in the United States.

In the context of a 2010 examination of the ICE Trust, an industry self-regulatory body, Gary Gensler, the chairman of the Commodity Futures Trading Commission which regulates most derivatives, was quoted saying that the derivatives marketplace as it functions now "adds up to higher costs to all Americans." More oversight of the banks in this market is needed, he also said. Additionally, the report said, "[t]he Department of Justice is looking into derivatives, too. The department's antitrust unit is actively investigating 'the possibility of anticompetitive practices in the credit derivatives clearing, trading and information services industries,' according to a department spokeswoman."

For legislators and committees responsible for financial reform related to derivatives in the United States and elsewhere, distinguishing between hedging and speculative derivatives activities has been a nontrivial challenge. The distinction is critical because regulation should help to isolate and curtail speculation with derivatives, especially for "systemically significant" institutions whose default could be large enough to threaten the entire financial system. At the same time, the legislation should allow for responsible parties to hedge risk without unduly tying up working capital as collateral that firms may better employ elsewhere in their operations and investment. In this regard, it is important to distinguish between financial (e.g. banks) and non-financial end-users of derivatives (e.g. real estate development companies) because these firms' derivatives usage is inherently different. More importantly, the reasonable collateral that secures these different counterparties can be very different.

The distinction between these firms is not always straight forward (e.g. hedge funds or even some private equity firms do not neatly fit either category). Finally, even financial users must be differentiated, as 'large' banks may classified as "systemically significant" whose derivatives activities must be more tightly monitored and restricted than those of smaller, local and regional banks.

Over-the-counter dealing will be less common as the Dodd–Frank Wall Street Reform and Consumer Protection Act comes into effect. The law mandated the clearing of certain swaps at registered exchanges and imposed various restrictions on derivatives. To implement Dodd-Frank, the CFTC developed new rules in at least 30 areas. The Commission determines which swaps are subject to mandatory clearing and whether a derivatives exchange is eligible to clear a certain type of swap contract.

Nonetheless, the above and other challenges of the rule-making process have delayed full enactment of aspects of the legislation relating to derivatives. The challenges are further complicated by the necessity to orchestrate globalized financial reform among the nations that comprise the world's major financial markets, a primary responsibility of the Financial Stability Board whose progress is ongoing.

In the U.S., by February 2012 the combined effort of the SEC and CFTC had produced over 70 proposed and final derivatives rules. However, both of them had delayed adoption of a number of derivatives regulations because of the burden of other rulemaking, litigation and opposition to the rules, and many core definitions (such as the terms "swap," "security-based swap," "swap dealer," "security-based swap dealer," "major swap participant" and "major security-based swap participant") had still not been adopted. SEC Chairman Mary Schapiro opined: "At the end of the day, it probably does not make sense to harmonize everything [between the SEC and CFTC rules] because some of these products are quite different and certainly the market structures are quite different."

In November 2012, the SEC and regulators from Australia, Brazil, the European Union, Hong Kong, Japan, Ontario, Quebec, Singapore, and Switzerland met to discuss reforming the OTC derivatives market, as had been agreed by leaders at the 2009 G-20 Pittsburgh summit in September 2009.

In December 2012, they released a joint statement to the effect that they recognised that the market is a global one and "firmly support the adoption and enforcement of robust and consistent standards in and across jurisdictions", with the goals of mitigating risk, improving transparency, protecting against market abuse, preventing regulatory gaps, reducing the potential for arbitrage opportunities, and fostering a level playing field for market participants.

They also agreed on the need to reduce regulatory uncertainty and provide market participants with sufficient clarity on laws and regulations by avoiding, to the extent possible, the application of conflicting rules to the same entities and transactions, and minimizing the application of inconsistent and duplicative rules. At the same time, they noted that "complete harmonization – perfect alignment of rules across jurisdictions" would be difficult, because of jurisdictions' differences in law, policy, markets, implementation timing, and legislative and regulatory processes.

On December 20, 2013 the CFTC provided information on its swaps regulation "comparability" determinations. The release addressed the CFTC's cross-border compliance exceptions. Specifically it addressed which entity level and in some cases transaction-level requirements in six jurisdictions (Australia, Canada, the European Union, Hong Kong, Japan, and Switzerland) it found comparable to its own rules, thus permitting non-US swap dealers, major swap participants, and the foreign branches of US Swap Dealers and major swap participants in these jurisdictions to comply with local rules in lieu of Commission rules.

Reporting

Mandatory reporting regulations are being finalized in a number of countries, such as Dodd Frank Act in the US, the European Market Infrastructure Regulations (EMIR) in Europe, as well as regulations in Hong Kong, Japan, Singapore, Canada, and other countries. The OTC Derivatives Regulators Forum (ODRF), a group of over 40 world-wide regulators, provided trade repositories with a set of guidelines regarding data access to regulators, and the Financial Stability Board and CPSS IOSCO also made recommendations in with regard to reporting.

DTCC, through its "Global Trade Repository" (GTR) service, manages global trade repositories for interest rates, and commodities, foreign exchange, credit, and equity derivatives. It makes global trade reports to the CFTC in the U.S., and plans to do the same for ESMA in Europe and for regulators in Hong Kong, Japan, and Singapore. It covers cleared and uncleared OTC derivatives products, whether or not a trade is electronically processed or bespoke.

Glossary

- *Bilateral netting:* A legally enforceable arrangement between a bank and a counter-party that creates a single legal obligation covering all included individual contracts. This means that a bank's obligation, in the event of the default or insolvency of one of the parties, would be the net sum of all positive and negative fair values of contracts included in the bilateral netting arrangement.

- *Counterparty:* The legal and financial term for the other party in a financial transaction.
- *Credit derivative:* A contract that transfers credit risk from a protection buyer to a credit protection seller. Credit derivative products can take many forms, such as credit default swaps, credit linked notes and total return swaps.
- *Derivative:* A financial contract whose value is derived from the performance of assets, interest rates, currency exchange rates, or indexes. Derivative transactions include a wide assortment of financial contracts including structured debt obligations and deposits, swaps, futures, options, caps, floors, collars, forwards and various combinations thereof.
- *Exchange-traded derivative contracts:* Standardized derivative contracts (e.g., futures contracts and options) that are transacted on an organised futures exchange.
- *[Gross negative fair value:* The sum of the fair values of contracts where the bank owes money to its counter-parties, without taking into account netting. This represents the maximum losses the bank's counter-parties would incur if the bank defaults and there is no netting of contracts, and no bank collateral was held by the counter-parties.
- *Gross positive fair value:* The sum total of the fair values of contracts where the bank is owed money by its counter-parties, without taking into account netting. This represents the maximum losses a bank could incur if all its counter-parties default and there is no netting of contracts, and the bank holds no counter-party collateral.
- *High-risk mortgage securities:* Securities where the price or expected average life is highly sensitive to interest rate changes, as determined by the U.S. Federal Financial Institutions Examination Council policy statement on high-risk mortgage securities.
- *Notional amount:* The nominal or face amount that is used to calculate payments made on swaps and other risk management products. This amount generally does not change hands and is thus referred to as notional.

- *Over-the-counter (OTC) derivative contracts:* Privately negotiated derivative contracts that are transacted off organised futures exchanges.
- *Structured notes:* Non-mortgage-backed debt securities, whose cash flow characteristics depend on one or more indices and / or have embedded forwards or options.
- *Total risk-based capital:* The sum of tier 1 plus tier 2 capital. Tier 1 capital consists of common shareholders equity, perpetual preferred shareholders equity with noncumulative dividends, retained earnings, and minority interests in the equity accounts of consolidated subsidiaries. Tier 2 capital consists of subordinated debt, intermediate-term preferred stock, cumulative and long-term preferred stock, and a portion of a bank's allowance for loan and lease losses.

The Securities Markets

Primary and Secondary Market: Public securities markets are either primary or secondary markets. In the primary market, the money for the securities is received by the issuer of the securities from investors, typically in an initial public offering (IPO). In the secondary market, the securities are simply assets held by one investor selling them to another investor, with the money going from one investor to the other.

An initial public offering is when a company issues public stock newly to investors, called an "IPO" for short. A company can later issue more new shares, or issue shares that have been previously registered in a shelf registration. These later new issues are also sold in the primary market, but they are not considered to be an IPO but are often called a "secondary offering". Issuers usually retain investment banks to assist them in administering the IPO, obtaining SEC (or other regulatory body) approval of the offering filing, and selling the new issue. When the investment bank buys the entire new issue from the issuer at a discount to resell it at a markup, it is called a firm commitment underwriting. However, if the investment bank considers the risk too great for an underwriting, it may only assent to a best effort agreement, where the investment bank will simply do its best to sell the new issue.

For the primary market to thrive, there must be a secondary market, or aftermarket that provides liquidity for the investment security—where holders of securities can sell them to other investors for cash. Otherwise, few people would purchase primary issues, and, thus, companies and governments would be restricted in raising equity capital (money) for their operations. Organised exchanges constitute the main secondary markets. Many smaller issues and most debt securities trade in the decentralized, dealer-based over-the-counter markets.

In Europe, the principal trade organisation for securities dealers is the International Capital Market Association. In the U.S., the principal trade organisation for securities dealers is the Securities Industry and Financial Markets Association, which is the result of the merger of the Securities Industry Association and the Bond Market Association. The Financial Information Services Division of the Software and Information Industry Association (FISD/SIIA) represents a round-table of market data industry firms, referring to them as Consumers, Exchanges, and Vendors. In India the equivalent organisation is the securities exchange board of India (SEBI).

Public Offer and Private Placement

In the primary markets, securities may be offered to the public in a public offer. Alternatively, they may be offered privately to a limited number of qualified persons in a private placement. Sometimes a combination of the two is used. The distinction between the two is important to securities regulation and company law. Privately placed securities are not publicly tradable and may only be bought and sold by sophisticated qualified investors. As a result, the secondary market is not nearly as liquid as it is for public (registered) securities.

Another category, sovereign bonds, is generally sold by auction to a specialised class of dealers.

Listing and OTC Dealing

Securities are often listed in a stock exchange, an organised and officially recognised market on which securities can be bought and sold. Issuers may seek listings for their securities to attract investors, by ensuring there is a liquid and regulated market that investors can buy and sell securities in.

Growth in informal electronic trading systems has challenged the traditional business of stock exchanges. Large volumes of securities are also bought and sold "over the counter" (OTC). OTC dealing involves buyers and sellers dealing with each other by telephone or electronically on the basis of prices that are displayed electronically, usually by commercial information vendors such as Super Derivatives, Reuters and Bloomberg.

There are also eurosecurities, which are securities that are issued outside their domestic market into more than one jurisdiction. They are generally listed on the Luxembourg Stock Exchange or admitted to listing in London. The reasons for listing eurobonds include regulatory and tax considerations, as well as the investment restrictions.

Market

London is the centre of the eurosecurities markets. There was a huge rise in the eurosecurities market in London in the early 1980s. Settlement of trades in eurosecurities is currently effected through two European computerized clearing/depositories called Euroclear (in Belgium) and Clearstream (formerly Cedelbank) in Luxembourg.

The main market for Eurobonds is the EuroMTS, owned by BorsaItaliana and Euronext. There are ramp up market in Emergent countries, but it is growing slowly.

Physical Nature of Securities

Certificated Securities: Securities that are represented in paper (physical) form are called certificated securities. They may be *bearer* or *registered.*

DRS Securities

Securities may also be held in the Direct Registration System (DRS), which is a method of recording shares of stock in book-entry form. Book-entry means the company's transfer agent maintains the shares on the owner's behalf without the need for physical share certificates. Shares held in un-certificated book-entry form have the same rights and privileges as shares held in certificated form.

Bearer Securities

Bearer securities are completely negotiable and entitle the holder to the rights under the security (e.g. to payment if it is a debt security, and voting if it is an equity security). They are transferred by delivering the instrument from person to person. In some cases, transfer is by endorsement, or signing the back of the instrument, and delivery.

Regulatory and fiscal authorities sometimes regard bearer securities negatively, as they may be used to facilitate the evasion of regulatory restrictions and tax. In the United Kingdom, for example, the issue of bearer securities was heavily restricted firstly by the *Exchange Control Act* 1947 until 1953. Bearer securities are very rare in the United States because of the negative tax implications they may have to the issuer and holder.

Registered Securities

In the case of registered securities, certificates bearing the name of the holder are issued, but these merely represent the securities. A person does not automatically acquire legal ownership by having possession of the certificate. Instead, the issuer (or its appointed agent) maintains a register in which details of the holder of the securities are entered and updated as appropriate. A transfer of registered securities is effected by amending the register.

Non-Certificated Securities and Global Certificates

Modern practice has developed to eliminate both the need for certificates and maintenance of a complete security register by the issuer. There are two general ways this has been accomplished.

Non-Certificated Securities

In some jurisdictions, such as France, it is possible for issuers of that jurisdiction to maintain a legal record of their securities electronically.

In the United States, the current "official" version of Article 8 of the Uniform Commercial Code permits non-certificated securities. However, the "official" UCC is a mere draft that must be enacted individually by each U.S. state. Though all 50 states (as well as the District of Columbia and the U.S. Virgin Islands) have enacted some form of Article 8, many of them still appear to use older versions of Article 8, including some that did not permit non-certificated securities.

Global Certificates, Book Entry Interests, Depositories

To facilitate the electronic transfer of interests in securities without dealing with inconsistent versions of Article 8, a system has developed whereby issuers deposit a single global certificate representing all the outstanding securities of a class or series with a universal depository. This depository is called The Depository Trust Company, or DTC. DTC's parent, Depository Trust & Clearing Corporation (DTCC), is a non-profit cooperative owned by approximately thirty of the largest Wall Street players that typically act as brokers or dealers in securities. These thirty banks are called the DTC participants. DTC, through a legal nominee, owns each of the global securities on behalf of all the DTC participants.

All securities traded through DTC are in fact held, in electronic form, on the books of various intermediaries between the ultimate owner, e.g. a retail investor, and the DTC participants. For example, Mr. Smith may hold 100 shares of Coca Cola, Inc. in his brokerage account at local broker Jones & Co. brokers. In turn, Jones & Co. may hold 1000 shares of Coca Cola on behalf of Mr. Smith and nine other customers. These 1000 shares are held by Jones & Co. in an account with Goldman Sachs, a DTC participant, or in an account at another DTC participant. Goldman Sachs in turn may hold millions of Coca Cola shares on its books on behalf of hundreds of brokers similar to Jones & Co. Each day, the DTC participants settle their accounts with the other DTC participants and adjust the number of shares held on their books for the benefit of customers like Jones & Co. Ownership of securities in this fashion is called beneficial ownership. Each intermediary holds on behalf of someone beneath him in the chain. The ultimate owner is called the beneficial owner. This is also referred to as owning in "Street name".

Among brokerages and mutual fund companies, a large amount of mutual fund share transactions take place among intermediaries as opposed to shares being sold and redeemed directly with the transfer agent of the fund. Most of these intermediaries such as brokerage firms clear the shares electronically through the National Securities Clearing Corp. or "NSCC", a subsidiary of DTCC.

Other Depositories: Euroclear and Clearstream

Besides DTC, two other large securities depositories exist, both in Europe: Euroclear and Clearstream.

Divided and Undivided Security

The terms "divided" and "undivided" relate to the proprietary nature of a security.

Each divided security constitutes a separate asset, which is legally distinct from each other security in the same issue. Pre-electronic bearer securities were divided. Each instrument constitutes the separate covenant of the issuer and is a separate debt.

With undivided securities, the entire issue makes up one single asset, with each of the securities being a fractional part of this undivided whole. Shares in the secondary markets are always undivided. The issuer owes only one set of obligations to shareholders under its memorandum, articles of association and company law. A share represents an undivided fractional part of the issuing company. Registered debt securities also have this undivided nature.

Fungible and Non-Fungible Security

The terms "fungible" and "non-fungible" are a feature of assets. If an asset is fungible, this means that if such an asset is lent, or placed with a custodian, it is customary for the borrower or custodian to be obliged at the end of the loan or custody arrangement to return assets equivalent to the original asset, rather than the specific identical asset. In other words, the redelivery of fungibles is equivalent and not *in specie*. For example, if an owner of 100 shares of IBM transfers custody of those shares to another party to hold for a purpose, at the end of the arrangement, the holder need simply provide the owner with 100 shares of IBM identical to those received. Cash is also an example of a fungible asset. The exact currency notes received need not be segregated and returned to the owner.

Undivided securities are always fungible by logical necessity. Divided securities may or may not be fungible, depending on market practice. The clear trend is towards fungible arrangements.

Regulation

In the US, the public offer and sale of securities must be either registered pursuant to a registration statement that is filed with the U.S. Securities and Exchange Commission (SEC) or are offered and sold pursuant to an exemption therefrom. Dealing in securities is regulated by both federal authorities (SEC) and state securities departments. In addition, the brokerage industry is supposedly self policed by Self Regulatory Organisations (SROs), such as the Financial Industry Regulatory Authority (FINRA), formerly the National Association of Securities Dealers (or NASD) or the MSRB.

With respect to investment schemes that do not fall within the traditional categories of securities listed in the definition of a security (Sec. 2(a)(1) of the 33 act and Sec. 3(a)(10) of the 34 act) the US Courts have developed a broad definition for securities that must then be registered with the SEC. When determining if there a is an "investment contract" that must be registered the courts look for an investment of money, a common enterprise and expectation of profits to come primarily from the efforts of others.

Capital Structure and the Prediction of Bankruptcy

The recent bankruptcies of Enron and Worldcom have underlined the importance of default prediction both in academia and in industry. It now seems more necessary than ever to develop early warning systems that can help prevent or avert corporate default and that facilitate the selection of firms to collaborate with or invest in. Research on default prediction has been conducted for many decades and a very large number of empirical studies has been published since the pioneering work of Beaver (1966, 1968) and Altman (1968). The initial approach to predicting corporate failure has been to apply a statistical classification technique (usually discriminant analysis) to a sample containing both failed and non-failed firms. Examples of such studies are Deakin (1972) and Altman et al. (1977). After that, emphasis shifted toward probit or logit analysis. Martin (1977) and Ohlson (1980) were among the first to apply these techniques, followed by e.g. Wiginton (1980), Zmijewski (1984), Zavgren (1985), Aziz and Lawson (1989), Lennox (1999) and Westgaard& Van der Wijst (2001)). Other statistical techniques have also been introduced, such as recursive partitioning (Frydman et al. (1985)), catastrophe theory (Gregory et al. (1991)), multidimensional scaling (Mar Molinero and Ezzamel (1991)), neural networks (Tam and Kiang (1992)), multinominallogit models (Johnsen and Melicher (1994)), multicriteria decision aid methodology (Zopounidis and Doumpos, 1999) and rough sets (Dimitras et al., 1999). Reviews studies can be found in Jones (1987), Karels and Prakash (1987) and Dimitras et al. (1996).

The general conclusions from this extensive research effort seem to be that each study by itself provides a reasonable discrimination between failed and non-failed firms, but also, and perhaps more significantly, that the various studies hardly show any agreement on what factors are important for failure prediction. Indeed, it can be said that more than 30 years of empirical research on bankruptcy prediction failed to produce agreement on which variables are good predictors and why. This discord of conclusions can, of course, partly be attributed to the fact that the studies refer to different periods, countries and industries. Another factor may be that virtually all of these studies lack a theoretical framework to guide the empirical research effort. In the absence of a theory that provides testable hypotheses, each empirical result has to be evaluated on its own merits and one can only hope that patterns emerge from the multitude of results. This is obviously not the case in the default prediction.

This paper addresses the theoretical underpinnings of bankruptcy prediction, taking the well-known neo-classical theory of capital structure as a starting point. Thus, it follows an alternative approach compared to the well-known Merton model (Merton, 1974), that is based on option pricing theory and that is elaborated into the KMV model. The origins of a capital structure based default theory lie, on the one hand, in models that relate the risk of ruin to the valuation of corporate claims). A later elaboration can be found in Scott (1981). On the other hand, they lie in the models of optimal capital structure that were developed in the wake of the famous Modigliani-Miller irrelevance theorem (Modigliani and Miller (1958, 1963), Baxter (1967),

Kraus and Litzenberger (1973), Scott (1976), and Kim (1978)). Practically all models of optimal capital structure use a default (or bankruptcy) condition in the derivation of optimal capital structure. This condition captures the essence of the default decision: it obtains when the value of the various cash flows available to firm are insufficient to cover the debt obligations. With this, the theory derives properties of the optimal capital structure in its comparative statics, which are the basis for empirical analyses. Surprisingly, these models are seldom, if ever, rewritten to explicitly state the probability of bankruptcy and its characteristics, i.e. how it is influenced by the determinants of optimal capital structure. Since the early eighties, this line of theoretical research appears to be completely outstripped by the option based default theories. This paper aims to contribute to a capital structure based default theory by demonstrating its feasibility in a simple setting, i.e. by using a simple theoretical models and limited empirical analysis.

The organisation of this paper is as follows. Section 2 firstly restates a simple model of optimal capital structure and subsequently rewrites the model to elicit the determinants of the probability of default. Testable hypotheses are formulated on the basis of the comparative statics of the model. These hypotheses are tested empirically on Norwegian firm data from the period 1995-2001. Section 3 describes the data and methodology, section 4 presents and discusses the results. Conclusions are formulated in section 5.

Default Probabilities in a Capital Structurev Framework

A Simple Model of Optimal Capital Structure

The model used here is a simple, single period model of optimal capital structure. The model allows only two market imperfections: taxes and bankruptcy costs. This suffices to capture the essence of the so-called trade-off theory, in which optimal capital structures are set as a trade-off between tax advantages and expected bankruptcy costs. The model is adopted from Van der Wijst (1989), in which a family of related models is elaborated.

The major assumptions of the model are as follows. Capital markets are assumed to be costless and competitive. Corporate profits are taxed at a fixed rate and according to a wealth tax system that allows the deduction of all payments to the debt holders, including principal repayments, from the firm's taxable income. However, there are no other tax deductible items or tax shields and there are no personal taxes. All market participants are assumed to be insatiable and to act rationally. The firm's set of income generating assets is assumed to be fixed; i.e. all investment decisions are already made but the financing decision not. Firms only issue equity and debt. Debt claims are only subject to the risk of default. Finally, investors are assumed to be risk neutral and to have limited liability.

In this setting, a firm's cash flow is the only source that can be used to cover the obligations to the debt holders. Consequently, if these obligations exceed the firm's cash flow, the firm defaults and is declared bankrupt. Thus, the bankruptcy condition, *b*, is:

$$b = \tilde{x} < R \tag{1}$$

where $\tilde{x}$ is a random variable representing the firm's cash flow before interest and taxes and R is the payment to the debtholders, is assumed to be normally distributed with mean m_x and standard deviation s_x . If, at the end of the period, b obtains, stockholders are protected by limited liability and receive nothing. Otherwise they receive the cash flow after taxes and interest. The end of period value of equity, Y_e, is:

$$\begin{aligned} Y_e &= 0 \quad \text{if } \tilde{x} < b \\ Y_e &= (1-\tau)(\tilde{x}-R) \quad \text{if } \tilde{x} \geq b \end{aligned} \tag{2}$$

where *t* is the corporate tax rate. For risk neutral investors, the equilibrium value of equity, V_e.,is the present value, discounted at the risk free interest rate, of the expectation of Y_e, :

$$V_e = \frac{E(Y_e)}{(1+r)} = \frac{(1-\tau)\int_b^{\infty}(\tilde{x}-R)f(\tilde{x})d\tilde{x}}{(1+r)} \tag{3}$$

where *r* is the risk free interest rate. The debt holders' value at the end of the period, Y_d, can be derived in a similar way. If the bankruptcy condition obtains, the firm is transferred to the debtholders, which means that they receive the cash flow minus the bankruptcy costs. Limited liability prevents them from having to accept a negative cash flow. So the end of period value of debt is:

$$\begin{aligned} Y_d &= 0 \text{ if } \tilde{x} \leq 0 \\ Y_d &= \tilde{x} - B(\tilde{x}) \text{ if } 0 < \tilde{x} < b \\ Y_d &= R \text{ if (b=R)} \end{aligned} \tag{4}$$

were $B(\tilde{x})$ is the amount of bankruptcy costs as a function of the cash flow $\tilde{x}$[1]. The equilibrium value of the debt is the present value of the expectation of Y_d:

$$V_d = \frac{\int_0^b (\tilde{x} - B(\tilde{x}))f(\tilde{x})d\tilde{x} + R(1-F)}{(1+r)} \tag{5}$$

where F is defined as the probability to default: $F = \int_{-\infty}^{b} f(\tilde{x})d\tilde{x}$. Since it is defined as a cumulative density function, the probability of default will always be between 0 and 1.

The total value of the firm is found by adding V_e and V_d, which, after rearranging terms, is:

$$V = \frac{\int_0^\infty \tilde{x}f(\tilde{x})d\tilde{x} - \tau\int_b^\infty \tilde{x}f(\tilde{x})d\tilde{x} - \int_0^b B(\tilde{x})f(\tilde{x})d\tilde{x} + \tau R(1-F)}{(1+r)} \tag{6}$$

Optimal capital structure and debt capacity are found by differentiating V and V_d with respect to R:

$$\frac{\partial V}{\partial R} = \frac{\tau(1-F) - B(R)f(R)}{(1+r)} \tag{7}$$

$$\frac{\partial V_d}{\partial R} = \frac{(1-F) - B(R)f(R)}{(1+r)} \tag{8}$$

Where B(R) and f(R) are the bankruptcy cost function and the pdf of the cash flow respectively, both evaluated at the point of optimal capital structure.

Setting equation (8) equal to zero gives the maximum amount of debt the debt holders are willing to supply, which is the firm's debt capacity. Equation (7) set equal to zero gives the amount of debt that maximizes the value of the firm, i.e. the optimal capital structure. It can be shown that for normally distributed cash flows the second order conditions for (7) and (8) are satisfied. Because the corporate tax rate, t, has a value between zero and one, the amount of debt in the optimal capital structure is less than the amount debt holders are willing to supply. This means that equation (8) does not limit the amount of debt the company can obtain, i.e. optimal capital structure is reached before debt capacity. Rewriting equation (7) gives:

$$\frac{\tau(1-F)}{(1+r)} = \frac{B(R)f(R)}{(1+r)} \tag{9}$$

The left hand side represents the present value of the marginal expected tax saving, while the right hand side represents the present value of marginal bankruptcy costs. Thus, the optimal capital structure is reached as the marginal benefits of debt financing equal the marginal costs. A more extensive discussion of the model and further computational details including comparative statics can be found in Van der Wijst (1989).

The Bankruptcy Probability Model

In this section, the capital structure model is reformulated as a bankruptcy probability model and further analysed. Equation (9) represents the optimal choice of capital structure as a function of the tax rate, bankruptcy costs and the distributional properties of the cash flow including the probability of default. Rearranging the terms of equation (9) gives an expression for the probability of default:

$$F = 1 - \frac{B(R)f(R)}{\tau} \tag{10}$$

where all variables are as defined before.

Note that (2.10) reflects the consequences for the probability of default of the decision to maximize the value of the firm using capital structure as an instrument. The default probability itself is neither a goal variable (to be minimized or optimised) nor a direct instrument. The default probability is, of course, manipulated indirectly by choosing levels of R. In equation (10) the default probability is dependent on the tax rate, bankruptcy costs and the distributional properties of the cash flow. To further analyse the model, its comparative statics are calculated. These show the effect on the probability of default, F, of changes in the variables in the model. The comparative statics of the model are given below, some more detailed calculations are appended.

- The default probability F depends on the debt level in the following way:

$$\frac{\partial F}{\partial R} = -\frac{f(R)}{\tau}\left[\frac{B(R)(\mu_x - R)}{\sigma_x^2} + B'(R)\right] < 0 \quad \text{if} \quad \mu_x \geq R \tag{11}$$

Since f(R), the corporate tax rate, the bankruptcy costs, the variance of the cash flow and the first derivative of the bankruptcy costs are all positive, (11) is only strictly negative if $\mu_x \geq R$. Otherwise the sign depends on the relative sizes of the other variables and cannot be determined unambiguously. This means that the effect of leverage on the probability on default cannot be determined unambiguously, and in the range where it can be determined unambiguously its influence is contrary to what conventional wisdom predicts.

- The change in F due to a change in the tax rate is:

$$\frac{\partial F}{\partial \tau} = \frac{B(R)f(R)}{\tau^2} > 0 \tag{12}$$

Both the bankruptcy costs, f(R) and t, the corporate tax rate, are positive. This means that an increase in the corporate tax rate will increase the probability of default. It makes debt financing more attractive on the margin, leading to more debt in the optimal capital structure and higher default probabilities.

- Derivation of F with respect to the bankruptcy costs gives:

$$\frac{\partial F}{\partial B(R)} = -\frac{f(R)}{\tau} < 0 \tag{13}$$

Since f(R) and t are both positive, (13) will be negative. An increase in the bankruptcy costs makes debt financing less attractive on the margin, leading to less debt in the optimal capital structure which reduces the probability of default.

- The change in the standard deviation of the cash flow will affect the probability of default as follows:

$$\frac{\partial F}{\partial \sigma_x} = -\frac{B(R)\frac{\partial f}{\partial \sigma_x}}{\tau} = \frac{f(R)B(R)}{\tau}\left[\frac{1}{\sigma_x} - \frac{(R-\mu_x)^2}{\sigma_x^3}\right] \tag{14}$$

Although (14) looks a bit complicated at first sight, f(R), B(R), τ and σ_x are all positive, so the equation within the square brackets will determine the sign of (14). This can be narrowed down to:

$$\begin{aligned} &\sigma_x^2 - (R-\mu_x)^2 < 0 \quad \text{if}\, R-\mu > \sigma \\ &= 0 \qquad \text{if}\ R-\mu = \sigma \\ &> 0 \qquad \text{if}\ R-\mu_x < \sigma_x \end{aligned} \tag{15}$$

Thus, the comparative static of the standard deviation of the cash flow depends on whether the difference between the expected earnings and the debt obligations is larger or smaller than the standard deviation in earnings.

- Finally, a change in the expectation of the future cash flows m_x on F is:

$$\frac{\partial F}{\partial \mu_x} = -\frac{B(R)\frac{\partial f}{\partial \mu_x}}{\tau} = \frac{f(R)B(R)}{\tau\sigma_x^2}(\mu_x - R) > 0 \ \text{if}\, \mu_x > R \tag{16}$$

$$= 0 \text{ if } \mu_x = R$$

$$< 0 \text{ if } \mu_x < R$$

Since f(R), the bankruptcy costs B(R), the tax rate and the variance of the cash flow are all positive, the sign of (16) depends on the relation between the expectation of the cash flow and the level of debt.

The comparative statics of the default probability model are summarised in Table below.

Table : *The influence of the variables in the model on the probability of default*

Comparative statics: $\frac{\partial F}{\partial ..}$	Expected effect on F
R, debt	Positive or Indetermined
τ, tax rate	Positive
B(R), bankruptcy costs	Negative
σ, std.dev. of cash flow	Positive or Negative
μ, expected cash flow	Positive or Negative

The most striking aspect of table is, of course, that neither capital structure nor the distributional properties of the cash flow (expectation and variance) have a straightforward effect on the probability of default. A comparable conclusion was reached in the comparative statics analysis of the optimal capital structure model (i.e. the probability of default has an ambiguous influence on optimal capital structure). Similar results are occasionally reported on in the literature (Kale et al., 1991) without attracting much attention.

This challenges the conventional wisdom that the probability of default increases, other things equal, with leverage and cash flow variance and decreases with cash flow expectation. Note that is not possible to make assumptions regarding R, μ_x and σ_x that bring all comparative statics in line with conventional wisdom. If leverage and cash flow expectation are to have the 'conventional wisdom' effect, it must be assumed that μ_x<R, but this would give cash flow variance a negative effect, contrary to conventional wisdom.

More research is necessary to determine whether these ambiguous results spring from the extreme ends of the distribution or the central area. At present, we can only formulate hypotheses for the tax rate and the bankruptcy costs, which are hypothesized to have a positive resp, negative effect on default probability. These hypotheses are tested in section 4 using the data described in the next section.

Data and Methodology

Dataset: The data used in this study come from a dataset that comprises all Norwegian limited liability companies (AS Companies) for the period 1995-2000. Companies with total assets or total sales less than 100 000 Norwegian Kroner (approximately $12.500) are excluded from our analysis. This is done to exclude non-operative companies established for e.g. tax advantages only. Second, all companies in our analysis must have delivered their financial statements for every year between 1995 and 2000. Companies that are about to go bankrupt or have gone bankrupt will in many cases not hand in their financial statements in time or even not hand them in at all. Using these selection criteria we are left with roughly 70,000 companies and among these are 149 companies that went bankrupt in the year 2000. 149 companies is a small number compared to the total number of 4,661 companies that went bankrupt in 2000. The reason is the strong restriction we put on the data, demanding that all companies have accounting data available for all years between 1995 and 2000. A random sample of 1394 non-bankrupt companies was selected for the analysis in addition to the 149 bankrupt companies. The construction of the dataset for this study is rather crude and the procedure is chosen for convenience only.

Empirical Model and Proxy Variables

Many variables in the theoretical models refer to future expected values that cannot be measured directly. Instead, empirical proxy variables have to be used, taken from the available accounting data. The proxy variables used in the analysis are:

- *Debt:* the level of debt divided by total assets: DEBT/TA
- *Taxes:* observed tax rate, the amount of tax paid over earnings: TAX/EBIT
- Cash flow expectation (μ_x): accounting cash flow $CF = \dfrac{\text{net profit} + \text{depreciation}}{\text{total assets}}$.
- Standard deviation of cash flow (σ_x): standard deviation of CF calculated over 1995-2000
- Bankruptcy costs B(x): approximated by the size of the company (ln(sales))

Since these variables are straightforward (transformations of) accounting numbers they do not need much discussion. With the exception of cash flow standard deviation, they refer to the year 2001.

The leverage and cash flow variables are included in the analysis without any explicit hypothesis regarding their influence. The tax rate (TAX/EBIT) is hypothesized to be positively related to the probability of default. Bankruptcy costs are generally assumed to be inversely related to size, i.e. bankruptcy costs as a fraction of firm value decreases with size. In our model, bankruptcy costs have a negative effect on the probability of default, so this leads to the hypothesis that size is positively related to default probability. In addition to these 5 financial variables, 8 dummy variables for industrial classification (first digit NACE code, explained in appendix A) are included to capture the effect of omitted variables, if any, that would otherwise disturb the analysis.

Estimation Procedure

The analytical technique used for this study should allow for a binary dependent variable and the testing of the hypotheses formulated in the previous subsection. The latter requirement prohibits the use of classification techniques as discriminant analysis, as the discriminant function coefficients are not unique, only their ratios are). The binary dependent variable essentially rules out usual regression analysis, including the linear probability model. Linear functions are inherently unbounded, while probabilities are bounded by 0 and 1. This makes logit and probit analysis the most obvious candidates for the 'regression' analysis of dichotomous variables. Both models always return values between 0 and 1.

The logit model solves the problem of the bounded dependent variable by transforming the probabilities in such a way that they are no longer bounded. The upper bound is removed by transforming the probability p to the odds ratio p/(1-p). The lower bound is removed by taking the logarithm of the odds ratio: ln(p/(1-p)).

The logit model is linear in the log-odds and this makes the coefficients somewhat easier to interpret than those of the probit model. However, both models are very close and rarely lead to different qualitative conclusions, so that it is difficult to distinguish between them statistically. As a general proposition, the question of the choice between them is unresolved (Greene, 1993). Without decisive arguments pro or contra, logit analysis is used to estimate the influence of the above mentioned variables on the probability of default

The logit model formulated here for the Norwegian data contains a two state dependent variable (state 1 = declared bankrupt in 2001, state 2 = not bankrupt in 2001). The independent variables are the

5 proxy variables described in section 3.2 plus the 8 industry dummies. The logistic regression analysis is performed with the statistical software SPSS).

Logistic Regression Results

The results of the analysis are presented in table presented, where the estimated coefficients and their significance are given. The significance level is calculated with the Wald statistic, that has a chi-square distribution. For variables with a single degree of freedom, as is the case here, the Wald statistic is the square of the ratio of the coefficient to its standard error. Using a 5% significance level, the coefficient of the tax rate is seen to be positive, but not significantly so. The hypothesis regarding the tax rate is not supported in the data, but not rejected either. The analysis provides support for the hypothesized effect of size (measured as ln(sales)) as a proxy for bankruptcy costs: the coefficient is significantly positive.

For the other variables, no unequivocal hypotheses could be derived from the theory, but the results are seen to be in line with what could be expected according to conventional wisdom. Leverage and cash flow standard deviation have a significantly positive effect on default probability, cash flow itself has a significantly negative effect. Only one industry dummy is significantly different from zero, indicating that the other variables to a large extend capture the inter-industry differences in default probability.

As a measure for 'goodness of fit' the Nagelkerke R^2 is used. This statistic measures the proportion of explained "variation" in the logistic model. It is similar in intent to the R^2 in a linear regression model, although the variation in a logistic regression model must be defined differently). According to this measure, the logistic regression model explains 17.4% of the "variation" in the outcome variable. So it must be concluded that the variables used here give an only partial explanation of the probability of default.

Table: *Estimated parameters of the model (significance level in parentheses).*

Variable	*Parameter*
Constant	-3.349(0.000)
Debt / TA	0.485(0.020)
Tax / earnings	0.000(0.354)
Cash flow	-1.459(0.000)

Table conts...

Variable	*Parameter*
Standard dev. of cash flow	0.926(0.005)
ln (sales) (bankr. costs)	0.116(0.046)
Dummy for sector 2	0.259(0.625)
Dummy for sector 3	-0.089(0.896)
Dummy for sector 4	0.026(0.959)
Dummy for sector 5	-0.420(0.372)
Dummy for sector 6	-1.064(0.085)
Dummy for sector 7	-1.329(0.015)
Dummy for sector 8	0.225(0.739)
Dummy for sector 9	-1.252(0.167)
R^2 (Nagelkerke)	0.174

Conclusions

The purpose of this paper is to contribute to a theory of default that is based on capital structure theory, by demonstrating its feasibility in a simple setting. As a preliminary conclusion it can be said that the approach is indeed feasible, but that it clearly has its limitations. One limitation is that some undesirable aspects of the capital structure model are transferred into default probability model. More specifically, the model shows no straightforward relationship between default probability on the one hand and leverage and cash flow characteristics (expectation and variance) on the other. Conventional wisdom generally assumes that such a straightforward relationship exists. In addition, the models appeared to have a limited explanatory power, even if the variables for which no hypothesis could be formulated are included in the empirical analysis. On the other hand, the advantages of a theory based methodology have become apparent along the way: it provides a clear frame of reference in which the results can be evaluated and directions for future research can be specified. This by itself can be a valuable contribution compared to the multitude of theory-less empirical studies and a useful addition to default theory based on option pricing.

Organic Composition of Capital

The organic composition of capital (OCC) is a concept created by Karl Marx in his critique of political economy and used in Marxian economics as a theoretical alternative to neo-classical concepts of factors of production, production functions, capital productivity and capital-output ratios. It is normally defined as the ratio of constant capital (capital invested in plant, equipment and materials) to variable capital (capital invested in the labour-costs involved in hiring employees). The concept does not apply to *all* capital assets, only to capital invested in production (i.e. production capital). The neoclassical concept synonymous to increasing organic composition of capital is capital deepening.

Marx first referred to the idea in 1847 and discussed it in detail in *Capital Vol. 1*, chapter 25 ("The General law of Capitalist Accumulation"]). In *Capital Vol. 3* Marx demonstrates that the organic composition of capital decisively influences industrial profitability.

According to Marx, the OCC expresses the specific form which the capitalist mode of production gives to the relationship between means of production and labour power, determining the productivity of labour and the creation of a surplus product. This relationship has both technical and social aspects, reflecting the fact that simultaneously consumable use values and commercial exchange-values are being produced.

Marx calls this capital composition "organic", because it refers to the relationship between "living" and "dead" (or inert) elements in a capital investment. The "living element" is employed labour actively at work. The "dead" parts are the tools, materials and equipment worked with, which are the results of past labour.

Marx argues that a rising organic composition of capital is a necessary effect of capital accumulation and competition in the sphere of production, at least in the long term. This means that the share of constant capital in the total capital outlay increases, and that labour input per product unit declines.

Definition

The concept is introduced in chapter 25 of Das Kapital, where Marx writes:

"In this chapter we consider the influence of the growth of capital on the lot of the labouring class. The most important factor in this inquiry is the composition of capital and the changes it undergoes in the course of the process of accumulation. The composition of capital is to be understood in a two-fold sense. On the side of value, it is determined by the proportion in which it is divided into constant capital or value of the means of production, and variable capital or value of labour-power, the sum total of wages. On the side of material, as it functions in the process of production, all capital is divided into means of production and living labour-power. This latter composition is determined by the relation between the mass of the means of production employed, on the one hand, and the mass of labour necessary for their employment on the other. I call the former the value-composition, the latter the technical composition of capital. Between the two there is a strict correlation. To express this, I call the value-composition of capital, in so far as it is determined by its technical composition and mirrors the changes of the latter, the organic composition of capital."

In his discussion, Marx leaves out of account components of capital other than labour-power and means of production invested in, such as the faux frais of production (incidental expenses).

The full importance of the OCC emerges in chapter 8 of the third volume of Das Kapital

Ratios

The value composition of capital (VCC) is usually expressed as a ratio of constant capital to variable capital, or $\frac{c}{v}$. Other measures are also used in the Marxian literature. One is $\frac{c}{s+v}$. This is the ratio of constant capital to newly produced value (roughly, what modern economists call "value added"), i.e., surplus-value + variable capital and close to the concept of a capital/output ratio. Less common is the measure used by Paul M. Sweezy, i.e., $\frac{c}{c+v}$, the ratio of constant capital to the total capital invested.

The total capital tied up by a capitalist enterprise of course includes more than fixed assets, materials and wages/salaries; it also includes liquid funds, reserves and other financial assets. For instance, an employer must normally reserve funds to pay for ongoing operating expenses, until these are recouped from product sales.

4

New Stock Offerings and Stockholder's Returns

Initial Public Offering

An initial public offering (IPO) or stock market launch is a type of public offering where shares of stock in a company are sold to the general public, on a securities exchange, for the first time. Through this process, a private company transforms into a public company. Initial public offerings are used by companies to raise expansion capital, to possibly monetize the investments of early private investors, and to become publicly traded enterprises.

A company selling shares is never required to repay the capital to its public investors. After the IPO, when shares trade freely in the open market, money passes between public investors. Although an IPO offers many advantages, there are also significant disadvantages, chief among these the costs associated with the process and the requirement to disclose certain information that could prove helpful to competitors, or create difficulties with vendors.

Details of the proposed offering are disclosed to potential purchasers in the form of a lengthy document known as a prospectus. Most companies undertake an IPO with the assistance of an investment banking firm acting in the capacity of an underwriter. Underwriters provide several services, including help with correctly assessing the value of shares (share price), and establishing a public market for shares (initial sale).

Alternative methods such as the dutch auction have also been explored. In terms of size and public participation, the most notable example of this method is the Google IPO. China has recently emerged as a major IPO market, with several of the largest IPOs taking place in that country.

History

The earliest form of a company which issued public shares was the *publicani* during the Roman Republic. Like modern joint-stock companies, the *publicani* were legal bodies independent of their members whose ownership was divided into shares, or *parties*. There is evidence that these shares were sold to public investors and traded in a type of over-the-counter market in the Forum, near the Temple of Castor and Pollux. The shares fluctuated in value, encouraging the activity of speculators, or *quaestors*. Mere evidence remains of the prices for which *partes* were sold, the nature of initial public offerings, or a description of stock market behaviour. *Publicanis* lost favour with the fall of the Republic and the rise of the Empire.

In March 1602 the "Vereenigde Oost-Indische Compagnie (VOC), or Dutch East India Company was formed. The VOC was the first modern company to issue public shares, and it is this issuance, at the beginning of the 17th century, that is considered the first modern IPO. The company had an original paid-up share capital of 6,424,588 guilders. The ability to raise this large sum is attributable to the decision taken by the owners to open up access to share ownership to a wide public. Everyone living in the United Provinces had an opportunity to participate in the Company. Each share was worth 3000 guilders (roughly equivalent to US$1,500). All the shares were tradable, and the shareholders received receipts for the purchase. A share certificate documenting payment and ownership such as we know today was not issued but ownership was instead entered in the company's share register.

Reasons for Listing

Advantages

When a company lists its securities on a public exchange, the money paid by the investing public for the newly issued shares goes directly to the company (primary offering) as well as to any early private investors who opt to sell all or a portion of their holdings (secondary offering) as part of the larger IPO. An IPO, therefore, allows a company to tap into a wide pool of potential investors to provide itself with capital for future growth, repayment of debt, or working capital. A company selling common shares is never required to repay the capital to its public investors. Those investors must endure the unpredictable nature of the open market to price and trade their shares. After the IPO, when shares trade freely in the open market, money passes between public investors. For early private investors who choose to sell shares as part of the IPO process, the IPO represents an opportunity to monetize their investment. After the IPO, once shares trade in the open market, investors holding large blocks of shares can either sell those shares piecemeal in the open market, or sell a large block of shares directly to the public, at a fixed price, through a secondary market offering. This type of offering is not dilutive, since no new shares are being created.

Once a company is listed, it is able to issue additional common shares in a number of different ways, one of which is the follow-on offering. This method provides capital for various corporate purposes through the issuance of equity without incurring any debt. This ability to quickly raise potentially large amounts of capital from the marketplace is a key reason many companies seek to go public.

An IPO accords several benefits to the previously private company:

- Enlarging and diversifying equity base
- Enabling cheaper access to capital
- Increasing exposure, prestige, and public image
- Attracting and retaining better management and employees through liquid equity participation
- Facilitating acquisitions (potentially in return for shares of stock)
- Creating multiple financing opportunities: equity, convertible debt, cheaper bank loans, etc.

Disadvantages

There are several disadvantages to completing an initial public offering:

- Significant legal, accounting and marketing costs, many of which are ongoing
- Requirement to disclose financial and business information
- Meaningful time, effort and attention required of senior management
- Risk that required funding will not be raised
- Public dissemination of information which may be useful to competitors, suppliers and customers.
- Loss of control and stronger agency problems due to new shareholders

Procedure

Advance Planning

Planning is crucial to a successful IPO. One book suggests the following 7 advance planning steps: (1) develop an impressive management and professional team; (2) grow the company's business with an eye to the public marketplace; (3) obtain audited financial statements using IPO-accepted accounting principles; (4) clean up the company's act; (5) establish antitakeover defences; (6) develop good corporate governance; (7) create insider bail-out opportunities and take advantage of IPO windows.

Retention of Underwriters

IPOs generally involve one or more investment banks known as "underwriters". The company offering its shares, called the "issuer", enters into a contract with a lead underwriter to sell its shares to the public. The underwriter then approaches investors with offers to sell those shares.

A large IPO is usually underwritten by a "syndicate" of investment banks, the largest of which take the position of "lead underwriter". Upon selling the shares, the underwriters retain a portion of the proceeds as their fee. This fee is called an underwriting spread. The spread is calculated as a discount from the price of the shares sold (called the gross spread). Components of an underwriting spread in an initial public offering (IPO) typically include the following (on a per share basis): Manager's fee, Underwriting fee—earned by members of the syndicate, and the Concession—earned by the broker-dealer selling the shares.

The Manager would be entitled to the entire underwriting spread. A member of the syndicate is entitled to the underwriting fee and the concession. A broker dealer who is not a member of the syndicate but sells shares would receive only the concession, while the member of the syndicate who provided the shares to that broker dealer would retain the underwriting fee. Usually, the managing/lead underwriter, also known as the bookrunner, typically the underwriter selling the largest proportions of the IPO, takes the highest portion of the gross spread, up to 8% in some cases.

Multinational IPOs may have many syndicates to deal with differing legal requirements in both the issuer's domestic market and other regions. For example, an issuer based in the E.U. may be represented by the main selling syndicate in its domestic market, Europe, in addition to separate syndicates or selling groups for US/

Canada and for Asia. Usually, the lead underwriter in the main selling group is also the lead bank in the other selling groups.

Because of the wide array of legal requirements and because it is an expensive process, IPOs also typically involve one or more law firms with major practices in securities law, such as the Magic Circle firms of London and the white shoe firms of New York City.

Financial historians Richard Sylla and Robert E. Wright have shown that before 1860 most early U.S. corporations sold shares in themselves directly to the public without the aid of intermediaries like investment banks. The direct public offering or DPO, as they term it, was not done by auction but rather at a share price set by the issuing corporation. In this sense, it is the same as the fixed price public offers that were the traditional IPO method in most non-US countries in the early 1990s. The DPO eliminated the agency problem associated with offerings intermediated by investment banks. There has recently been a movement based on crowd funding to revive the popularity of Direct Public Offerings.

Allocation and Pricing

The sale (allocation and pricing) of shares in an IPO may take several forms. Common methods include:

- Best efforts contract
- Firm commitment contract
- All-or-none contract
- Bought deal

Public offerings are sold to both institutional investors and retail clients of the underwriters. A licensed securities salesperson (Registered Representative in the USA and Canada) selling shares of a public offering to his clients is paid a portion of the selling concession (the fee paid by the issuer to the underwriter) rather than by his client. In some situations, when the IPO is not a "hot" issue (undersubscribed), and where the salesperson is the client's advisor, it is possible that the financial incentives of the advisor and client may not be aligned.

The issuer usually allows the underwriters an option to increase the size of the offering by up to 15% under certain circumstance known as the greenshoe or overallotment option. This option is always exercised when the offering is considered a "hot" issue, by virtue of being oversubscribed.

In the USA, clients are given a preliminary prospectus, known as a red herring prospectus, during the initial quiet period. The red herring prospectus is so named because of a bold red warning statement printed on its front cover. The warning states that the offering information is incomplete, and may be changed. The actual wording can vary, although most roughly follow the format exhibited on the Facebook IPO red herring. During the quiet period, the shares cannot be offered for sale. Brokers can, however, take indications of interest from their clients. At the time of the stock launch, after the Registration Statement has become effective, indications of interest can be converted to buy orders, at the discretion of the buyer. Sales can only be made through a final prospectus cleared by the Securities and Exchange Commission.

Before legal actions initiated by New York Attorney General Eliot Spitzer, which later became known as the Global Settlement enforcement agreement, some large investment firms had initiated favourable research coverage of companies in an effort to aid Corporate Finance departments and retail divisions engaged in the marketing of new issues. The central issue in that enforcement agreement had been judged in court previously. It involved the conflict of interest between the investment banking and analysis departments of ten of the largest investment firms in the United States. The investment firms involved in the settlement had all engaged in actions and practices that had allowed the inappropriate influence of their research analysts by their investment bankers seeking lucrative fees. A typical violation addressed by the settlement was the case of CSFB and Salomon Smith Barney, which were alleged to have engaged in inappropriate spinning of "hot" IPOs and issued fraudulent research reports in violation of various sections within the Securities Exchange Act of 1934.

Pricing of IPO

A company planning an IPO typically appoints a lead manager, known as a bookrunner, to help it arrive at an appropriate price at which the shares should be issued. There are two primary ways in which the price of an IPO can be determined. Either the company, with the help of its lead managers, fixes a price ("fixed price method"), or the price can be determined through analysis of confidential investor demand data compiled by the bookrunner ("book building").

Historically, some IPOs both globally and in the United States have been underpriced. The effect of "initial underpricing" an IPO is to generate additional interest in the stock when it first becomes publicly traded. Flipping, or quickly selling shares for a profit, can lead to significant gains for investors who have been allocated shares of the IPO at the offering price. However, underpricing an IPO results in lost potential capital for the issuer. One extreme example is theglobe.com IPO which helped fuel the IPO "mania" of the late 90's internet era. Underwritten by Bear Stearns on November 13, 1998, the IPO was priced at $9 per share. The share price quickly increased 1000% after the opening of trading, to a high of $97. Selling pressure from institutional flipping eventually drove the stock back down, and it closed the day at $63. Although the company did raise about $30 million from the offering it is estimated that with the level of demand for the offering and the volume of trading that took place the company might have left upwards of $200 million on the table.

The danger of overpricing is also an important consideration. If a stock is offered to the public at a higher price than the market will pay, the underwriters may have trouble meeting their commitments to sell shares. Even if they sell all of the issued shares, the stock may fall in value on the first day of trading. If so, the stock may lose its marketability and hence even more of its value. This could result in losses for investors, many of whom being the most favoured clients of the underwriters. Perhaps the best known example of this is the Facebook IPO in 2012.

Underwriters, therefore, take many factors into consideration when pricing an IPO, and attempt to reach an offering price that is low enough to stimulate interest in the stock, but high enough to raise an adequate amount of capital for the company. The process of determining an optimal price usually involves the underwriters ("syndicate") arranging share purchase commitments from leading institutional investors.

Some researchers (e.g. Geoffrey C., and C. Swift, 2009) believe that the underpricing of IPOs is less a deliberate act on the part of issuers and/or underwriters, than the result of an over-reaction on the part of investors (Friesen & Swift, 2009). One potential method for determining underpricing is through the use of IPO Underpricing Algorithms.

Dutch Auction

A Dutch Auction allows shares of an initial public offering to be allocated based only on price aggressiveness, with all successful bidders paying the same price per share. One version of the Dutch auction is OpenIPO, which is based on an auction system designed by Nobel Prize-winning economist William Vickrey. This auction method ranks bids from highest to lowest, then accepts the highest bids that allow all shares to be sold, with all winning bidders paying the same price.

It is similar to the model used to auction Treasury bills, notes, and bonds since the 1990s. Before this, Treasury bills were auctioned through a discriminatory or pay-what-you-bid auction, in which the various winning bidders each paid the price (or yield) they bid, and thus the various winning bidders did not all pay the same price. Both discriminatory and uniform price or "Dutch" auctions have been used for IPOs in many countries, although only uniform price auctions have been used so far in the US. Large IPO auctions include Japan Tobacco, Singapore Telecom, BAA Plc and Google (ordered by size of proceeds).

A variation of the Dutch Auction has been used to take a number of U.S. companies public including Morningstar, Interactive Brokers Group, Overstock.com, Ravenswood Winery, Clean Energy Fuels, and Boston Beer Company. In 2004, Google used the Dutch Auction system for its Initial Public Offering. Traditional U.S. investment banks have shown resistance to the idea of using an auction process to engage in public securities offerings. The auction method allows for equal access to the allocation of shares and eliminates the favourable treatment accorded important clients by the underwriters in conventional IPOs. In the face of this resistance, the Dutch Auction is still a little used method in U.S. public offerings, although there have been hundreds of auction IPOs in other countries.

In determining the success or failure of a Dutch Auction, one must consider competing objectives. If the objective is to reduce risk, a traditional IPO may be more effective because the underwriter manages the process, rather than leaving the outcome in part to random chance in terms of who chooses to bid or what strategy each bidder chooses to follow. From the viewpoint of the investor, the Dutch Auction allows everyone equal access. Moreover, some forms of the Dutch Auction allow the underwriter to be more active in coordinating bids and even communicating general auction trends to some bidders during the bidding period. Some have also argued that a uniform price auction is more effective at price discovery, although the theory behind this is based on the assumption of independent private values (that the value of IPO shares to each bidder is entirely independent of their value to others, even though the shares will shortly be traded on the aftermarket). Theory that incorporates assumptions more appropriate to IPOs does not find that sealed bid auctions are an effective form of price discovery, although possibly some modified form of auction might give a better result.

In addition to the extensive international evidence that auctions have not been popular for IPOs, there is no U.S. evidence to indicate that the Dutch Auction fares any better than the traditional IPO in an unwelcoming market environment. A Dutch Auction IPO by WhiteGlove Health, Inc., announced in May 2011 was postponed in September of that year, after several failed attempts to price. An article in the *Wall Street Journal* cited the reasons as "Broader stock-market volatility and uncertainty about the global economy have made investors wary of investing in new stocks."

Quiet Period

Under American securities law, there are two time windows commonly referred to as "quiet periods" during an IPO's history. The first and the one linked above is the period of time following the filing of the company's S-1 but before SEC staff declare the registration statement effective. During this time, issuers, company insiders, analysts, and other parties are legally restricted in their ability to discuss or promote the upcoming IPO (U.S. Securities and Exchange Commission, 2005).

The other "quiet period" refers to a period of 40 calendar days following an IPO's first day of public trading. During this time, insiders and any underwriters involved in the IPO are restricted from issuing any earnings forecasts or research reports for the company. Regulatory changes enacted by the SEC as part of the Global Settlement enlarged the "quiet period" from 25 days to 40 days on July 9, 2002. When the quiet period is over, generally the underwriters will initiate research coverage on the firm. For a company with less than $1B in revenue, this quiet period was reduced to 25 days by the JOBS act of 2012. Additionally, the NASDAQ and NYSE have approved a rule mandating a 10-day quiet period after a Secondary Offering and a 15-day quiet period both before and after expiration of a "lock-up agreement" for a securities offering.

Delivery of Shares

Not all IPOs are eligible for delivery settlement through the DTC system, which would then either require the physical delivery of the stock certificates to the clearing agent bank's custodian, or a delivery versus payment (DVP) arrangement with the selling group brokerage firm.

Stag Profit (Flipping)

"Stag profit" is a situation in the stock market before and immediately after a company's Initial public offering (or any new issue of shares). A "stag" is a party or individual who subscribes to the new issue expecting the price of the stock to rise immediately upon the start of trading. Thus, stag profit is the financial gain accumulated by the party or individual resulting from the value of the shares rising. This term is more popular in the United Kingdom than in the United States. In the US, such investors are usually called flippers, because they get shares in the offering and then immediately turn around "flipping" or selling them on the first day of trading.

Documents under seal in a decade-long lawsuit concerning eToys.com's IPO but obtained by *New York Times* Wall Street Business columnist Joe Nocera alleged that IPOs managed by Goldman Sachs and other investment bankers involved asking for kickbacks from their institutional clients who made large profits flipping IPOs which Goldman had intentionally undervalued. Depositions in the lawsuit alleged that clients willingly complied with these demands because they understood it was necessary in order to participate in future hot issues. *Reuters* Wall Street correspondent Felix Salmon retracted his earlier, more conciliatory, statements on the subject and said he believed that the depositions show that companies going public and their initial consumer stockholders are both defrauded by this practice, which may be widespread throughout the IPO finance industry. The case is ongoing, and the allegations remain unproven.

Direct Public Offering

A Direct Public Offering (DPO) is a method by which a business can offer stock directly to the public.

Description

A DPO is similar to an initial public offering (IPO) in that stock is sold to investors, but unlike an IPO, a company uses a DPO to raise capital directly and without a firm underwriting from an investment banking firm or broker-dealer. A DPO will generally have a sponsoring FINRA broker, but in the case of a DPO, the FINRA broker does not guarantee full subscription of the offering. In this instance, the broker merely assures compliance with all applicable Securities and Exchange Commission (SEC) rules that the offering must comply with. Following registration with the SEC and subject to compliance with state blue sky laws, a company can sell its shares directly to anyone, even non-accredited investors, including customers, employees, suppliers, distributors, family, friends and others.

Not all DPOs require registration with the SEC. Some offerings will qualify for an exemption from the federal registration requirements. The most commonly used exemptions are for intrastate offerings and offerings under $1 million (the Rule 504 exemption). In such cases, state level registration is generally required. State level registration is usually less onerous and time consuming than federal registration.

Some law firms and other service providers offer to manage a DPO within twelve months, for less than $100,000. The process and time required to become public is similar to the process utilised by large companies to complete an IPO, except that many DPOs are marketed via internet advertising and ads direct to consumers.

Offerings that do not require federal registration can be done more cheaply and quickly - costs can range from $25,000-$50,000 and it can take as little as one month to complete the process.

Direct public offerings are primarily utilised by small to medium size companies who are unable to attract the interest of an investment banking firm to represent them in a traditional initial public offering. Investment bankers represent companies which can attract and support large financing from which they can earn a commission.

Direct public offerings are now being issued on crowdfunding platform sites. This style of DPO combines the success of WIT capital and platforms like Kickstarter. Many companies offer software and services to facilitate electronic DPOs on their websites.

Pros and Cons

The advantages of a direct public offering include: broader access to investment capital, the ability to utilise stock to complete acquisitions and stock options to attract and retain employees, enhanced credibility and providing early investors with liquidity.

The disadvantages of a direct public offering include: the company must raise its own capital without the assistance of professional financiers, the process has significant cost which offsets any capital raised, it takes management time and attention from business operations and there are ongoing financial and legal reporting requirements.

Requirements

Any company following the applicable rules and regulations can go public by direct public offering. There are no sales, profit, asset or other traditional requirements or qualifications.

Companies interested in completing a direct public offering must have:

1. a complete set of internally generated financial statements
2. financial statements audited by a qualified accounting firm

3. a registration statement filed and declared effective by the Securities and Exchange Commission

After the Securities and Exchange Commission declares a registration statement effective and subject to compliance with state blue sky laws, a company may sell its shares to the public using a variety of methods. Upon completion of the public offering, the company may find a market maker to file an application for a trading symbol and stock listing.

Some companies attempt to organise their financial statements, audit and legal filings on their own, but many utilise direct public offering services offered by a consulting firm.

Alternative Public Offering

An alternative public offering (APO) is the combination of a reverse merger with a simultaneous private investment of public equity (PIPE). It allows companies an alternative to an initial public offering (IPO) as a means of going public while raising capital.

Overview

There are two parts that comprise an APO: the reverse merger and the PIPE. In the reverse merger, the private company becomes public by merging with or being acquired by a public "shell" company. The shell company is a public company that has no assets or liabilities. When the private company and public shell merge, the combined entity thereafter trades under the previously private company's name rather than the shell company's name as it did before.

What differentiates an APO from a reverse merger is the simultaneous PIPE raise. A PIPE is when a publicly traded company sells its stock to investors in a privately negotiated transaction. The stock is normally sold at a discount to current market value and investors are normally acquiring unregistered "restricted" stock. The typical PIPE investor is an institutional investor such as a hedge fund or mutual fund. PIPEs are usually completed by investment banks who act as "Placement Agent" in the transaction.

Process

An APO is a quick transaction compared to an initial public offering (IPO). At the closing of an APO, the public shell and private company sign merger documents to complete the reverse merger; file a 8K with the Securities and Exchange Commission (SEC), which is the required public disclosure of transaction; file a registration statement with the SEC to register the PIPE shares; release PIPE funds from escrow; and issue a press release announcing the completion of the transaction. The company's stock now begins trading on the OTCBB, reflecting the new valuation.

A company can close an APO in as little as 30 – 45 days. After the close of an APO, the company is funded and has exactly the same SEC disclosure requirements as an IPO. Approximately 3 to 4 months after the completion of the APO, the company's registration statement should clear comments and "go effective" with the SEC. When this is accomplished the company can then submit its application to obtain a listing on NASDAQ, AMEX, or NYSE. Listing approval for the exchanges typically takes about one month. At this point analyst research coverage begins and the company focuses on IR efforts, non-deal roadshow, conferences etc.

At the conclusion of a successful APO transaction, a company has received equity funding and has a base of institutional investors. The company has the sponsorship of an investment bank and is exchange listed with analyst coverage. There is now a true market value for the company and the company is positioned to raise additional capital in PIPE transactions.

Benefits

Companies want to become public through an APO for several reasons. The public shell company already has shareholders, so after the APO is complete, the formerly private company typically already meets the shareholder requirements for NASDAQ and AMEX; 400 and 300 respectively. A company that goes public through an IPO must sell its stock to a large number of shareholders in order to meet these requirements necessitating a broad marketing and roadshow process. Unlike an IPO, there is no public disclosure required until the transaction closes. Customers, suppliers, employees, and press are unaware until closing. Therefore, a private company can pursue going public through an APO and understand what kind of investor response and valuation they will receive without having to make the "leap of faith" requirement of an IPO. With an IPO a company must publicly announce its intentions and file with the SEC at the beginning of the process. It is only after clearing comments with the SEC and after going on the roadshow that a company learns what kind of investor response and valuation it will receive.

The APO model owes much of its success to the involvement of the Investment Bank as the gatekeeper that standalone reverse mergers never had. In a traditional reverse merger, anyone could simply buy a shell and go public whether or not they had sufficient financial performance to justify being a public company. With an APO, the investment bank would not raise capital for a company that it did not believe would be successful in the marketplace. This is why the APO has such a high success rate. The investment bank also brings research, trading and liquidity to the company's stock after the transaction closes. Investment banks find the APO process appealing because they can receive the same fees and breakage for raising the capital as they do in an IPO in a much condensed period of time and to a significantly smaller number of investors.

PIPE investors are attracted to the APO because they get to buy stock at a negotiated discount to the projected public market value of a company. In addition, because the company completed a reverse merger and is now public, there is a guaranteed exit defined upfront if they wish to get out. After a company completes an APO, potential investors will be inclined to invest in additional PIPE raises for the company because the public company has had SEC disclosures from day one including audited financial statements, Sarbanes-Oxley, 10Qs, 8Ks, etc. Many tier 1 hedge funds are active investors in APO and many investment banks support the process. There are many tier 2 and tier 3 banks that are active in APO business.

Disadvantages

Investors expect a discount on stock since they are buying restricted securities and thus this is a more expensive cost of capital to the company. The aftermarket of an APO typically takes 6–12 months to develop and thus there is minimal stock liquidity immediately at closing.

Public Offering

A public offering is the offering of securities of a company or a similar corporation to the public. Generally, the securities are to be listed on a stock exchange. In most jurisdictions, a public offering requires the issuing company to publish a prospectus detailing the terms and rights attached to the offered security, as well as information on the company itself and its finances. Many other regulatory requirements surround any public offering and they vary according to jurisdiction.

Initial public offering (IPO) is one type of public offering. Not all public offerings are IPOs. An IPO occurs only when a company offers its shares (not other securities) for the first time for public ownership and trading, an act making it a public company. However, public offerings are also made by already-listed companies. The company issues additional securities to the public, adding to those currently being traded. For example, a listed company with 8 million shares outstanding can offer to the public another 2 million shares. This is a public offering but not an IPO. Once the transaction is complete, the company will have 10 million shares outstanding. Non-initial public offering of equity is also called seasoned equity offering.

A shelf prospectus is often used by companies in exactly that situation. Instead of drafting one before each public offering, the company can file a single prospectus detailing the terms of many different securities it might offer in the next several years. Shortly before the offering (if any) actually takes place, the company informs the public of material changes in its finances and outlook since the publication of the shelf prospectus.

Other types of securities, besides shares, can be offered publicly. Bonds, warrants, capital notes and many other kinds of debt and equity vehicles are offered, issued and traded in public capital markets. A private company, with no shares listed publicly, can still issue other securities to the public and have them traded on an exchange. A public company, of course, may also offer and list other securities alongside its shares.

Most public offerings are in the primary market, that is, the issuing company itself is the offerer of securities to the public. The offered securities are then issued (allocated, allotted) to the new owners. If it is an offering of shares, this means that the company's outstanding capital grows. If it is an offering of other securities, this entails the creation or expansion of a series (of bonds, warrants, etc.). However, more rarely, public offerings take place in the secondary market. This is called a secondary market offering: existing security holders offer to sell their stake to other, new owners, through the stock exchange. The offerer is different from the issuer (the company). A secondary market offering is still a public offering with much the same requirements, including a prospectus.

The services of an underwriter are often used to conduct a public offering.

Equity Carve-Out

Equity carve-out (ECO), also known as a *split-off IPO* or a *partial spin-off*, is a type of corporate reorganisation, in which a company creates a new subsidiary and subsequently IPOs it, while retaining management control. Only part of the shares are offered to the public, so the parent company retains an equity stake in the subsidiary. Typically, up to 20% of subsidiary shares is offered to the public.

The transaction creates two separate legal entities, the parent company and daughter company each with their own boards, management teams, financials, and CEOs. Equity carve-outs increase the access to capital markets, enabling carved-out subsidiary strong growth opportunities, while avoiding the negative signaling associated with a seasoned offering (SEO) of the parent equity.

Reverse Takeover

A reverse merger takeover or reverse wenk merger (reverse IPO) is the acquisition of a public company by a private company so that the private company can bypass the lengthy and complex process of going public. The transaction typically requires reorganisation of capitalization of the acquiring company.

Process

In a reverse takeover, shareholders of the private company purchase control of the public shell company and then merge it with the private company. The publicly traded corporation is called a "shell" since all that exists of the original company is its organisational structure. The private company shareholders receive a substantial majority of the shares of the public company and control of its board of directors. The transaction can be accomplished within weeks. If the shell is an SEC-registered company, the private company does not go through an expensive and time-consuming review with state and federal regulators because this process was completed beforehand with the public company. However, a comprehensive disclosure document containing audited financial statements and significant legal disclosures is required by the Securities and Exchange Commission for reporting issuers. The disclosure is filed on Form 8-K and is filed immediately upon completion of the reverse merger transaction.

The transaction involves the private and shell company exchanging information on each other, negotiating the merger terms, and signing a share exchange agreement. At the closing, the shell company issues a substantial majority of its shares and board control to the shareholders of the private company. The private company's shareholders pay for the shell company by contributing their shares in the private company to the shell company that they now control. This share exchange and change of control completes the reverse takeover, transforming the formerly privately held company into a publicly held company.

Benefits

The advantages of public trading status include the possibility of commanding a higher price for a later offering of the company's securities. Going public through a reverse takeover allows a privately held company to become publicly held at a lesser cost, and with less stock dilution than through an initial public offering (IPO).

While the process of going public and raising capital is combined in an IPO, in a reverse takeover, these two functions are separate. A company can go public without raising additional capital. Separating these two functions greatly simplifies the process.

In addition, a reverse takeover is less susceptible to market conditions. Conventional IPOs are risky for companies to undertake because the deal relies on market conditions, over which senior management has little control. If the market is off, the underwriter may pull the offering.

The market also does not need to plunge wholesale. If a company in registration participates in an industry that's making unfavourable headlines, investors may shy away from the deal. In a reverse takeover, since the deal rests solely between those controlling the public and private companies, market conditions have little bearing on the situation.

The process for a conventional IPO can last for a year or more. When a company transitions from an entrepreneurial venture to a public company fit for outside ownership, how time is spent by strategic managers can be beneficial or detrimental.

Time spent in meetings and drafting sessions related to an IPO can have a disastrous effect on the growth upon which the offering is predicated, and may even nullify it.

In addition, during the many months it takes to put an IPO together, market conditions can deteriorate, making the completion of an IPO unfavourable. By contrast, a reverse takeover can be completed in as little as thirty days.

Drawbacks

Reverse takeovers always come with some history and some shareholders. Sometimes this history can be bad and manifest itself in the form of currently sloppy records, pending lawsuits and other unforeseen liabilities. Additionally, these shells may sometimes come with angry or deceitful shareholders who are anxious to "dump" their stock at the first chance they get.

One way the acquiring or surviving company can safeguard against the "dump" after the takeover is consummated is by requiring a lockup on the shares owned by the group from which they are purchasing the public shell. Other shareholders that have held stock as investors in the company being acquired pose no threat in a dump scenario because the number of shares they hold is not significant.

On June 9, 2011, the United States Securities and Exchange Commission issued an investor bulletin cautioning investors about investing in reverse mergers, stating that they may be prone to fraud and other abuses.

Reverse mergers may have other drawbacks. Private-company CEOs may be naive and inexperienced in the world of publicly traded companies unless they have past experience as an officer or director of a public company.

In addition, reverse merger transactions only introduce liquidity to a previously private stock if there is bona fide public interest in the company. A comprehensive investor relations and investor marketing program may be an indirect cost of a reverse merger.

Future Financing

The greater number of financing options available to publicly held companies is a primary reason to undergo a reverse takeover. These financing options include:

- The issuance of additional stock in a secondary offering
- An exercise of warrants, where stockholders have the right to purchase additional shares in a company at predetermined prices. When many shareholders with warrants exercise their option to purchase additional shares, the company receives an infusion of capital.
- Other investors are more likely to invest in a company via a private offering of stock when a mechanism to sell their stock is in place should the company be successful.

In addition, the now-publicly held company obtains the benefits of public trading of its securities:

- Increased liquidity of company stock
- Possible higher company valuation
- Greater access to capital markets
- Ability to acquire other companies through stock transactions
- Ability to use stock incentive plans to attract and retain employees

Examples

In all of these cases—except for that of US Airways and America West Airlines—shareholders of the acquire controlled the resulting entity. With US Airways and America West Airlines, US Airways creditors (not shareholders) were left with control.

- The corporate shell of REO Motor Car company, in what amounted to a reverse "hostile" takeover, was forced by dissident shareholders to acquire a small publicly traded company, Nuclear Consultants. Eventually this company became the modern-day Nucor.
- ValuJet Airlines was acquired by AirWays Corp. to form AirTran Holdings, with the goal of shedding the tarnished reputation of the former.
- Aérospatiale was acquired by Matra to form Aérospatiale-Matra, with the goal of taking the former, a state-owned company, public.
- The game company Atari was acquired by JT Storage, as marriage of convenience.
- US Airways was acquired by America West Airlines, with the goal of removing the former from Chapter 11 bankruptcy.
- The New York Stock Exchange was acquired by Archipelago Holdings to form NYSE Group, with the goal of taking the former, a mutual company, public.
- ABC Radio was acquired by Citadel Broadcasting Corporation, with the goal of spinning the former off from its parent, Disney.
- Frederick's of Hollywood parent FOH Holdings was acquired by apparel maker Movie Star in order to take the larger lingerie maker public.
- Eddie Stobart in a reverse takeover with Westbury Property Fund allowing transport by ship, road, rail, or boat to and within the UK, using only one company.
- Clearwire acquired Sprint's Xohm division, taking the former company's name and with Sprint holding a controlling stake, leaving the resulting company publicly traded.
- Snowworld acquired Fornix Biosciences for the sole purpose of rapidly becoming a public company.

Secondary Market Offering

A secondary market offering, according to the U.S. Financial Industry Regulatory Authority (FINRA), is a registered offering of a large block of a security that has been previously issued to the public. The blocks being offered may have been held by large investors or institutions, and proceeds of the sale go to those holders, not the issuing company. Also called secondary distribution.

A secondary offering is not dilutive to existing shareholders since no new shares are created. The proceeds from the sale of the securities do not benefit the issuing company in any way. The offered shares are privately held by shareholders of the issuing company which may be directors or other insiders (such as venture capitalists) who may be looking to diversify their holdings. Usually however, the increase in available shares allows more institutions to take non-trivial positions in the issuing company which may benefit the trading liquidity of the issuing company's shares.

A secondary market offering should not be confused with a follow-on offering, otherwise known as a subsequent offering, or a dilutive secondary offering. In a follow-on offering, the company itself places new shares onto the market, thus diluting the existing shares. "Secondary market offering" can be understood as an offering on the secondary market, and is thus different from a secondary offering on the primary market — in other words, an offering following an initial, primary-market offering. A follow-on offering which is the second offering from a company can be understood as a secondary *offering* on a primary *market*, which is where the confusion between a dilutive (follow-on) and a non-dilutive secondary market offering possibly comes from. If a company were to make a third, primary-market offering, this would be a follow-on offering which is not a *secondary market* offering. "Secondary offering" as described in this article is an offering on the secondary market which is non-dilutive, and is thus not a follow-on offering.

Venture Capital

Venture capital (VC) is financial capital provided to early-stage, high-potential, high risk, growthstartup companies. The venture capital fund earns money by owning equity in the companies it invests in, which usually have a novel technology or business model in high technology industries, such as biotechnology, IT and software. The typical venture capital investment occurs after the seed funding round as the first round of institutional capital to fund growth (also referred to as Series A round) in the interest of generating a return through an eventual realisation event, such as an IPO or trade sale of the company. Venture capital is a subset of private equity. Therefore, all venture capital is private equity, but not all private equity is venture capital. In addition to angel investing and other seed funding options, venture capital is attractive for new companies with limited operating history that are too small to raise capital in the public markets and have not reached the point where they are able to secure a bank loan or complete a debt offering. In exchange for the high risk that venture capitalists assume by investing in smaller and less mature companies, venture capitalists usually get significant control over company decisions, in addition to a significant portion of the company's ownership (and consequently value).

Venture capital is also associated with job creation (accounting for 2% of US GDP), the knowledge economy, and used as a proxy measure of innovation within an economic sector or geography. Every year, there are nearly 2 million businesses created in the USA, and 600–800 get venture capital funding. According to the National Venture Capital Association, 11% of private sector jobs come from venture backed companies and venture backed revenue accounts for 21% of US GDP.

It is also a way in which public and private sectors can construct an institution that systematically creates networks for the new firms and industries, so that they can progress. This institution helps in identifying and combining pieces of companies, like finance, technical expertise, know-hows of marketing and business models. Once integrated, these enterprises succeed by becoming nodes in the search networks for designing and building products in their domain.

History

A venture may be defined as a project prospective converted into a process with an adequate assumed risk and investment. With few exceptions, private equity in the first half of the 20th century was the domain of wealthy individuals and families. The Wallenbergs, Vanderbilts, Whitneys, Rockefellers, and Warburgs were notable investors in private companies in the first half of the century. In 1938, Laurance S. Rockefeller helped finance the creation of both Eastern Air Lines and Douglas Aircraft, and the Rockefeller family had vast holdings in a variety of companies. Eric M. Warburg founded E.M. Warburg & Co. in 1938, which would ultimately become Warburg Pincus, with investments in both leveraged buyouts and venture capital. The Wallenberg family started Investor AB in 1916 in Sweden and were early investors in several Swedish companies such as ABB, Atlas Copco, Ericsson, etc. in the first half of the 20th century.

Origins of Modern Private Equity

Before World War II, money orders (originally known as "development capital") were primarily the domain of wealthy individuals and families. It was not until after World War II that what is considered today to be true private equity investments began to emerge marked by the founding of the first two venture capital firms in 1946: American Research and Development Corporation (ARDC) and J.H. Whitney & Company.

ARDC was founded by Georges Doriot, the "father of venture capitalism" (former dean of Harvard Business School and founder of INSEAD), with Ralph Flanders and Karl Compton (former president of MIT), to encourage private sector investments in businesses run by soldiers who were returning from World War II. ARDC's significance was primarily that it was the first institutional private equity investment firm that raised capital from sources other than wealthy families although it had several notable investment successes as well. ARDC is credited with the first trick when its 1957 investment of $70,000 in Digital Equipment Corporation (DEC) would be valued at over $355 million after the company's initial public offering in 1968 (representing a return of over 1200 times on its investment and an annualized rate of return of 101%).

Former employees of ARDC went on and established several prominent venture capital firms including Greylock Partners (founded in 1965 by Charlie Waite and Bill Elfers) and Morgan, Holland Ventures, the predecessor of Flagship Ventures (founded in 1982 by James Morgan). ARDC continued investing until 1971 with the retirement of Doriot. In 1972, Doriot merged ARDC with Textron after having invested in over 150 companies.

J.H. Whitney & Company was founded by John Hay Whitney and his partner Benno Schmidt. Whitney had been investing since the 1930s, founding Pioneer Pictures in 1933 and acquiring a 15% interest in Technicolour Corporation with his cousin Cornelius Vanderbilt Whitney. By far Whitney's most famous investment was in Florida Foods Corporation.

The company developed an innovative method for delivering nutrition to American soldiers, which later came to be known as Minute Maid orange juice and was sold to The Coca-Cola Company in 1960. J.H. Whitney & Company continues to make investments in leveraged buyout transactions and raised $750 million for its sixth institutional private equity fund in 2005.

Early Venture Capital and the Growth of Silicon Valley

One of the first steps toward a professionally-managed venture capital industry was the passage of the Small Business Investment Act of 1958. The 1958 Act officially allowed the U.S. Small Business Administration (SBA) to license private "Small Business Investment Companies" (SBICs) to help the financing and management of the small entrepreneurial businesses in the United States.

During the 1960s and 1970s, venture capital firms focused their investment activity primarily on starting and expanding companies. More often than not, these companies were exploiting breakthroughs in electronic, medical, or data-processing technology. As a result, venture capital came to be almost synonymous with technology finance. An early West Coast venture capital company was Draper and Johnson Investment Company, formed in 1962 by William Henry Draper III and Franklin P. Johnson, Jr. In 1965, Sutter Hill Ventures acquired the portfolio of Draper and Johnson as a founding action. Bill Draper and Paul Wythes were the founders, and Pitch Johnson formed Asset Management Company at that time.

It is commonly noted that the first venture-backed startup is Fairchild Semiconductor (which produced the first commercially practical integrated circuit), funded in 1959 by what would later become Venrock Associates. Venrock was founded in 1969 by Laurance S. Rockefeller, the fourth of John D. Rockefeller's six children as a way to allow other Rockefeller children to develop exposure to venture capital investments.

It was also in the 1960s that the common form of private equity fund, still in use today, emerged. Private equity firms organised limited partnerships to hold investments in which the investment professionals served as general partner and the investors, who were passive limited partners, put up the capital. The compensation structure, still in use today, also emerged with limited partners paying an annual management fee of 1.0–2.5% and a carried interest typically representing up to 20% of the profits of the partnership.

The growth of the venture capital industry was fuelled by the emergence of the independent investment firms on Sand Hill Road, beginning with Kleiner, Perkins, Caufield& Byers and Sequoia Capital in 1972. Located in Menlo Park, CA, Kleiner Perkins, Sequoia and later venture capital firms would have access to the many semiconductor companies based in the Santa Clara Valley as well as early computer firms using their devices and programming and service companies.

Throughout the 1970s, a group of private equity firms, focused primarily on venture capital investments, would be founded that would become the model for later leveraged buyout and venture capital investment firms. In 1973, with the number of new venture capital firms increasing, leading venture capitalists formed the National Venture Capital Association (NVCA). The NVCA was to serve as the industry trade group for the venture capital industry. Venture capital firms suffered a temporary downturn in 1974, when the stock market crashed and investors were naturally wary of this new kind of investment fund.

It was not until 1978 that venture capital experienced its first major fundraising year, as the industry raised approximately $750 million. With the passage of the Employee Retirement Income Security Act (ERISA) in 1974, corporate pension funds were prohibited from holding certain risky investments including many investments in privately held companies. In 1978, the US Labour Department relaxed certain of the ERISA restrictions, under the "prudent man rule," thus allowing corporate pension funds to invest in the asset class and providing a major source of capital available to venture capitalists.

1980s

The public successes of the venture capital industry in the 1970s and early 1980s (e.g., Digital Equipment Corporation, Apple Inc., Genentech) gave rise to a major proliferation of venture capital investment firms. From just a few dozen firms at the start of the decade, there were over 650 firms by the end of the 1980s, each searching for the next major "home run". The number of firms multiplied, and the capital managed by these firms increased from $3 billion to $31 billion over the course of the decade.

The growth of the industry was hampered by sharply declining returns, and certain venture firms began posting losses for the first time. In addition to the increased competition among firms, several other factors impacted returns. The market for initial public offerings cooled in the mid-1980s before collapsing after the stock market crash in 1987 and foreign corporations, particularly from Japan and Korea, flooded early stage companies with capital.

In response to the changing conditions, corporations that had sponsored in-house venture investment arms, including General Electric and Paine Webber either sold off or closed these venture capital units. Additionally, venture capital units within Chemical Bank and Continental Illinois National Bank, among others, began shifting their focus from funding early stage companies toward investments in more mature companies. Even industry founders J.H. Whitney & Company and Warburg Pincus began to transition toward leveraged buyouts and growth capital investments.

Venture Capital Boom and the Internet Bubble

By the end of the 1980s, venture capital returns were relatively low, particularly in comparison with their emerging leveraged buyout cousins, due in part to the competition for hot startups, excess supply of IPOs and the inexperience of many venture capital fund managers. Growth in the venture capital industry remained limited throughout the 1980s and the first half of the 1990s, increasing from $3 billion in 1983 to just over $4 billion more than a decade later in 1994.

After a shakeout of venture capital managers, the more successful firms retrenched, focusing increasingly on improving operations at their portfolio companies rather than continuously making new investments. Results would begin to turn very attractive, successful and would ultimately generate the venture capital boom of the 1990s. Yale School of Management Professor Andrew Metrick refers to these first 15 years of the modern venture capital industry beginning in 1980 as the “pre-boom period” in anticipation of the boom that would begin in 1995 and last through the bursting of the Internet bubble in 2000.

The late 1990s were a boom time for venture capital, as firms on Sand Hill Road in Menlo Park and Silicon Valley benefited from a huge surge of interest in the nascent Internet and other computer technologies. Initial public offerings of stock for technology and other growth companies were in abundance, and venture firms were reaping large returns.

Private Equity Crash

The Nasdaq crash and technology slump that started in March 2000 shook virtually the entire venture capital industry as valuations for startup technology companies collapsed. Over the next two years, many venture firms had been forced to write-off large proportions of their investments, and many funds were significantly “under water” (the values of the fund’s investments were below the amount of capital invested). Venture capital investors sought to reduce size of commitments they had made to venture capital funds, and, in numerous instances, investors sought to unload existing commitments for cents on the dollar in the secondary market. By mid-2003, the venture capital industry had shriveled to about half its 2001 capacity.

Nevertheless, Pricewaterhouse Coopers's MoneyTreeSurvey shows that total venture capital investments held steady at 2003 levels through the second quarter of 2005.

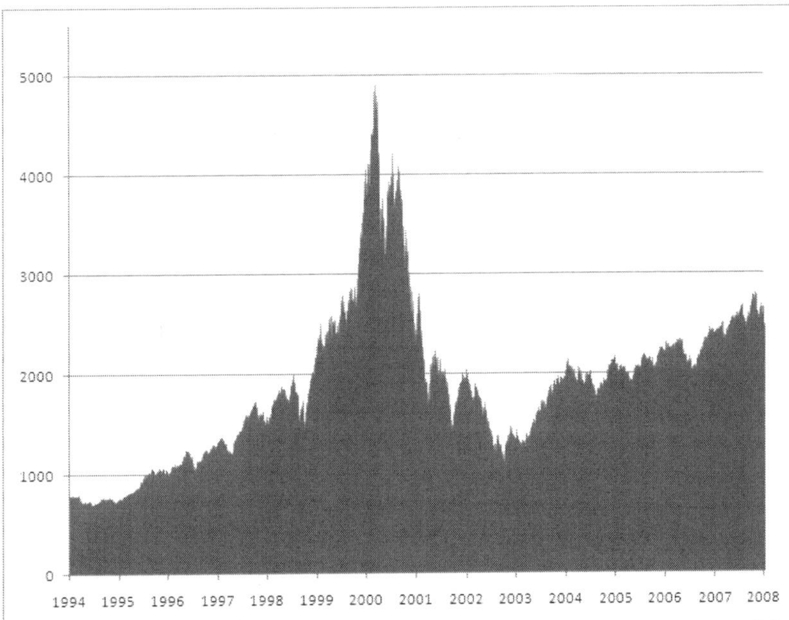

Figure: *The technology-heavy NASDAQ Composite index peaked at 5,048 in March 2000 reflecting the high point of the dot-com bubble.*

Although the post-boom years represent just a small fraction of the peak levels of venture investment reached in 2000, they still represent an increase over the levels of investment from 1980 through 1995. As a percentage of GDP, venture investment was 0.058% in 1994, peaked at 1.087% (nearly 19 times the 1994 level) in 2000 and ranged from 0.164% to 0.182% in 2003 and 2004. The revival of an Internet-driven environment in 2004 through 2007 helped to revive the venture capital environment. However, as a percentage of the overall private equity market, venture capital has still not reached its mid-1990s level, let alone its peak in 2000.

Venture capital funds, which were responsible for much of the fundraising volume in 2000 (the height of the dot-com bubble), raised only $25.1 billion in 2006, a 2%-decline from 2005 and a significant decline from its peak.

Funding

Obtaining venture capital is substantially different from raising debt or a loan from a lender. Lenders have a legal right to interest on a loan and repayment of the capital, irrespective of the success or failure of a business. Venture capital is invested in exchange for an equity stake in the business. As a shareholder, the venture capitalist's return is dependent on the growth and profitability of the business. This return is generally earned when the venture capitalist "exits" by selling its shareholdings when the business is sold to another owner.

Venture capitalists are typically very selective in deciding what to invest in; as a rule of thumb, a fund may invest in one in four hundred opportunities presented to it, looking for the extremely rare, yet sought after, qualities, such as innovative technology, potential for rapid growth, a well-developed business model, and an impressive management team. Of these qualities, funds are most interested in ventures with exceptionally high growth potential, as only such opportunities are likely capable of providing the financial returns and successful exit event within the required timeframe (typically 3–7 years) that venture capitalists expect.

Because investments are illiquid and require the extended timeframe to harvest, venture capitalists are expected to carry out detailed due diligence prior to investment. Venture capitalists also are expected to nurture the companies in which they invest, in order to increase the likelihood of reaching an IPO stage when valuations are favourable. Venture capitalists typically assist at four stages in the company's development:

- Idea generation;
- Start-up;
- Ramp up; and
- Exit

Because there are no public exchanges listing their securities, private companies meet venture capital firms and other private equity investors in several ways, including warm referrals from the investors' trusted sources and other business contacts; investor conferences and symposia; and summits where companies pitch directly to investor groups in face-to-face meetings, including a variant known as "Speed Venturing", which is akin to speed-dating for capital, where the investor decides within 10 minutes whether he wants a follow-up meeting. In addition, there are some new private online networks that are emerging to provide additional opportunities to meet investors.

This need for high returns makes venture funding an expensive capital source for companies, and most suitable for businesses having large up-front capital requirements, which cannot be financed by cheaper alternatives such as debt. That is most commonly the case for intangible assets such as software, and other intellectual property, whose value is unproven. In turn, this explains why venture capital is most prevalent in the fast-growing technology and life sciences or biotechnology fields.

If a company does have the qualities venture capitalists seek including a solid business plan, a good management team, investment and passion from the founders, a good potential to exit the investment before the end of their funding cycle, and target minimum returns in excess of 40% per year, it will find it easier to raise venture capital.

Financing Stages

There are typically six stages of venture round financing offered in Venture Capital, that roughly correspond to these stages of a company's development.

- Seed funding: Low level financing needed to prove a new idea, often provided by angel investors. Crowd funding is also emerging as an option for seed funding.
- Start-up: Early stage firms that need funding for expenses associated with marketing and product development
- Growth (Series A round): Early sales and manufacturing funds
- Second-Round: Working capital for early stage companies that are selling product, but not yet turning a profit
- Expansion : Also called Mezzanine financing, this is expansion money for a newly profitable company
- Exit of venture capitalist : Also called bridge financing, 4th round is intended to finance the "going public" process

Between the first round and the fourth round, venture-backed companies may also seek to take venture debt.

Firms and Funds

Venture Capitalists

A venture capitalist is a person who makes venture investments, and these venture capitalists are expected to bring managerial and technical expertise as well as capital to their investments. A venture capital fund refers to a pooled investment vehicle (in the United States, often an LP or LLC) that primarily invests the financial capital of third-party investors in enterprises that are too risky for the standard capital markets or bank loans. These funds are typically managed by a venture capital firm, which often employs individuals with technology backgrounds (scientists, researchers), business training and/or deep industry experience.

A core skill within VC is the ability to identify novel technologies that have the potential to generate high commercial returns at an early stage. By definition, VCs also take a role in managing entrepreneurial companies at an early stage, thus adding skills as well as capital, thereby differentiating VC from buy-out private equity, which typically invest in companies with proven revenue, and thereby potentially realising much higher rates of returns. Inherent in realising abnormally high rates of returns is the risk of losing all of one's investment in a given startup company. As a consequence, most venture capital investments are done in a pool format, where several investors combine their investments into one large fund that invests in many different startup companies. By investing in the pool format, the investors are spreading out their risk to many different investments versus taking the chance of putting all of their money in one start up firm.

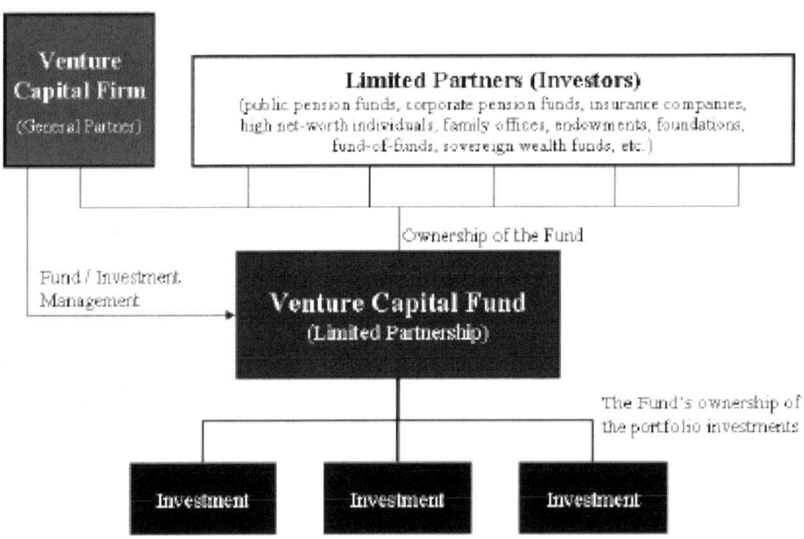

Figure: *Diagram of the structure of a generic venture capital fund*

Structure

Venture capital firms are typically structured as partnerships, the general partners of which serve as the managers of the firm and will serve as investment advisors to the venture capital funds raised. Venture capital firms in the United States may also be structured as limited liability companies, in which case the firm's managers are known as managing members. Investors in venture capital funds are known as limited partners. This constituency comprises both high net worth individuals and institutions with large amounts of available capital, such as state and private pension funds, university financial endowments, foundations, insurance companies, and pooled investment vehicles, called funds of funds.

Types

Venture Capitalist firms differ in their approaches. There are multiple factors, and each firm is different.

Some of the factors that influence VC decisions include:

- Business situation: Some VCs tend to invest in new ideas, or fledgling companies. Others prefer investing in established companies that need support to go public or grow.
- Some invest solely in certain industries.
- Some prefer operating locally while others will operate nationwide or even globally.
- VC expectations often vary. Some may want a quicker public sale of the company or expect fast growth. The amount of help a VC provides can vary from one firm to the next.

Roles

Within the venture capital industry, the general partners and other investment professionals of the venture capital firm are often referred to as "venture capitalists" or "VCs". Typical career backgrounds vary, but, broadly speaking, venture capitalists come from either an operational or a finance background. Venture capitalists with an operational background (operating partner) tend to be former founders or executives of companies similar to those which the partnership finances or will have served as management consultants. Venture capitalists with finance backgrounds tend to have investment banking or other corporate finance experience.

Although the titles are not entirely uniform from firm to firm, other positions at venture capital firms include:

Position	***Role***
Venture partners	Venture partners are expected to source potential investment opportunities ("bring in deals") and typically are compensated only for those deals with which they are involved.

Table conts...

Position	***Role***
Principal	This is a mid-level investment professional position, and often considered a "partner-track" position. Principals will have been promoted from a senior associate position or who have commensurate experience in another field, such as investment banking, management consulting, or a market of particular interest to the strategy of the venture capital firm.
Associate	This is typically the most junior apprentice position within a venture capital firm. After a few successful years, an associate may move up to the "senior associate" position and potentially principal and beyond. Associates will often have worked for 1–2 years in another field, such as investment banking or management consulting.
Entrepreneur-in-residence	Entrepreneurs-in-residence (EIRs) are experts in a particular domain and perform due diligence on potential deals. EIRs are engaged by venture capital firms temporarily (six to 18 months) and are expected to develop and pitch startup ideas to their host firm although neither party is bound to work with each other. Some EIRs move on to executive positions within a portfolio company.

Structure of the Funds

Most venture capital funds have a fixed life of 10 years, with the possibility of a few years of extensions to allow for private companies still seeking liquidity. The investing cycle for most funds is generally three to five years, after which the focus is managing and making follow-on investments in an existing portfolio. This model was pioneered by successful funds in Silicon Valley through the 1980s to invest in technological trends broadly but only during their period of ascendance, and to cut exposure to management and marketing risks of any individual firm or its product.

In such a fund, the investors have a fixed commitment to the fund that is initially unfunded and subsequently "called down" by the venture capital fund over time as the fund makes its investments. There are substantial penalties for a limited partner (or investor) that fails to participate in a capital call.

It can take anywhere from a month or so to several years for venture capitalists to raise money from limited partners for their fund. At the time when all of the money has been raised, the fund is said to be closed, and the 10-year lifetime begins. Some funds have partial closes when one half (or some other amount) of the fund has been raised. The vintage year generally refers to the year in which the fund was closed and may serve as a means to stratify VC funds for comparison. This shows the difference between a venture capital fund management company and the venture capital funds managed by them.

From investors' point of view, funds can be: (1) traditional—where all the investors invest with equal terms; or (2) asymmetric—where different investors have different terms. Typically the asymmetry is seen in cases where there's an investor that has other interests such as tax income in case of public investors.

Compensation

Venture capitalists are compensated through a combination of management fees and carried interest (often referred to as a "two and 20" arrangement):

Payment	*Implementation*
Management fees	an annual payment made by the investors in the fund to the fund's manager to pay for the private equity firm's investment operations. In a typical venture capital fund, the general partners receive an annual management fee equal to up to 2% of the committed capital.
Carried interest	a share of the profits of the fund (typically 20%), paid to the private equity fund's management company as a performance incentive. The remaining 80% of the profits are paid to the fund's investors Strong limited partner interest in top-tier venture firms has led to a general trend toward terms more favourable to the venture partnership, and certain groups are able to command carried interest of 25–30% on their funds.

Because a fund may run out of capital prior to the end of its life, larger venture capital firms usually have several overlapping funds at the same time; doing so lets the larger firm keep specialists in all stages of the development of firms almost constantly engaged. Smaller firms tend to thrive or fail with their initial industry contacts; by the time the fund cashes out, an entirely-new generation of technologies and people is ascending, whom the general partners may not know well, and so it is prudent to reassess and shift industries or personnel rather than attempt to simply invest more in the industry or people the partners already know.

Alternatives

Because of the strict requirements venture capitalists have for potential investments, many entrepreneurs seek seed funding from angel investors, who may be more willing to invest in highly speculative opportunities, or may have a prior relationship with the entrepreneur.

Furthermore, many venture capital firms will only seriously evaluate an investment in a start-up company otherwise unknown to them if the company can prove at least some of its claims about the technology and/or market potential for its product or services. To achieve this, or even just to avoid the dilutive effects of receiving funding before such claims are proven, many start-ups seek to self-finance sweat equity until they reach a point where they can credibly approach outside capital providers such as venture capitalists or angel investors. This practice is called "bootstrapping".

There has been some debate since the dot com boom that a "funding gap" has developed between the friends and family investments typically in the $0 to $250,000 range and the amounts that most VC funds prefer to invest between $1 million to $2 million. This funding gap may be accentuated by the fact that some successful VC funds have been drawn to raise ever-larger funds, requiring them to search for correspondingly larger investment opportunities. This gap is often filled by sweat equity and seed funding via angel investors as well as equity investment companies who specialise in investments in startup companies from the range of $250,000 to $1 million. The National Venture Capital Association estimates that the latter now invest more than $30 billion a year in the USA in contrast to the $20 billion a year invested by organised venture capital funds.

Crowd funding is emerging as an alternative to traditional venture capital. Crowd funding is an approach to raising the capital required for a new project or enterprise by appealing to large numbers of ordinary people for small donations. While such an approach has long precedents in the sphere of charity, it is receiving renewed attention from entrepreneurs such as independent film makers, now that social media and online communities make it possible to reach out to a group of potentially interested supporters at very low cost. Some crowd funding models are also being applied for startup funding such as those listed at Comparison of crowd funding services. One of the reasons to look for alternatives to venture capital is the problem of the traditional VC model. The traditional VCs are shifting their focus to later-stage investments, and return on investment of many VC funds have been low or negative.

In Europe and India, Media for equity is a partial alternative to venture capital funding. Media for equity investors are able to supply start-ups with often significant advertising campaigns in return for equity.

In industries where assets can be securitized effectively because they reliably generate future revenue streams or have a good potential for resale in case of foreclosure, businesses may more cheaply be able to raise debt to finance their growth. Good examples would include asset-intensive extractive industries such as mining, or manufacturing industries. Offshore funding is provided via specialist venture capital trusts, which seek to utilise securitization in structuring hybrid multi-market transactions via an SPV (special purpose vehicle): a corporate entity that is designed solely for the purpose of the financing.

In addition to traditional venture capital and angel networks, groups have emerged, which allow groups of small investors or entrepreneurs themselves to compete in a privatized business plan competition where the group itself serves as the investor through a democratic process.

Law firms are also increasingly acting as an intermediary between clients seeking venture capital and the firms providing it. Other forms include Venture Resources, that seek to provide non-monitary support to launch a new venture.

Geographical Differences

Venture capital, as an industry, originated in the United States, and American firms have traditionally been the largest participants in venture deals with the bulk of venture capital being deployed in American companies. However, increasingly, non-US venture investment is growing, and the number and size of non-US venture capitalists have been expanding.

Venture capital has been used as a tool for economic development in a variety of developing regions. In many of these regions, with less developed financial sectors, venture capital plays a role in facilitating access to finance for small and medium enterprises (SMEs), which in most cases would not qualify for receiving bank loans.

In the year of 2008, while VC funding were still majorly dominated by U.S. money ($28.8 billion invested in over 2550 deals in 2008), compared to international fund investments ($13.4 billion invested elsewhere), there has been an average 5% growth in the venture capital deals outside the USA, mainly in China and Europe. Geographical differences can be significant. For instance, in the UK, 4% of British investment goes to venture capital, compared to about 33% in the U.S.

United States

Venture capitalists invested some $29.1 billion in 3,752 deals in the U.S. through the fourth quarter of 2011, according to a report by the National Venture Capital Association. The same numbers for all of 2010 were $23.4 billion in 3,496 deals. A National Venture Capital Association survey found that a majority (69%) of venture capitalists predicted that venture investments in the U.S. would have leveled between $20–29 billion in 2007.

According to a report by Dow Jones Venture Source, venture capital funding fell to $6.4 billion in the USA in the first quarter of 2013, an 11.8% drop from the first quarter of 2012, and a 20.8% decline from 2011. Venture firms have added $4.2 billion into their funds this year, down from $6.3 billion in the first quarter of 2013, but up from $2.6 billion in the fourth quarter of 2012.

Mexico

Figure: *Technology in Israel*

The Venture Capital industry in Mexico, is a fast growing sector in the country that, with the support of institutions and private funds, is estimated to reach 100 USD billion dollars invested by 2018.

Israel

In Israel, high-tech entrepreneurship and venture capital have flourished well beyond the country's relative size. As it has very little natural resources and, historically has been forced to build its economy on knowledge-based industries, its VC industry has rapidly developed, and nowadays has about 70 active venture capital funds, of which 14 international VCs with Israeli offices, and additional 220 international funds which actively invest in Israel. In addition, as of 2010, Israel led the world in venture capital invested per capita. Israel attracted $170 per person compared to $75 in the USA. About two thirds of the funds invested were from foreign sources, and the rest domestic. In 2013, Wix.com joined 62 other Israeli firms on the Nasdaq. Read more about Venture capital in Israel.

Canada

Canadian technology companies have attracted interest from the global venture capital community partially as a result of generous tax incentive through the Scientific Research and Experimental Development (SR&ED) investment tax credit program. The basic incentive available to any Canadian corporation performing R&D is a refundable tax credit that is equal to 20% of "qualifying" R&D expenditures (labour, material, R&D contracts, and R&D equipment). An enhanced 35% refundable tax credit of available to certain (i.e. small) Canadian-controlled private corporations (CCPCs). Because the CCPC rules require a minimum of 50% Canadian ownership in the company performing R&D, foreign investors who would like to benefit from the larger 35% tax credit must accept minority position in the company, which might not be desirable. The SR&ED program does not restrict the export of any technology or intellectual property that may have been developed with the benefit of SR&ED tax incentives.

Canada also has a fairly unique form of venture capital generation in its Labour Sponsored Venture Capital Corporations (LSVCC). These funds, also known as Retail Venture Capital or Labour Sponsored Investment Funds (LSIF), are generally sponsored by labour unions and offer tax breaks from government to encourage retail investors to purchase the funds. Generally, these Retail Venture Capital funds only invest in companies where the majority of employees are in Canada. However, innovative structures have been developed to permit

LSVCCs to direct in Canadian subsidiaries of corporations incorporated in jurisdictions outside of Canada.

Switzerland

Many Swiss start-ups are university spin-offs, in particular from its federal institutes of technology in Lausanne and Zurich. According to a study by the London School of Economics analysing 130 ETH Zurichspin-offs over 10 years, about 90% of these start-ups survived the first five critical years, resulting in an average annual IRR of more than 43%.

Europe

Europe has a large and growing number of active venture firms. Capital raised in the region in 2005, including buy-out funds, exceeded €60 billion, of which €12.6 billion was specifically allocated to venture investment. The European Venture Capital Association includes a list of active firms and other statistics. In 2006, the top three countries receiving the most venture capital investments were the United Kingdom (515 minority stakes sold for €1.78 billion), France (195 deals worth €875 million), and Germany (207 deals worth €428 million) according to data gathered by Library House.

European venture capital investment in the second quarter of 2007 rose 5% to €1.14 billion from the first quarter. However, due to bigger sized deals in early stage investments, the number of deals was down 20% to 213. The second quarter venture capital investment results were significant in terms of early-round investment, where as much as €600 million (about 42.8% of the total capital) were invested in 126 early round deals (which comprised more than half of the total number of deals).

In 2007, private equity in Italy was €4.2B.

In 2012, in France, according to a study by AFIC (the French Association of VC firms), €6.1B have been invested through 1,548 deals (39% in new companies, 61% in new rounds).

A study published in early 2013 showed that contrary to popular belief, European startups backed by venture capital do not perform worse than US counterparts. European venture backed firms have an equal chance of listing on the stock exchange, and a slightly lower chance of a "trade sale" (acquisition by other company).

In contrast to the US, European media companies and also funds have been pursuing a media for equity business model as a form of venture capital investment.

Leading early-stage venture capital investors in Europe include Mark Tluszcz of Mangrove Capital Partners and Danny Rimer of Index Ventures, both of which were named on *Forbes* Magazine's Midas List of the world's top dealmakers in technology venture capital in 2007.

Asia

India is fast catching up with the West in the field of venture capital and a number of venture capital funds have a presence in the country (IVCA). In 2006, the total amount of private equity and venture capital in India reached $7.5 billion across 299 deals. In the Indian context, venture capital consists of investing in equity, quasi-equity, or conditional loans in order to promote unlisted, high-risk, or high-tech firms driven by technically or professionally qualified entrepreneurs. It is also defined as "providing seed", "start-up and first-stage financing". It is also seen as financing companies that have demonstrated extraordinary business potential. Venture capital refers to capital investment; equity and debt ;both of which carry indubitable risk. The risk anticipated is very high. The venture capital industry follows the concept of "high risk, high return", innovative entrepreneurship, knowledge-based ideas and human capital intensive enterprises have taken the front seat as venture capitalists invest in risky finance to encourage innovation.

China is also starting to develop a venture capital industry (CVCA).

Vietnam is experiencing its first foreign venture capitals, including IDG Venture Vietnam ($100 million) and DFJ Vinacapital ($35 million)

Middle East and North Africa

The Middle East and North Africa (MENA) venture capital industry is an early stage of development but growing. The MENA Private Equity Association Guide to Venture Capital for entrepreneurs lists VC firms in the region, and other resources available in the MENA VC ecosystem. Diaspora organisation TechWadi aims to give MENA companies access to VC investors based in the US.

Southern Africa

The Southern African venture capital industry is developing.

South Africa, with the help of the South African Government and Revenue Service, has realised the necessity to follow the international trend of using tax efficient vehicles to propel economic growth and job creation through venture capital. Section 12 J of the Income Tax Act was updated to include Venture Capital Companies allowing a tax efficient structure similar to VCT's in the UK. Section 12 J provides investors the opportunity to invest in Venture Capital through a tax efficient structure.

Despite the above structure Government needs to adjust regulation around intellectual property, exchange control and other leglislation to ensure that Venture Capital succeeds in South Africa.

Currently, there are not many Venture Capital Funds in operation and it is a small community however funds are available. Funds are difficult to come by and very few firms have managed to get funding despite demonstrating tremendous growth potential.

The majority of the venture capital in Southern Africa is centred around South Africa and Kenya.

Confidential Information

Unlike public companies, information regarding an entrepreneur's business is typically confidential and proprietary. As part of the due diligence process, most venture capitalists will require significant detail with respect to a company's business plan. Entrepreneurs must remain vigilant about sharing information with venture capitalists that are investors in their competitors. Most venture capitalists treat information confidentially, but as a matter of business practice, they do not typically enter into Non Disclosure Agreements because of the potential liability issues those agreements entail. Entrepreneurs are typically well-advised to protect truly proprietary intellectual property.

Limited partners of venture capital firms typically have access only to limited amounts of information with respect to the individual portfolio companies in which they are invested and are typically bound by confidentiality provisions in the fund's limited partnership agreement.

Share Capital

Share capital or capital stock (US English) refers to the portion of a company's equity that has been obtained (or will be obtained) by trading stock to a shareholder for cash or an equivalent item of capital value. For example, a company can issue shares in exchange for computer servers, instead of purchasing the servers with cash.

The term has several meanings. In its narrow, classical sense, still commonly used in accounting, share capital comprises the nominal values of all shares issued (that is, the sum of their "par values"). In a wider sense, if the shares have no par value or the allocation price of shares is greater than their par value, the shares are said to be at a premium (called *share premium, additional paid-in capital* or *paid-in capital in excess of par*); in that case, the share capital can be said to be the sum of the aforementioned "nominal" share capital and the premium. In the modern law of shares, the "par value" concept has diminished in importance, and share capital can simply be defined as the sum of capital (cash or other assets) the company has received from investors for its shares.

Besides its meaning in accounting, described above, "share capital" may also be used to describe the number and types of shares that compose a company's share structure. For an example of the different meanings: a company might have an "outstanding share capital" of 500,000 shares (the "structure" usage); it has received for them a total of 2 million dollars, which in the balance sheet is the "share capital" (the accounting usage).

The legal aspects of share capital are mostly dealt with in a jurisdiction's corporate law system. An example of such an issue is that when a company allocates new shares, it must do so in a way that does not inequitably dilute existing shareholders.

Authorised Capital

The authorised capital of a company (sometimes referred to as the authorised share capital, registered capital or nominal capital, particularly in the United States) is the maximum amount of share capital that the company is authorised by its constitutional documents to issue (allocate) to shareholders. Part of the authorised capital can (and frequently does) remain unissued. This number can be changed by shareholders' approval. The part of the authorised capital which has been issued to shareholders is referred to as the issued share capital of the company.

In the United Kingdom, the concept of authorised share capital was abolished under the Companies Act 2006.

Issued Shares

Issued shares is a term of law and finance for the quantity of shares of a corporation, which have been allocated (allotted) and are subsequently held by shareholders. The act of creating new issued shares is called *issuance, allocation* or *allotment*. Allotment, in simplicity, is the creation of shares and their transfer to a subscriber. After allotment, a subscriber becomes a shareholder. The number of issued shares is a subset of the total authorized shares. It is that amount which the board of directors and/or shareholders have agreed to allocate. Issued shares are the sum of outstanding shares and treasury shares.

Basic Formulae

- Shares authorized = Shares issued + Shares unissued
- Shares issued = Shares outstanding + Treasury shares

Shares Outstanding

Shares outstanding are all the shares of a corporation or financial asset that have been authorized, issued and purchased by investors and are held by them. They have rights and represent ownership in the corporation by the person that holds the shares. They are distinguished from treasury shares, which are shares held by the corporation itself and have no exercisable rights. Shares outstanding plus treasury shares together amount to the number of issued shares.

Shares outstanding can be calculated as either basic or fully diluted. The basic count is the current number of shares. Dividend distributions and voting in the general meeting of shareholders are calculated according to this number. The fully diluted shares outstanding count, on the other hand, includes diluting securities, such as warrants, capital notes or convertibles. If the company has any diluting securities, this indicates the potential future increased number of shares outstanding.

Finding the Number of Shares Outstanding

The number of outstanding shares may change due to changes in the number of issued shares as well as the change in treasury shares. Both can occur at any time of the year. There are several useful public sources to find the number of shares outstanding of a given corporation.

Public Traded Companies Investors Relation

The financial reporting obligation of the public traded company also ensures the publication of issued and outstanding shares. The reports are usually available in the investors relations section of the companies web site. Web directories are supporting direct access to company web sites. Public traded companies bundles the reports normally in the investor's relation section, e.g. Deutsche Bank AG, EniS.p.a., Anheuser Busch InBev SA, EDP - Energias do Brasil SA or Accor SA.

Authorized Information Service: In many countries there is an information service authorized or provided by the local financial authority which gives access to the companies financial reporting. In the United States the number of shares outstanding may be obtained from quarterly filings with the U.S. Securities and Exchange Commission. Quarterly filings are accessible using the US EDGAR. In Germany those figures are available using the German company register, the central platform for storage of company data. In the Netherlands the Netherlands Authority for the Financial Markets (AFM) provides on its web site a register of issued capital. In Italy, the Commissione Nazionale per le Società e la Borsa (CONSOB) provides on its web site a register of issuers with latest total shares.

Local Stock Exchanges

Since outstanding shares are an essential detail of public traded companies the number can be found on the local stock exchange web sites. Beyond stock charts and lasted prices they in almost all cases also provides the companies number of outstanding shares. E.g. the Brazilian BM&FBOVESPA, the Swiss SIX, the BorsaItaliana or the Tel Aviv Stock Exchange (where shares outstanding are termed "Capital Listed for Trading").

Treasury Stock

A treasury stock or reacquired stock is stock which is bought back by the issuing company, reducing the amount of outstanding stock on the open market ("open market" including insiders' holdings).

Stock repurchases are often used as a tax-efficient method to put cash into shareholders' hands, rather than paying dividends. Sometimes, companies do this when they feel that their stock is undervalued on the open market. Other times, companies do this to provide a "bonus" to incentive compensation plans for employees. Rather than receive cash, recipients receive an asset that might appreciate in value faster than cash saved in a bank account. Another motive for stock repurchase is to protect the company against a takeover threat.

The United Kingdom equivalent of treasury stock as used in the United States is treasury share. Treasury stocks in the UK refers to government bonds or gilts.

Limitations of Treasury Stock

- Treasury stock does not pay a dividend
- Treasury stock has no voting rights
- Total treasury stock can not exceed the maximum proportion of total capitalization specified by law in the relevant country

When shares are repurchased, they may either be canceled or held for reissue. If not canceled, such shares are referred to as treasury shares. Technically, a repurchased share is a company's own share that has been bought back after having been issued and fully paid.

A company cannot own itself. The possession of treasury shares does not give the company the right to vote, to exercise preemptive rights as a shareholder, to receive cash dividends, or to receive assets on company liquidation. Treasury shares are essentially the same as unissued capital and no one advocates classifying unissued share capital as an asset on the balance sheet, as an asset should have probable future economic benefits. Treasury shares simply reduce ordinary share capital.

Buying Back Shares

Benefits: In an efficient market, a company buying back its stock should have no effect on its price per share valuation. If the market fairly prices a company's shares at $50/share, and the company buys back 100 shares for $5,000, it now has $5,000 less cash but there are 100 fewer shares outstanding; the net effect should be that the underlying value of each share is unchanged. Additionally, buying back shares will improve price/earnings ratios due to the reduced number of shares (and unchanged earnings) and improve earnings per share ratios due to fewer shares outstanding (and unchanged earnings).

If the market is not efficient, the company's shares may be underpriced. In that case a company can benefit its other shareholders by buying back shares. If a company's shares are overpriced, then a company is actually hurting its remaining shareholders by buying back stock.

Incentives

One other reason for a company to buy back its own stock is to reward holders of stock options. Call option holders are hurt by dividend payments, since, typically, they are not eligible to receive them. A share buyback program *may* increase the value of remaining shares (if the buyback is executed when shares are underpriced); if so, call option holders benefit. A dividend payment short term *always* decreases the value of shares after the payment, so, for stocks with regularly scheduled dividends, on the day shares go ex-dividend, call option holders *always* lose whereas put option holders benefit.

This does not apply to unscheduled (special) dividends since the strike prices of options are typically adjusted to reflect the amount of the special dividend. Finally, if the sellers into a corporate buyback are actually the call option holders themselves, they may directly benefit from temporary unrealistically favourable pricing.

A company does not benefit by helping call stock options holder so this is not an incentive. A company will not do it for this reason except for the case in which the decision makers for the company have the incentive of profiting which is indeed illegal.

After Buyback

The company can either retire (cancel) the shares (however, retired shares are not listed as treasury stock on the company's financial statements) or hold the shares for later resale. Buying back stock reduces the number of outstanding shares. Accompanying the decrease in the number of shares outstanding is a reduction in company assets, in particular, cash assets, which are used to buy back shares.

Accounting for Treasury Stock

On the balance sheet, treasury stock is listed under shareholders' equity as a negative number. The accounts may be called "Treasury stock" or "equity reduction".

One way of accounting for treasury stock is with the cost method. In this method, the paid-in capital account is reduced in the balance sheet when the treasury stock is bought. When the treasury stock is sold back on the open market, the paid-in capital is either debited or credited if it is sold for more or less than the initial cost respectively.

Another common way for accounting for treasury stock is the par value method. In the par value method, when the stock is purchased back from the market, the books will reflect the action as a retirement of the shares. Therefore, common stock is debited and treasury stock is credited. However, when the treasury stock is resold back to the market the entry in the books will be the same as the cost method.

In either method, any transaction involving treasury stock cannot increase the amount of retained earnings. If the treasury stock is sold for more than cost, then the paid-in capital treasury stock is the account that is increased, not retained earnings. In auditing financial statements, it is a common practice to check for this error to detect possible attempts to "cook the books."

United States Regulations

In the United States, buybacks are covered by multiple laws under the auspices of the Securities and Exchange Commission.

United Kingdom Regulations

In the UK, the Companies Act 1955 disallowed companies from holding their own shares. However, the Companies Act 1993 later repealed this.

Stock Valuation

In financial markets, stock valuation is the method of calculating theoretical values of companies and their stocks. The main use of these methods is to predict future market prices, or more generally, potential market prices, and thus to profit from price movement – stocks that are judged *undervalued* (with respect to their theoretical value) are bought, while stocks that are judged *overvalued* are sold, in the expectation that undervalued stocks will, on the whole, rise in value, while overvalued stocks will, on the whole, fall.

In the view of fundamental analysis, stock valuation based on fundamentals aims to give an estimate of their intrinsic value of the stock, based on predictions of the future cash flows and profitability of the business. Fundamental analysis may be replaced or augmented by market criteria – what the market will pay for the stock, without any necessary notion of intrinsic value.

These can be combined as "predictions of future cash flows/profits (fundamental)", together with "what will the market pay for these profits?" These can be seen as "supply and demand" sides – what underlies the supply (of stock), and what drives the (market) demand for stock?

In the view of others, such as John Maynard Keynes, stock valuation is not a *prediction* but a *convention,* which serves to facilitate investment and ensure that stocks are liquid, despite being underpinned by an illiquid business and its illiquid investments, such as factories.

Fundamental Criteria (Fair Value)

The most theoretically sound stock valuation method, called income valuation or the discounted cash flow (DCF) method, involves discounting of the profits (dividends, earnings, or cash flows) the stock will bring to the stockholder in the foreseeable future, and a final value on disposal. The discounted rate normally includes a risk premium which is commonly based on the capital asset pricing model.

In July 2010, a Delaware court ruled on appropriate inputs to use in discounted cash flow analysis in a dispute between shareholders and a company over the proper fair value of the stock. In this case the shareholders' model provided value of $139 per share and the company's model provided $89 per share. Contested inputs included the terminal growth rate, the equity risk premium, and beta.

Stock Valuation Methods

Stocks have two types of valuations. One is a value created using some type of cash flow, sales or fundamental earnings analysis. The other value is dictated by how much an investor is willing to pay for a particular share of stock and by how much other investors are willing to sell a stock for (in other words, by supply and demand). Both of these values change over time as investors change the way they analyze stocks and as they become more or less confident in the future of stocks.

The fundamental valuation is the valuation that people use to justify stock prices. The most common example of this type of valuation methodology is P/E ratio, which stands for Price to Earnings Ratio. This form of valuation is based on historic ratios and statistics and aims to assign value to a stock based on measurable attributes. This form of valuation is typically what drives long-term stock prices.

The other way stocks are valued is based on supply and demand. The more people that want to buy the stock, the higher its price will be. And conversely, the more people that want to sell the stock, the lower the price will be. This form of valuation is very hard to understand or predict, and it often drives the short-term stock market trends.

There are many different ways to value stocks. The key is to take each approach into account while formulating an overall opinion of the stock. If the valuation of a company is lower or higher than other similar stocks, then the next step would be to determine the reasons.

Earnings Per Share (EPS)

EPS is the net income available to common shareholders of the company divided by the number of shares outstanding. Usually there will be two types of EPS listed: a GAAP (Generally Accepted Accounting Principles) EPS and a Pro Forma EPS, which means that the income has been adjusted to exclude any one time items as well as some non-cash items like amortization of goodwill or stock option expenses.

The most important thing to look for in the EPS figure is the overall quality of earnings. Make sure the company is not trying to manipulate their EPS numbers to make it look like they are more profitable.

Also, look at the growth in EPS over the past several quarters / years to understand how volatile their EPS is, and to see if they are an underachiever or an overachiever. In other words, have they consistently beaten expectations or are they constantly restating and lowering their forecasts?

The EPS number that most analysts use is the pro forma EPS. To compute this number, use the net income that excludes any one-time gains or losses and excludes any non-cash expenses like stock options or amortization of goodwill. Then divide this number by the number of fully diluted shares outstanding. Historical EPS figures and forecasts for the next 1–2 years can be found by visiting free financial sites such as Yahoo Finance.

Through fundamental investment research, one can determine their own EPS forecasts and apply other valuation techniques below.

Price to Earnings (P/E)

Now that the analyst has several EPS figures (historical and forecasts), the analyst will be able to look at the most common valuation technique used, the price to earnings ratio, or P/E. To compute this figure, one divides the stock price by the annual EPS figure. For example, if the stock is trading at $10 and the EPS is $0.50, the P/E is 20 times. A complete analysis of the P/E multiple includes a look at the historical and forward ratios.

Historical P/Es are computed by taking the current price divided by the sum of the EPS for the last four quarters, or for the previous year. Historical trends of the P/E should also be considered by viewing a chart of its historical P/E over the last several years (one can find this on most finance sites like Yahoo Finance). Specifically consider what range the P/E has traded in so as to determine whether the current P/E is high or low versus its historical average.

Forward P/Es reflect the future growth of the company into the future. Forward P/Es are computed by taking the current stock price divided by the sum of the EPS estimates for the next four quarters, or for the EPS estimate for next calendar or fiscal year or two.

P/Es change constantly. If there is a large price change in a stock, or if the earnings (EPS) estimates change, the ratio is recomputed.

Growth Rate

Valuations rely very heavily on the expected growth rate of a company. One must look at the historical growth rate of both sales and income to get a feeling for the type of future growth expected. However, companies are constantly changing, as well as the economy, so solely using historical growth rates to predict the future is not an acceptable form of valuation. Instead, they are used as guidelines for what future growth could look like if similar circumstances are encountered by the company. Calculating the future growth rate requires personal investment research. This may take form in listening to the company's quarterly conference call or reading a press release or other company article that discusses the company's growth guidance. However, although companies are in the best position to forecast their own growth, they are often far from accurate, and unforeseen events could cause rapid changes in the economy and in the company's industry.

For any valuation technique, it is important to look at a range of forecast values. For example, if the company being valued has been growing earnings between 5 and 10% each year for the last 5 years, but believes that it will grow 15 –20% this year, a more conservative growth rate of 10–15% would be appropriate in valuations. Another example would be for a company that has been going through restructuring. It may have been growing earnings at 10–15% over the past several quarters or years because of cost cutting, but their sales growth could be only 0–5%. This would signal that their earnings growth will probably slow when the cost cutting has fully taken effect. Therefore, forecasting an earnings growth closer to the 0–5% rate would be more appropriate rather than the 15–20%. Nonetheless, the growth rate method of valuations relies heavily on gut feel to make a forecast. This is why analysts often make inaccurate forecasts, and also why familiarity with a company is essential before making a forecast.

Price Earnings to Growth (PEG) Ratio

This valuation technique has really become popular over the past decade or so. It is better than just looking at a P/E because it takes three factors into account; the price, earnings, and earnings growth rates. To compute the PEG ratio, the Forward P/E is divided by the expected earnings growth rate (one can also use historical P/E and historical growth rate to see where it has traded in the past). This will yield a ratio that is usually expressed as a percentage. The theory goes that as the percentage rises over 100% the stock becomes more and more overvalued, and as the PEG ratio falls below 100% the stock becomes more and more undervalued. The theory is based on a belief that P/E ratios should approximate the long-term growth rate of a company's earnings. Whether or not this is true will never be proven and the theory is therefore just a rule of thumb to use in the overall valuation process.

Here is an example of how to use the PEG ratio to compare stocks. Stock A is trading at a forward P/E of 15 and expected to grow at 20%. Stock B is trading at a forward P/E of 30 and expected to grow at 25%. The PEG ratio for Stock A is 75% (15/20) and for Stock B is 120% (30/25). According to the PEG ratio, Stock A is a better purchase because it has a lower PEG ratio, or in other words, you can purchase its future earnings growth for a lower relative price than that of Stock B.

Sum of Perpetuities Method

The PEG ratio is a special case in the Sum of Perpetuities Method (SPM) equation. A generalized version of the Walter model (1956), SPM considers the effects of dividends, earnings growth, as well as the risk profile of a firm on a stock's value. Derived from the compound interest formula using the present value of a perpetuity equation, SPM is an alternative to the Gordon Growth Model. The variables are:

- P is the value of the stock or business
- E is a company's earnings
- G is the company's constant growth rate
- K is the company's risk adjusted discount rate
- D is the company's dividend payment

$$P = \left(\frac{E * G}{K^2}\right) + \left(\frac{D}{K}\right)$$

In a special case where K is equal to 10%, and the company does not pay dividends, SPM reduces to the PEG ratio.

$$Z = \frac{\dfrac{P}{H[P / E]} - E12}{stdev(E12)}$$

Additional models represent the sum of perpetuities in terms of earnings, growth rate, the risk-adjusted discount rate, and accounting book value.

Nerbrand Z

Given that investments are subject to revisions of future expectations the Nerbrand Z utilises uncertainty of consensus estimates to assess how much earnings forecasts can be revised in standard deviation terms before P/E ratios return to normalised levels. This calculation is best done with I/B/E/S consensus estimates. The market tends to focus on the 12 month forward P/E level, but this ratio is dependent on earnings estimates which are never homogenous. Hence there is a standard deviation of 12 month forward earnings estimates.

The Nerbrand z is therefore expressed as

where H[P/E] = normalised P/E, e.g. a 5 year historical average of 12 month forward P/E ratios.

E12 = mean 12 month forward earnings estimates

stdev(E12) = standard deviation of 12 month forward earnings estimates.

A negative number indicates that earnings are likely to be downgraded before valuations normalise. As such, a negative number indicates a valuation adjusted earnings buffer. For example, if the 12 month forward mean EPS forecast is \$10, the price of the equity is \$100, the historical average P/E ratio is 15, and the standard deviation of EPS forecast is 2, then the Nerbrand Z is -1.67. That is, 12 month forward consensus earnings estimates could be downgraded by 1.67 standard deviation before P/E ratio would go back to 15.

Return on Invested Capital (ROIC)

This valuation technique measures how much money the company makes each year per dollar of invested capital. Invested Capital is the amount of money invested in the company by both stockholders and debtors. The ratio is expressed as a percent and one looks for a percent that approximates the level of growth that expected. In its simplest definition, this ratio measures the investment return that management is able to get for its capital. The higher the number, the better the return.

To compute the ratio, take the pro forma net income (same one used in the EPS figure mentioned above) and divide it by the invested capital. Invested capital can be estimated by adding together the stockholders equity, the total long and short term debt and accounts payable, and then subtracting accounts receivable and cash (all of these numbers can be found on the company's latest quarterly balance sheet). This ratio is much more useful when comparing it to other companies being valued.

Return on Assets (ROA)

Similar to ROIC, ROA, expressed as a percent, measures the company's ability to make money from its assets. To measure the ROA, take the pro forma net income divided by the total assets. However, because of very common irregularities in balance sheets (due to things like Goodwill, write-offs, discontinuations, etc.) this ratio is not always a good indicator of the company's potential. If the ratio is higher or lower than expected, one should look closely at the assets to see what could be over or understating the figure.

Price to Sales (P/S)

This figure is useful because it compares the current stock price to the annual sales. In other words, it describes how much the stock costs per dollar of sales earned. To compute it, take the current stock price divided by the annual sales per share. The annual sales per share should be calculated by taking the net sales for the last four quarters divided by the fully diluted shares outstanding (both of these figures can be found by looking at the press releases or quarterly reports). The price to sales ratio is useful, but it does not take into account any debt the company has. For example, if a company is heavily financed by debt instead of equity, then the sales per share will seem high (the P/S will be lower). All things equal, a lower P/S ratio is better. However, this ratio is best looked at when comparing more than one company.

Market Cap

Market cap, which is short for market capitalization, is the value of all of the company's stock. To measure it, multiply the current stock price by the fully diluted shares outstanding. Remember, the market cap is only the value of the stock. To get a more complete picture, look at the enterprise value.

Enterprise Value (EV)

Enterprise value is equal to the total value of the company, as it is trading for on the stock market. To compute it, add the market cap and the total net debt of the company. The total net debt is equal to total long and short term debt plus accounts payable, minus accounts receivable, minus cash. The enterprise value is the best approximation of what a company is worth at any point in time because it takes into account the actual stock price instead of balance sheet prices. When analysts say that a company is a "billion dollar" company, they are often referring to its total enterprise value. Enterprise value fluctuates rapidly based on stock price changes.

EV to Sales

This ratio measures the total company value as compared to its annual sales. A high ratio means that the company's value is much more than its sales. To compute it, divide the EV by the net sales for the last four quarters. This ratio is especially useful when valuing companies that do not have earnings, or that are going through unusually rough times. For example, if a company is facing restructuring and it is currently losing money, then the P/E ratio would be irrelevant. However, by applying an EV to Sales ratio, one could compute what that company could trade for when its restructuring is over and its earnings are back to normal.

EBITDA

EBITDA stands for earnings before interest, taxes, depreciation and amortization. It is one of the best measures of a company's cash flow and is used for valuing both public and private companies. To compute EBITDA, use a company's income statement, take the net income and then add back interest, taxes, depreciation, amortization and any other non-cash or one-time charges. This leaves you with a number that approximates how much cash the company is producing. EBITDA is a very popular figure because it can easily be compared across companies, even if not all of the companies are profitable.

EV to EBITDA

This is perhaps one of the best measurements of whether or not a company is cheap or expensive. To compute, divide the EV by EBITDA. The higher the number, the more expensive the company is. However, remember that more expensive companies are often valued higher because they are growing faster or because they are a higher quality company. With that said, the best way to use EV/ EBITDA is to compare it to that of other similar companies.

Approximate Valuation Approaches

Average Growth Approximation

Assuming that two stocks have the same earnings growth, the one with a lower P/E is a better value. The P/E method is perhaps the most commonly used valuation method in the stock brokerage industry. By using comparison firms, a target price/earnings (or P/ E) ratio is selected for the company, and then the future earnings of the company are estimated. The valuation's fair price is simply estimated earnings times target P/E. This model is essentially the same model as Gordon's model, if k-g is estimated as the dividend payout ratio (D/E) divided by the target P/E ratio.

Constant Growth Approximation

The Gordon model or *Gordon's growth model* is the best known of a class of discounted dividend models. It assumes that dividends will increase at a constant growth rate (less than the discount rate) forever. The valuation is given by the formula:

$$P = D \cdot \sum_{i=1}^{\infty} \left(\frac{1+g}{1+k} \right)^i = D \cdot \frac{1+g}{k-g}.$$

and the following table defines each symbol:

Symbol	*Meaning*	*Units*
P	*estimated stock price*	\$ or € or £
D	*last dividend paid*	\$ or € or £
k	*discount rate*	%
g	*the growth rate of the dividends*	%

Limited High-Growth Period Approximation

When a stock has a significantly higher growth rate than its peers, it is sometimes assumed that the earnings growth rate will be sustained for a short time (say, 5 years), and then the growth rate will revert to the mean. This is probably the most rigorous approximation that is practical.

While these DCF models are commonly used, the uncertainty in these values is hardly ever discussed. Note that the models diverge for $k = g$ and hence are extremely sensitive to the difference of dividend growth to discount factor. One might argue that an analyst can justify any value (and that would usually be one close to the current price supporting his call) by fine-tuning the growth/discount assumptions.

Implied Growth Models

One can use the Gordon model or the limited high-growth period approximation model to impute an implied growth estimate. To do this, one takes the average P/E and average growth for a comparison index, uses the current (or forward) P/E of the stock in question, and calculates what growth rate would be needed for the two valuation equations to be equal. This yields an estimate of the "break-even" growth rate for the stock's current P/E ratio. (Note : we are using earnings not dividends here because dividend policies vary and may be influenced by many factors including tax treatment).

Imputed Growth Acceleration Ratio

Subsequently, one can divide this imputed growth estimate by recent historical growth rates. If the resulting ratio is greater than one, it implies that the stock would need to experience accelerated growth relative to its prior recent historical growth to justify its current P/E (higher values suggest potential overvaluation). If the resulting ratio is less than one, it implies that either the market expects growth to slow for this stock or that the stock could sustain its current P/E with lower than historical growth (lower values suggest potential undervaluation). Comparison of the IGAR across stocks in the same industry may give estimates of relative value. IGAR averages across an industry may give estimates of relative expected changes in industry growth (e.g. the market's imputed expectation that an industry is about to "take-off" or stagnate). Naturally, any differences in IGAR between stocks in the same industry may be due to differences in fundamentals, and would require further specific analysis.

Market Criteria (Potential Price)

Some feel that if the stock is listed in a well organised stock market, with a large volume of transactions, the listed price will be close to the estimated fair value. This is called the efficient market hypothesis.

On the other hand, studies made in the field of behavioural finance tend to show that deviations from the fair price are rather common, and sometimes quite large.

Thus, in addition to fundamental economic criteria, market criteria also have to be taken into account market-based valuation. Valuing a stock requires not just an estimate its fair value, but also to determine its potential price range, taking into account market behaviour aspects. One of the behavioural valuation tools is the stock image, a coefficient that bridges the theoretical fair value and the market price.

Keynes's View

In the view of noted economist John Maynard Keynes, stock valuation is not an *estimate* of the fair value of stocks, but rather a *convention,* which serves to provide the necessary stability and liquidity for investment, so long as the convention does not break down:

Certain classes of investment are governed by the average expectation of those who deal on the Stock Exchange as revealed in the price of shares, rather than by the genuine expectations of the professional entrepreneur. How then are these highly significant daily, even hourly, revaluations of existing investments carried out in practice?

In practice, we have tacitly agreed, as a rule, to fall back on what is, in truth, a convention. The essence of this convention – though it does not, of course, work out so simply – lies in assuming that the existing state of affairs will continue indefinitely, except in so far as we have specific reasons to expect a change.

Nevertheless the above conventional method of calculation will be compatible with a considerable measure of continuity and stability in our affairs, so long as we can rely on the maintenance of the convention. ...

Thus investment becomes reasonably 'safe' for the individual investor over short periods, and hence over a succession of short periods however many, if he can fairly rely on there being no breakdown in the convention and on his therefore having an opportunity to revise his judgment and change his investment, before there has been time for much to happen. Investments which are 'fixed' for the community are thus made 'liquid' for the individual.

— *The General Theory,* Chapter 12

Bond (Finance)

In finance, a bond is an instrument of indebtedness of the bond issuer to the holders. It is a debt security, under which the issuer owes the holders a debt and, depending on the terms of the bond, is obliged to pay them interest (the coupon) and/or to repay the principal at a later date, termed the maturity date. Interest is usually payable at fixed intervals (semiannual, annual, sometimes monthly). Very often the bond is negotiable, i.e. the ownership of the instrument can be transferred in the secondary market. This means that once the transfer agents at the bank medallion stamp the bond on the second market the bond is highly liquid.

Thus a bond is a form of loan or IOU: the *holder* of the bond is the lender (creditor), the *issuer* of the bond is the borrower (debtor), and the *coupon* is the interest. Bonds provide the borrower with external funds to finance long-term investments, or, in the case of government bonds, to finance current expenditure. Certificates of deposit (CDs) or short term commercial paper are considered to be money market instruments and not bonds: the main difference is in the length of the term of the instrument.

Bonds and stocks are both securities, but the major difference between the two is that (capital) stockholders have an equity stake in the company (i.e. they are investors), whereas bondholders have a creditor stake in the company (i.e. they are lenders). Being a creditor, bondholders have absolute priority and will be repaid before stockholders (who are owners) in the event of bankruptcy. Another difference is that bonds usually have a defined term, or maturity, after which the bond is redeemed, whereas stocks are typically outstanding indefinitely. An exception is an irredeemable bond, such as Consols, which is a perpetuity, i.e. a bond with no maturity.

Issuance

Bonds are issued by public authorities, credit institutions, companies and supranational institutions in the primary markets. The most common process for issuing bonds is through underwriting. When a bond issue is underwritten, one or more securities firms or banks, forming a syndicate, buy the entire issue of bonds from the issuer and re-sell them to investors. The security firm takes the risk of being unable to sell on the issue to end investors. Primary issuance is arranged by *bookrunners* who arrange the bond issue, have direct contact with investors and act as advisers to the bond issuer in terms of timing and price of the bond issue. The bookrunner is listed first among all underwriters participating in the issuance in the tombstone ads commonly used to announce bonds to the public. The bookrunners' willingness to underwrite must be discussed prior to any decision on the terms of the bond issue as there may be limited demand for the bonds.

In contrast, government bonds are usually issued in an auction. In some cases both members of the public and banks may bid for bonds. In other cases only market makers may bid for bonds. The overall rate of return on the bond depends on both the terms of the bond and the price paid. The terms of the bond, such as the coupon, are fixed in advance and the price is determined by the market.

In the case of an underwritten bond, the underwriters will charge a fee for underwriting. An alternative process for bond issuance, which is commonly used for smaller issues and avoids this cost, is the private placement bond. Bonds are sold directly to buyers and may not be tradeable in the bond market.

Historically an alternative practice of issuance was for the borrowing government authority to issue bonds over a period of time, usually at a fixed price, with volumes sold on a particular day dependent on market conditions. This was called a *tap issue* or *bond tap*.

Features

Principal

Nominal, principal, par or face amount is the amount on which the issuer pays interest, and which, most commonly, has to be repaid at the end of the term. Some structured bonds can have a redemption amount which is different from the face amount and can be linked to performance of particular assets such as a stock or commodity index, foreign exchange rate or a fund. This can result in an investor receiving less or more than his original investment at maturity.

Maturity

The issuer has to repay the nominal amount on the maturity date. As long as all due payments have been made, the issuer has no further obligations to the bond holders after the maturity date. The length of time until the maturity date is often referred to as the term or tenor or maturity of a bond. The maturity can be any length of time, although debt securities with a term of less than one year are generally designated money market instruments rather than bonds. Most bonds have a term of up to 30 years. Some bonds have been issued with terms of 50 years or more, and historically there have been some issues with no maturity date (irredeemables). In the market for United States Treasury securities, there are three categories of bond maturities:

- short term (bills): maturities between one to five year; (instruments with maturities less than one year are called Money Market Instruments)
- medium term (notes): maturities between six to twelve years;
- long term (bonds): maturities greater than twelve years.

Coupon

The coupon is the interest rate that the issuer pays to the holder. Usually this rate is fixed throughout the life of the bond. It can also vary with a money market index, such as LIBOR, or it can be even more exotic. The name "coupon" arose because in the past, paper bond certificates were issued which had coupons attached to them, one for each interest payment. On the due dates the bondholder would hand in the coupon to a bank in exchange for the interest payment. Interest can be paid at different frequencies: generally semi-annual, i.e. every 6 months, or annual.

Yield

The yield is the rate of return received from investing in the bond. It usually refers either to

- the current yield, or running yield, which is simply the annual interest payment divided by the current market price of the bond (often the clean price), or to

- the yield to maturity or redemption yield, which is a more useful measure of the return of the bond, taking into account the current market price, and the amount and timing of all remaining coupon payments and of the repayment due on maturity. It is equivalent to the internal rate of return of a bond.

Credit Quality

The "quality" of the issue refers to the probability that the bondholders will receive the amounts promised at the due dates. This will depend on a wide range of factors. High-yield bonds are bonds that are rated below investment grade by the credit rating agencies. As these bonds are more risky than investment grade bonds, investors expect to earn a higher yield. These bonds are also called *junk bonds.*

Market Price

The market price of a tradeable bond will be influenced amongst other things by the amounts, currency and timing of the interest payments and capital repayment due, the quality of the bond, and the available redemption yield of other comparable bonds which can be traded in the markets.

The price can be quoted as clean or dirty. ("Dirty" includes the present value of all future cash flows including accrued interest. Most often used in Europe.; "Clean" does not include accrued interest. Most often used in the U.S.)

The issue price at which investors buy the bonds when they are first issued will typically be approximately equal to the nominal amount. The net proceeds that the issuer receives are thus the issue price, less issuance fees. The market price of the bond will vary over its life: it may trade at a premium (above par, usually because market interest rates have fallen since issue), or at a discount (price below par, if market rates have risen or there is a high probability of default on the bond).

Others

- Indentures and Covenants — Anindenture is a formal debt agreement that establishes the terms of a bond issue, while covenants are the clauses of such an agreement. Covenants specify the rights of bondholders and the duties of issuers, such as actions that the issuer is obligated to perform or is prohibited from performing. In the U.S., federal and state securities and commercial laws apply to the enforcement of these agreements, which are construed by courts as contracts between issuers and bondholders. The terms may be changed only with great difficulty while the bonds are outstanding, with amendments to the governing document generally requiring approval by a majority (or super-majority) vote of the bondholders.

- Optionality: Occasionally a bond may contain an embedded option; that is, it grants option-like features to the holder or the issuer:
  - o Callability — Some bonds give the issuer the right to repay the bond before the maturity date on the call dates. These bonds are referred to as callable bonds. Most callable bonds allow the issuer to repay the bond at par. With some bonds, the issuer has to pay a premium, the so-called call premium. This is mainly the case for high-yield bonds. These have very strict covenants, restricting the issuer in its operations. To be free from these covenants, the issuer can repay the bonds early, but only at a high cost.
  - o Putability — Some bonds give the holder the right to force the issuer to repay the bond before the maturity date on the put dates. These are referred to as retractable or putable bonds.
  - o call dates and put dates—the dates on which callable and putable bonds can be redeemed early. There are four main categories.
    - A Bermudan callable has several call dates, usually coinciding with coupon dates.
    - A European callable has only one call date. This is a special case of a Bermudan callable.
    - An American callable can be called at any time until the maturity date.
    - A death put is an optional redemption feature on a debt instrument allowing the beneficiary of the estate of a deceased bondholder to put (sell) the bond (back to the issuer) at face value in the event of the bondholder's death or legal incapacitation. Also known as a "survivor's option".
- sinking fund provision of the corporate bond indenture requires a certain portion of the issue to be retired periodically. The entire bond issue can be liquidated by the maturity date. If that is not the case, then the remainder is called balloon

maturity. Issuers may either pay to trustees, which in turn call randomly selected bonds in the issue, or, alternatively, purchase bonds in open market, then return them to trustees.

Types

The following descriptions are not mutually exclusive, and more than one of them may apply to a particular bond.

- Fixed rate bonds have a coupon that remains constant throughout the life of the bond. A variation are stepped-coupon bonds, whose coupon increases during the life of the bond.
- Floating rate notes (FRNs, floaters) have a variable coupon that is linked to a reference rate of interest, such as LIBOR or Euribor. For example the coupon may be defined as three month USD LIBOR + 0.20%. The coupon rate is recalculated periodically, typically every one or three months.
- Zero-coupon bonds (zeros) pay no regular interest. They are issued at a substantial discount to par value, so that the interest is effectively rolled up to maturity (and usually taxed as such). The bondholder receives the full principal amount on the redemption date. An example of zero coupon bonds is Series E savings bonds issued by the U.S. government. Zero-coupon bonds may be created from fixed rate bonds by a financial institution separating ("stripping off") the coupons from the principal. In other words, the separated coupons and the final principal payment of the bond may be traded separately.
- High-yield bonds (junk bonds) are bonds that are rated below investment grade by the credit rating agencies. As these bonds are more risky than investment grade bonds, investors expect to earn a higher yield.
- Convertible bonds lets a bondholder exchange a bond to a number of shares of the issuer's common stock.
- Exchangeable bonds allows for exchange to shares of a corporation other than the issuer.
- Inflation-indexed bonds (linkers) (US) or Index-linked bond (UK), in which the principal amount and the interest payments are indexed to inflation. The interest rate is normally lower than for fixed rate bonds with a comparable maturity (this position briefly reversed itself for short-term UK bonds in December 2008). However, as the principal amount grows, the payments increase with inflation. The United Kingdom was

the first sovereign issuer to issue inflation linked gilts in the 1980s. Treasury Inflation-Protected Securities (TIPS) and I-bonds are examples of inflation linked bonds issued by the U.S. government.

- Other indexed bonds, for example equity-linked notes and bonds indexed on a business indicator (income, added value) or on a country's GDP.
- Asset-backed securities are bonds whose interest and principal payments are backed by underlying cash flows from other assets. Examples of asset-backed securities are mortgage-backed securities (MBS's), collateralized mortgage obligations (CMOs) and collateralized debt obligations (CDOs).
- Subordinated bonds are those that have a lower priority than other bonds of the issuer in case of liquidation. In case of bankruptcy, there is a hierarchy of creditors. First the liquidator is paid, then government taxes, etc. The first bond holders in line to be paid are those holding what is called senior bonds. After they have been paid, the subordinated bond holders are paid. As a result, the risk is higher. Therefore, subordinated bonds usually have a lower credit rating than senior bonds. The main examples of subordinated bonds can be found in bonds issued by banks, and asset-backed securities. The latter are often issued in tranches. The senior tranches get paid back first, the subordinated tranches later.
- Covered bond are backed by cash flows from mortgages or public sector assets. Contrary to asset-backed securities the assets for such bonds remain on the issuers balance sheet.
- Perpetual bonds are also often called perpetuities or 'Perps'. They have no maturity date. The most famous of these are the UK Consols, which are also known as Treasury Annuities or Undated Treasuries. Some of these were issued back in 1888 and still trade today, although the amounts are now insignificant. Some ultra-long-term bonds (sometimes a bond can last centuries: West Shore Railroad issued a bond which matures in 2361 (i.e. 24th century) are virtually perpetuities from a financial point of view, with the current value of principal near zero.
- Bearer bond is an official certificate issued without a named holder. In other words, the person who has the paper certificate can claim the value of the bond. Often they are registered by a number to prevent counterfeiting, but may be traded like

cash. Bearer bonds are very risky because they can be lost or stolen. Especially after federal income tax began in the United States, bearer bonds were seen as an opportunity to conceal income or assets. U.S. corporations stopped issuing bearer bonds in the 1960s, the U.S. Treasury stopped in 1982, and state and local tax-exempt bearer bonds were prohibited in 1983.

- Registered bond is a bond whose ownership (and any subsequent purchaser) is recorded by the issuer, or by a transfer agent. It is the alternative to a Bearer bond. Interest payments, and the principal upon maturity, are sent to the registered owner.
- A government bond, also called Treasury bond, is issued by a national government and is not exposed to default risk. It is characterized as the safest bond, with the lowest interest rate. A treasury bond is backed by the "full faith and credit" of the relevant government. For that reason, for the major OECD countries this type of bond is often referred to as risk-free.

Municipal bond is a bond issued by a state, U.S. Territory, city, local government, or their agencies. Interest income received by holders of municipal bonds is often exempt from the federal income tax and from the income tax of the state in which they are issued, although municipal bonds issued for certain purposes may not be tax exempt.

- Build America Bonds (BABs) are a form of municipal bond authorized by the American Recovery and Reinvestment Act of 2009. Unlike traditional US municipal bonds, which are usually tax exempt, interest received on BABs is subject to federal taxation. However, as with municipal bonds, the bond is tax-exempt within the US state where it is issued. Generally, BABs offer significantly higher yields (over 7 percent) than standard municipal bonds.
- Book-entry bond is a bond that does not have a paper certificate. As physically processing paper bonds and interest coupons became more expensive, issuers (and banks that used to collect coupon interest for depositors) have tried to discourage their use. Some book-entry bond issues do not offer the option of a paper certificate, even to investors who prefer them.
- Lottery bonds are issued by European and other states. Interest is paid as on a traditional fixed rate bond, but the issuer will redeem randomly selected individual bonds within the issue according to a schedule. Some of these redemptions will be for a higher value than the face value of the bond.

- War bond is a bond issued by a country to fund a war.
- Serial bond is a bond that matures in instalments over a period of time. In effect, a $100,000, 5-year serial bond would mature in a $20,000 annuity over a 5-year interval.
- Revenue bond is a special type of municipal bond distinguished by its guarantee of repayment solely from revenues generated by a specified revenue-generating entity associated with the purpose of the bonds. Revenue bonds are typically "non-recourse," meaning that in the event of default, the bond holder has no recourse to other governmental assets or revenues.
- Climate bond is a bond issued by a government or corporate entity in order to raise finance for climate change mitigation- or adaptation-related projects or programmes.
- Dual currency bonds
- Retail bond is a type of corporate bond with very low interest rates mostly designed for ordinary investors in the industry. They have become particularly attractive since the London Stock Exchange (LSE) launched an order book for retail bonds.
- Social impact bonds are an agreement for public sector entities to pay back private investors after meeting verified improved social outcome goals that result in public sector savings from innovative social program pilot projects.

Foreign Currencies

Some companies, banks, governments, and other sovereign entities may decide to issue bonds in foreign currencies as it may appear to be more stable and predictable than their domestic currency. Issuing bonds denominated in foreign currencies also gives issuers the ability to access investment capital available in foreign markets. The proceeds from the issuance of these bonds can be used by companies to break into foreign markets, or can be converted into the issuing company's local currency to be used on existing operations through the use of foreign exchange swap hedges. Foreign issuer bonds can also be used to hedge foreign exchange rate risk. Some foreign issuer bonds are called by their nicknames, such as the "samurai bond." These can be issued by foreign issuers looking to diversify their investor base away from domestic markets. These bond issues are generally governed by the law of the market of issuance, e.g., a samurai bond, issued by an investor based in Europe, will be governed by Japanese law. Not all of the following bonds are restricted for purchase by investors in the market of issuance.

- Eurodollar bond, a U.S. dollar-denominated bond issued by a non-U.S. entity outside the U.S
- Baklava bond, a bond denominated in Turkish Lira and issued by a domestic or foreign entity in the Turkish market
- Yankee bond, a US dollar-denominated bond issued by a non-US entity in the US market
- Kangaroo bond, an Australian dollar-denominated bond issued by a non-Australian entity in the Australian market
- Maple bond, a Canadian dollar-denominated bond issued by a non-Canadian entity in the Canadian market
- Samurai bond, a Japanese yen-denominated bond issued by a non-Japanese entity in the Japanese market
- Uridashi bond, a non-yen-demoninated bond sold to Japanese retail investors.
- Shibosai Bond, a private placement bond in Japanese market with distribution limited to institutions and banks.
- Shogun bond, a non-yen-denominated bond issued in Japan by a non-Japanese institution or government
- Bulldog bond, a pound sterling-denominated bond issued in London by a foreign institution or government.
- Matrioshka bond, a Russian rouble-denominated bond issued in the Russian Federation by non-Russian entities. The name derives from the famous Russian wooden dolls, Matrioshka, popular among foreign visitors to Russia
- Arirang bond, a Korean won-denominated bond issued by a non-Korean entity in the Korean market
- Kimchi bond, a non-Korean won-denominated bond issued by a non-Korean entity in the Korean market
- Formosa bond, a non-New Taiwan Dollar-denominated bond issued by a non-Taiwan entity in the Taiwan market
- Panda bond, a Chinese renminbi-denominated bond issued by a non-China entity in the People's Republic of China market
- Dim sum bond, a Chinese renminbi-denominated bond issued by a Chinese entity in Hong Kong. Enables foreign investors forbidden from investing in Chinese corporate debt in mainland China to invest in and be exposed to Chinese currency in Hong Kong.
- Huaso bond, a Chilean peso-denominated bond issued by a non-Chilean entity in the Chilean market.

- Thai Baht bond, issued by The Ministraty of Finance of The Lao People's Democratic Republic (Lao PDR) into the Thailand market.

Investing in Bonds

Bonds are bought and traded mostly by institutions like central banks, sovereign wealth funds, pension funds, insurance companies, hedge funds, and banks. Insurance companies and pension funds have liabilities which essentially include fixed amounts payable on predetermined dates.

They buy the bonds to match their liabilities, and may be compelled by law to do this. Most individuals who want to own bonds do so through bond funds. Still, in the U.S., nearly 10% of all bonds outstanding are held directly by households.

The volatility of bonds (especially short and medium dated bonds) is lower than that of equities (stocks). Thus bonds are generally viewed as safer investments than stocks, but this perception is only partially correct. Bonds do suffer from less day-to-day volatility than stocks, and bonds' interest payments are sometimes higher than the general level of dividend payments. Bonds are often liquid – it is often fairly easy for an institution to sell a large quantity of bonds without affecting the price much, which may be more difficult for equities – and the comparative certainty of a fixed interest payment twice a year and a fixed lump sum at maturity is attractive. Bondholders also enjoy a measure of legal protection: under the law of most countries, if a company goes bankrupt, its bondholders will often receive some money back (the recovery amount), whereas the company's equity stock often ends up valueless. However, bonds can also be risky but less risky than stocks:

- Fixed rate bonds are subject to *interest rate risk*, meaning that their market prices will decrease in value when the generally prevailing interest rates rise. Since the payments are fixed, a decrease in the market price of the bond means an increase in its yield. When the market interest rate rises, the market price of bonds will fall, reflecting investors' ability to get a higher interest rate on their money elsewhere — perhaps by purchasing a newly issued bond that already features the newly higher interest rate. This does not affect the interest payments to the bondholder, so long-term investors who want a specific amount at the maturity date do not need to worry about price swings in their bonds and do not suffer from interest rate risk.

Bonds are also subject to various other risks such as call and prepayment risk, credit risk, reinvestment risk, liquidity risk, event risk, exchange rate risk, volatility risk, inflation risk, sovereign risk and yield curve risk. Again, some of these will only affect certain classes of investors.

Price changes in a bond will immediately affect mutual funds that hold these bonds. If the value of the bonds in their trading portfolio falls, the value of the portfolio also falls. This can be damaging for professional investors such as banks, insurance companies, pension funds and asset managers (irrespective of whether the value is immediately "marked to market" or not).

If there is any chance a holder of individual bonds may need to sell his bonds and "cash out", interest rate risk could become a real problem (conversely, bonds' market prices would increase if the prevailing interest rate were to drop, as it did from 2001 through 2003. One way to quantify the interest rate risk on a bond is in terms of its duration. Efforts to control this risk are called immunization or hedging.

- Bond prices can become volatile depending on the credit rating of the issuer – for instance if the credit rating agencies like Standard & Poor's and Moody's upgrade or downgrade the credit rating of the issuer. An unanticipated downgrade will cause the market price of the bond to fall. As with interest rate risk, this risk does not affect the bond's interest payments (provided the issuer does not actually default), but puts at risk the market price, which affects mutual funds holding these bonds, and holders of individual bonds who may have to sell them.
- A company's bondholders may lose much or all their money if the company goes bankrupt. Under the laws of many countries (including the United States and Canada), bondholders are in line to receive the proceeds of the sale of the assets of a liquidated company ahead of some other creditors. Bank lenders, deposit holders (in the case of a deposit taking institution such as a bank) and trade creditors may take precedence.

There is no guarantee of how much money will remain to repay bondholders. As an example, after an accounting scandal and a Chapter 11 bankruptcy at the giant telecommunications company Worldcom, in 2004 its bondholders ended up being paid 35.7 cents on the dollar. In a bankruptcy involving reorganisation or recapitalization, as opposed to liquidation, bondholders may end up having the value of their bonds reduced, often through an exchange for a smaller number of newly issued bonds.

- Some bonds are callable, meaning that even though the company has agreed to make payments plus interest towards the debt for a certain period of time, the company can choose to pay off the bond early. This creates reinvestment risk, meaning the investor is forced to find a new place for his money, and the investor might not be able to find as good a deal, especially because this usually happens when interest rates are falling.

Bond Indices

A number of bond indices exist for the purposes of managing portfolios and measuring performance, similar to the S&P 500 or Russell Indexes for stocks. The most common American benchmarks are the Barclays Capital Aggregate (ex Lehman Aggregate), Citigroup BIG and Merrill Lynch Domestic Master. Most indices are parts of families of broader indices that can be used to measure global bond portfolios, or may be further subdivided by maturity and/or sector for managing specialised portfolios.

Bond Valuation

Bond valuation is the determination of the fair price of a bond. As with any security or capital investment, the theoretical fair value of a bond is the present value of the stream of cash flows it is expected to generate. Hence, the value of a bond is obtained by discounting the bond's expected cash flows to the present using an appropriate discount rate. In practice, this discount rate is often determined by reference to similar instruments, provided that such instruments exist. Various related yield-measures are calculated for the given price.

If the bond includes embedded options, the valuation is more difficult and combines option pricing with discounting. Depending on the type of option, the option price as calculated is either added to or subtracted from the price of the "straight" portion.

Bond Valuation

As above, the fair price of a "straight bond" (a bond with no embedded options) is usually determined by discounting its expected cash flows at the appropriate discount rate. The formula commonly applied is discussed initially. Although this present value relationship reflects the theoretical approach to determining the value of a bond, in practice its price is (usually) determined with reference to other, more liquid instruments. The two main approaches here, Relative pricing and Arbitrage-free pricing, are discussed next. Finally, where it is important to recognise that future interest rates are uncertain and that the discount rate is not adequately represented by a single fixed number - for example when an option is written on the bond in question - stochastic calculus may be employed.

Where the market price of bond is less than its face value (par value), the bond is selling at a discount. Conversely, if the market price of bond is greater than its face value, the bond is selling at a premium.

Present Value Approach

Below is the formula for calculating a bond's price, which uses the basic present value (PV) formula for a given discount rate: (This formula assumes that a coupon payment has just been made.)

$$P = \left(\frac{C}{1+i} + \frac{C}{(1+i)^2} + \ldots + \frac{C}{(1+i)^N}\right) + \frac{M}{(1+i)^N} = \left(\sum_{n=1}^{N} \frac{C}{(1+i)^n}\right) + \frac{M}{(1+i)^N} = C\left(\frac{1-(1+i)^{-N}}{i}\right) + M(1+i)^{-N}$$

where:

F = face values

i_F = contractual interest rate

C = F * i_F = coupon payment (periodic interest payment)

N = number of payments

i = market interest rate, or required yield, or observed / appropriate yield to maturity

M = value at maturity, usually equals face value

P = market price of bond.

Relative Price Approach

Under this approach - an extension of the above - the bond will be priced relative to a benchmark, usually a government security. Here, the yield to maturity on the bond is determined based on the bond's Credit rating relative to a government security with similar maturity or duration. The better the quality of the bond, the smaller the spread between its required return and the YTM of the benchmark. This required return is then used to discount the bond cash flows, replacing *i* in the formula above, to obtain the price.

Arbitrage-Free Pricing Approach

As distinct from the two related approaches above, a bond may be thought of as a "package of cash flows" - coupon or face - with each cash flow viewed as a zero-coupon instrument maturing on the date it will be received. Thus, rather than using a single discount rate, one should use multiple discount rates, discounting each cash flow at its own rate. Here, each cash flow is separately discounted at the same rate as a zero-coupon bond corresponding to the coupon date, and of equivalent credit worthiness (if possible, from the same issuer as the bond being valued, or if not, with the appropriate credit spread).

Under this approach, the bond price should reflect its "arbitrage-free" price, as any deviation from this price will be exploited and the bond will then quickly reprice to its correct level. Here, we apply the rational pricing logic relating to "Assets with identical cash flows". In detail: (1) the bond's coupon dates and coupon amounts are known with certainty. Therefore (2) some multiple (or fraction) of zero-coupon bonds, each corresponding to the bond's coupon dates, can be specified so as to produce identical cash flows to the bond. Thus (3) the bond price today must be equal to the sum of each of its cash flows discounted at the discount rate implied by the value of the corresponding ZCB. Were this not the case, (4) the arbitrageur could finance his purchase of whichever of the bond or the sum of the various ZCBs was cheaper, by short selling the other, and meeting his cash flow commitments using the coupons or maturing zeroes as appropriate. Then (5) his "risk free", arbitrage profit would be the difference between the two values.

Stochastic Calculus Approach

When modelling a bond option, or other interest rate derivative (IRD), it is important to recognise that future interest rates are uncertain, and therefore, the discount rate(s) referred to above, under all three cases - i.e. whether for all coupons or for each individual coupon - is not adequately represented by a fixed (deterministic) number. In such cases, stochastic calculus is employed.

The following is a partial differential equation (PDE) in stochastic calculus which is satisfied by any zero-coupon bond.

$$\frac{1}{2}\sigma(r)^2\frac{\partial^2 P}{\partial r^2}+[a(r)+\sigma(r)+\varphi(r,t)]\frac{\partial P}{\partial r}+\frac{\partial P}{\partial t}-rP=0$$

The solution to the PDE - given in - is:

$$P[t,T,r(t)]=E_t^*[e^{-R(t,T)}]$$

where E_t^* is the expectation with respect to risk-neutral probabilities, and $R(t,T)$ is a random variable representing the discount rate.

To actually determine the bond price, the analyst must choose the specific short rate model to be employed. The approaches commonly used are:

- the CIR model
- the Black-Derman-Toy model
- the Hull-White model
- the HJM framework
- the Chen model.

Note that depending on the model selected, a closed-form solution may not be available, and a lattice- or simulation-based implementation of the model in question is then employed.

Clean and Dirty Price

When the bond is not valued precisely on a coupon date, the calculated price, using the methods above, will incorporate accrued interest: i.e. any interest due to the owner of the bond since the previous coupon date. The price of a bond which includes this accrued interest is known as the "dirty price" (or "full price" or "all in price" or "Cash price"). The "clean price" is the price excluding any interest that has accrued. Clean prices are generally more stable over time than dirty prices.

This is because the dirty price will drop suddenly when the bond goes "ex interest" and the purchaser is no longer entitled to receive the next coupon payment. In many markets, it is market practice to quote bonds on a clean-price basis. When a purchase is settled, the accrued interest is added to the quoted clean price to arrive at the actual amount to be paid.

Yield and Price Relationships

Once the price or value has been calculated, various yields relating the price of the bond to its coupons can then be determined.

Yield to Maturity

The yield to maturity is the discount rate which returns the market price of a bond without embedded optionality; it is identical to (required return) in the above equation. YTM is thus the internal rate of return of an investment in the bond made at the observed price. Since YTM can be used to price a bond, bond prices are often quoted in terms of YTM.

To achieve a return equal to YTM, i.e. where it is the required return on the bond, the bond owner must:

- buy the bond at price P_0,
- hold the bond until maturity, and
- redeem the bond at par.

Coupon Yield

The coupon yield is simply the coupon payment (*C*) as a percentage of the face value (*F*).

$$Couponyield = \frac{C}{F}$$

Coupon yield is also called nominal yield.

Current Yield

The current yield is simply the coupon payment (C) as a percentage of the (*current*) bond price (P).

Current yield = C / P_0.

Relationship

The concept of current yield is closely related to other bond concepts, including yield to maturity, and coupon yield. The relationship between yield to maturity and the coupon rate is as follows:

- When a bond sells at a discount, YTM > current yield > coupon yield.
- When a bond sells at a premium, coupon yield > current yield > YTM.
- When a bond sells at par, YTM = current yield = coupon yield

Price Sensitivity

The sensitivity of a bond's market price to interest rate (i.e. yield) movements is measured by its duration, and, additionally, by its convexity.

Duration is a linear measure of how the price of a bond changes in response to interest rate changes. It is approximately equal to the percentage change in price for a given change in yield, and may be thought of as the elasticity of the bond's price with respect to discount rates. For example, for small interest rate changes, the duration is the approximate percentage by which the value of the bond will fall for a 1% per annum increase in market interest rate. So the market price of a 17-year bond with a duration of 7 would fall about 7% if the market interest rate (or more precisely the corresponding force of interest) increased by 1% per annum.

Convexity is a measure of the "curvature" of price changes. It is needed because the price is not a linear function of the discount rate, but rather a convex function of the discount rate. Specifically, duration can be formulated as the first derivative of the price with respect to the interest rate, and convexity as the second derivative (see: Bond duration closed-form formula; Bond convexity closed-form formula). Continuing the above example, for a more accurate estimate of sensitivity, the convexity score would be multiplied by the square of the change in interest rate, and the result added to the value derived by the above linear formula.

Accounting Treatment

In accounting for liabilities, any bond discount or premium must be amortized over the life of the bond. A number of methods may be used for this depending on applicable accounting rules. One possibility is that amortization amount in each period is calculated from the following formula:

$$n \in \{0,1,...,N-1\}$$

a_{n+1}= amortization amount in period number "n+1"

$$a_{n+1} = |iP - C|(1+i)^n$$

Bond Discount or Bond Premium = $|F-P| = a_1 + a_2 + ... + a_N$

Bond Discount or Bond Premium = $F|i - i_F|(\frac{1-(1+i)^{-N}}{i})$

Shareholder

A shareholder or stockholder is an individual or institution (including a corporation) that legally owns a share of stock in a public or private corporation. Shareholders are the owners of a limited company. They buy shares which represent part ownership of a company.

Stockholders are granted special privileges depending on the class of stock. These rights may include:

- The right to sell their shares.
- The right to vote on the directors nominated by the board.
- The right to nominate directors (although this is very difficult in practice because of minority protections) and propose shareholder resolutions.
- The right to dividends if they are declared.

- The right to purchase new shares issued by the company.
- The right to what assets remain after a liquidation.

Stockholders or shareholders are considered by some to be a subset of stakeholders, which may include anyone who has a direct or indirect interest in the business entity. For example, employees, suppliers, customers, the community, etc., are typically considered stakeholders because they contribute value and/or are impacted by the corporation.

Shareholders in the primary market who buy IPOs provide capital to corporations; however, the vast majority of shareholders are in the secondary market and provide no capital directly to the corporation.

Total Shareholder Return

Total Shareholder Return (TSR) (or simply Total Return) is a measure of the performance of different companies' stocks and shares over time. It combines share price appreciation and dividends paid to show the total return to the shareholder expressed as an annualized percentage. It is calculated by the growth in capital from purchasing a share in the company assuming that the dividends are reinvested each time they are paid. This growth is expressed as a percentage as the compound annual growth rate.

The main benefit of TSR is that allows the performance of shares to be compared even though some of the shares may have a high growth and low dividends and others may have low growth and high dividends.

Most stock market indices only use the growth of the prices of the companies making up the index. However, when they use TSR for the companies it is called a total return index or accumulation index. For example, corresponding to the S&P 500 index calculated by Standard and Poor's, there is the S&P 500 TR index.

In practice TSR is difficult to calculate since it involves knowing the price of the shares at the time the dividends are paid. However, as an approximation over one year it can be calculated as follows with:

$Price_{begin}$ = share price at beginning of year,

$Price_{end}$ = share price at end of year,

Dividends = dividends paid over year and

TSR = Total Shareholder Return, TSR is computed as

$$TSR = (Price_{end} - Price_{begin} + Dividends) / Price_{begin}$$

Shareholder Yield

The term shareholder yield captures the three ways in which the management of a public company can distribute cash to shareholders: cash dividends, stock repurchases and debt reduction.

Dividends are the most obvious form of distributing cash. Stock repurchases also increase shareholder value provided the shares purchased are cancelled or held in treasury but not used as a device to make up for dilution from option issuances to management and others. Reducing debt can also produce a de facto dividend; assuming the value of the firm remains the same, shareholder value is increased as debt is reduced.

To understand how debt reduction increases shareholder value, it is helpful to consider the 1958 paper by Nobel laureates Franco Modigliani and Merton H. Miller entitled *The Cost of Capital, Corporation Finance and the Theory of Investment*. This paper proved that a firm's value is independent of how it is financed, provided that one ignores the tax effect of debt interest. If Modigliani and Miller are correct, the use of free cash flow to repay debt results in a transfer of wealth from the debtor to the shareholder.

The term shareholder yield was coined by William W. Priest of Epoch Investment Partners in a paper in 2005 entitled *The Case for Shareholder Yield as a Dominant Driver of Future Equity Returns* as a way to look more holistically at how companies allocate and distribute cash rather than considering dividends in isolation.

5

Capital Structure and Executive Compensation

Executive Compensation

Executive compensation or executive pay is composed of the financial compensation and other non-financial awards received by an executive of a firm. It is typically a mixture of salary, bonuses, shares of or call options on the company stock, benefits, and perquisites, ideally configured to take into account government regulations, tax law, the desires of the organisation and the executive, and rewards for performance.

The three decades starting with the 1980s, saw a dramatic rise in executive pay relative to that of an average worker's wage in the United States, and to a lesser extent in a number of other countries. Observers differ as to whether this rise is a natural and beneficial result of competition for scarce business talent that can add greatly to stockholder value in large companies, or a socially harmful phenomenon brought about by social and political changes that have given executives greater control over their own pay. Executive pay is an important part of corporate governance, and is often determined by a company's board of directors.

Types

There are six basic tools of compensation or remuneration:

- salary
- short-term incentives (STIs), sometimes known as bonuses
- long-term incentive plans (LTIPs)

- employee benefits
- paid expenses (perquisites)
- insurance

In a modern corporation, the CEO and other top executives are often paid salary plus short-term incentives or bonuses. This combination is referred to as Total Cash Compensation (TCC). Short-term incentives usually are formula-driven and have some performance criteria attached depending on the role of the executive. For example, the Sales Director's performance related bonus may be based on incremental revenue growth turnover; a CEO's could be based on incremental profitability and revenue growth. Bonuses are after-the-fact (not formula driven) and often discretionary. Executives may also be compensated with a mixture of cash and shares of the company which are almost always subject to vesting restrictions (a long-term incentive). To be considered a long-term incentive the measurement period must be in excess of one year (3–5 years is common).

The vesting term refers to the period of time before the recipient has the right to transfer shares and realise value. Vesting can be based on time, performance or both. For example a CEO might get 1 million in cash, and 1 million in company shares (and share buy options used). Vesting can occur in two ways: "cliff vesting" (vesting occurring on one date), and "graded vesting" (which occurs over a period of time) and which maybe "uniform" (e.g., 20% of the options vest each year for 5 years) or "non-uniform" (e.g., 20%, 30% and 50% of the options vest each year for the next three years). Other components of an executive compensation package may include such perks as generous retirement plans, health insurance, a chauffeured limousine, an executive jet, and interest-free loans for the purchase of housing.

Stock Options

Executive stock option pay rose dramatically in the United States after scholarly support from University of Chicago educated Professors Michael C. Jensen and Kevin J. Murphy. Due to their publications in the Harvard Business Review 1990 and support from Wall Street and institutional investors, Congress passed a law making it cost effective to pay executives in equity.

Supporters of stock options say they align the interests of CEOs to those of shareholders, since options are valuable only if the stock price remains above the option's strike price. Stock options are now counted as a corporate expense (non-cash), which impacts a company's income statement and makes the distribution of options more transparent to shareholders. Critics of stock options charge that they are granted without justification as there is little reason to align the interests of CEOs with those of shareholders. Empirical evidence shows since the wide use of stock options, executive pay relative to workers has dramatically risen. Moreover, executive stock options contributed to the accounting manipulation scandals of the late 1990s and abuses such as the options backdating of such grants. Finally, researchers have shown that relationships between executive stock options and stock buybacks, implying that executives use corporate resources to inflate stock prices before they exercise their options.

Stock options also incentivize executives to engage in risk-seeking behaviour. This is because the value of a call option increases with increased volatility. Stock options also present a potential up-side gain (if the stock price goes up) for the executive, but no downside risk (if the stock price goes down, the option simply isn't exercised). Stock options therefore can incentivize excessive risk seeking behaviour that can lead to catastrophic corporate failure.

Restricted Stock

Executives are also compensated with restricted stock, which is stock given to an executive that cannot be sold until certain conditions are met and has the same value as the market price of the stock at the time of grant. As the size of stock option grants have been reduced, the number of companies granting restricted stock either with stock options or instead of, has increased. Restricted stock has its detractors, too, as it has value even when the stock price falls. As an alternative to straight time vested restricted stock, companies have been adding performance type features to their grants.

These grants, which could be called performance shares, do not vest or are not granted until these conditions are met. These performance conditions could be earnings per share or internal financial targets.

Levels

The levels of compensation in all countries has been rising dramatically over the past decades. Not only is it rising in absolute terms, but also in relative terms. In 2007, the world's highest paid chief executive officers and chief financial officers were American. They made 400 times more than average workers—a gap 20 times bigger than it was in 1965. In 2010 the highest paid CEO was Viacom's Philippe P. Dauman at $84.5 million The U.S. has the world's highest CEO's compensation relative to manufacturing production workers.

According to one 2005 estimate the U.S. ratio of CEO's to production worker pay is 39:1 compared to 31.8:1 in UK; 25.9:1 in Italy; 24.9:1 in New Zealand.

Controversy

The explosion in executive pay has become controversial, criticized by not only leftists but conservative establishmentarians such as Ben Bernanke Peter Drucker, John Bogle, Warren Buffett.

The idea that stock options and other alleged pay-for-performance are driven by economics has also been questioned. According to economist Paul Krugman, "Today the idea that huge paychecks are part of a beneficial system in which executives are given an incentive to perform well has become something of a sick joke. A 2001 article in *Fortune*, "The Great CEO Pay Heist" encapsulated the cynicism: You might have expected it to go like this: The stock isn't moving, so the CEO shouldn't be rewarded. But it was actually the opposite: The stock isn't moving, so we've got to find some other basis for rewarding the CEO.` And the article quoted a somewhat repentant Michael Jensen [a theorist for stock option compensation]: `I've generally worried these guys weren't getting paid enough. But now even I'm troubled.'"

Defenders of high executive pay say that the global war for talent and the rise of private equity firms can explain much of the increase in executive pay. For example, while in conservative Japan a senior executive has few alternatives to his current employer, in the United States it is acceptable and even admirable for a senior executive to jump to a competitor, to a private equity firm, or to a private equity portfolio company. Portfolio company executives take a pay cut but are routinely granted stock options for ownership of ten percent of the portfolio company, contingent on a successful tenure. Rather than signaling a conspiracy, defenders argue, the increase in executive pay is a mere byproduct of supply and demand for executive talent. However, U.S. executives make substantially more than their European and Asian counterparts.

United States

The U.S. Securities and Exchange Commission (SEC) has asked publicly traded companies to disclose more information explaining how their executives' compensation amounts are determined. The SEC has also posted compensation amounts on its website to make it easier for investors to compare compensation amounts paid by different companies. It is interesting to juxtapose SEC regulations related to executive compensation with Congressional efforts to address such compensation.

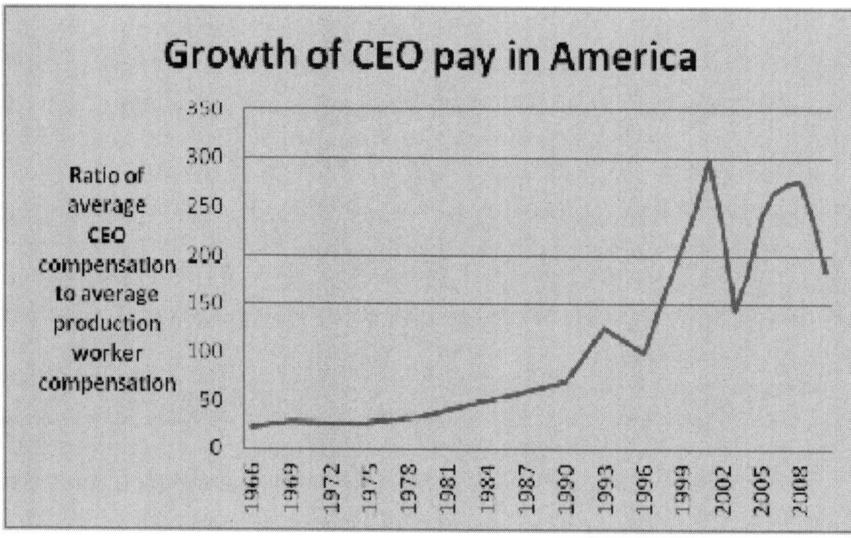

Figure: *Source: Economic Policy Institute. 2011.*

Since the 1990s, CEO compensation in the US has outpaced corporate profits, economic growth and the average compensation of all workers. Between 1980 and 2004, Mutual Fund founder John Bogle estimates total CEO compensation grew 8.5%/year compared, compared to corporate profit growth of 2.9%/year and per capita income growth of 3.1%. By 2006 CEOs made 400 times more than average workers—a gap 20 times bigger than it was in 1965. As a general rule, the larger the corporation the larger the CEO compensation package.

The share of corporate income devoted to compensating the five highest paid executives of (each) public firms more than doubled from 4.8% in 1993-1995 to 10.3% in 2001-2003. The pay for the five top-earning executives at each of the largest 1500 American companies for the ten years from 1994 to 2004 is estimated at approximately $500 billion in 2005 dollars.

As of late March 2012 USA Today's tally showed the median CEO pay of the S&P 500 for 2011 was $9.6 million.

Lower level executives also have fared well. About 40% of the top 0.1% income earners in the United States are executives, managers, or supervisors (and this doesn't include the finance industry) — far out of proportion to less than 5% of the working population that management occupations make up.

A study by University of Florida researchers found that highly paid CEOs improve company profitability as opposed to executives making less for similar jobs. However, a review of the experimental and quasi-experimental research relevant to executive compensation, by Philippe Jacquart and J. Scott Armstrong, found opposing results. In particular, the authors conclude that "the notion that higher pay leads to the selection of better executives is undermined by the prevalence of poor recruiting methods.

Moreover, higher pay fails to promote better performance. Instead, it undermines the intrinsic motivation of executives, inhibits their learning, leads them to ignore other stakeholders, and discourages them from considering the long-term effects of their decisions on stakeholders." Another study by Professors Lynne M. Andersson and Thomas S. Batemann published in the *Journal of Organisational Behaviour* found that highly paid executives are more likely to behave cynically and therefore show tendencies of unethical performance.

Australia

In Australia, shareholders can vote against the pay rises of board members, but the vote is non-binding. Instead the shareholders can sack some or all of the board members. Australia's corporate watchdog, the Australian Securities and Investments Commission has called on companies to improve the disclosure of their remuneration arrangements for directors and executives.

Canada

A 2012 report by the Canadian Centre for Policy Alternatives complained that the top 100 Canadian CEOs were paid an average of C$8.4 million in 2010, a 27% increase over 2009, this compared to C$44,366 earned by the average Canadian that year, 1.1% more than in 2009. The top three earners were automotive supplier Magna International Inc. founder Frank Stronach at C$61.8 million, co-CEO Donald Walker at C$16.7 million and former co-CEO Siegfried Wolf at C$16.5 million.

Europe

In 2008, Jean-Claude Juncker, president of the European Commission's "Eurogroup" of finance ministers, called excessive pay a "social scourge" and demanded action.

United Kingdom

Although executive compensation in the UK is said to be "dwarfed" by that of corporate America, it has caused public upset. In response to criticism of high levels of executive pay, the Compass organisation set up the High Pay Commission. Its 2011 report described the pay of executives as "corrosive".

In December 2011/January 2012 two of the country's biggest investors, Fidelity Worldwide Investment, and the Association of British Insurers, called for greater shareholder control over executive pay packages. Dominic Rossi of Fidelity Worldwide Investment stated, "Inappropriate levels of executive reward have destroyed public trust and led to a situation where all directors are perceived to be overpaid. The simple truth is that remuneration schemes have become too complex and, in some cases, too generous and out of line with the interests of investors." Two sources of public anger were Barclays, where senior executives were promised million-pound pay packages despite a 30% drop in share price; and Royal Bank of Scotland where the head of investment banking was set to earn a "large sum" after thousands of employees were made redundant.

Regulation

There are a number of strategies that could be employed as a response to the growth of executive compensation.

- As passed in the Swiss referendum "against corporate Rip-offs" of 2013, investors gain total control over executive compensation, and the executives of a board of directors. Institutional intermediaries must all vote in the interests of their beneficiaries and banks are prohibited from voting on behalf of investors.
- Disclosure of salaries is the first step, so that company stakeholders can know and decide whether or not they think remuneration is fair. In the UK, the Directors' Remuneration Report Regulations 2002 introduced a requirement into the old Companies Act 1985, the requirement to release all details of pay in the annual accounts. This is now codified in the Companies Act 2006. Similar requirements exist in most countries, including the U.S., Germany, and Canada.
- A say on pay - a non-binding vote of the general meeting to approve director pay packages, is practised in a growing number of countries. Some commentators have advocated a mandatory binding vote for large amounts (e.g. over $5 million). The aim is that the vote will be a highly influential signal to a board to not raise salaries beyond reasonable levels. The general meeting means shareholders in most countries. In most

European countries though, with two-tier board structures, a supervisory board will represent employees and shareholders alike. It is this supervisory board which votes on executive compensation.

- Another proposed reform is the bonus-malus system, where executives carry down-side risk in addition to potential up-side reward.
- Progressive taxation is a more general strategy that affects executive compensation, as well as other highly paid people. There has been a recent trend to cutting the highest bracket tax payers, a notable example being the tax cuts in the U.S. For example, the Baltic States have a flat tax system for incomes. Executive compensation could be checked by taxing more heavily the highest earners, for instance by taking a greater percentage of income over $200,000.
- Maximum wage is an idea which has been enacted in early 2009 in the United States, where they capped executive pay at $500,000 per year for companies receiving extraordinary financial assistance from the U.S. taxpayers. The argument is to place a cap on the amount that any person may legally make, in the same way as there is a floor of a minimum wage so that people can not earn too little.
- Debt Like Compensation - It has been widely accepted that the risk taking motivation of executives depends on its position in equity based compensation and risky debt. Adding debt like instrument as part of an executive compensation may reduce the risk taking motivation of executives. Therefore, as of 2011, there are several proposals to enforce financial institutions to use debt like compensation.
- Indexing Operating Performance is a way to make bonus targets business cycle independent. Indexed bonus targets move with the business cycle and are therefore fairer and valid for a longer period of time.
- Two strikes - In Australia an amendment to the *Corporations Amendment (Improving Accountability on Director and Executive Remuneration) Bill 2011* puts in place processes to trigger a re-election of a Board where a 25% "no" vote by shareholders to the company's remuneration report has been recorded in two consecutive annual general meetings. When the second "no" vote is recorded at an AGM, the meeting will be suspended and shareholders will be asked to vote on whether

a spill meeting is to be held. This vote must be upheld by at least a 50% majority for the spill (or re-election process) to be run. At a spill meeting all directors current at the time the remuneration report was considered are required to stand for re-election.

- Independent non-executive director setting of compensation is widely practised. An independent remuneration committee is an attempt to have pay packages set at arms' length from the directors who are getting paid.

Employee Stock Option

An employee stock option (ESO) is commonly viewed as a complex call option on the common stock of a company, granted by the company to an employee as part of the employee's remuneration package. Regulators and economists have since specified that "employee stock options" is a label that refers to compensation contracts between an employer and an employee that carries some characteristics of financial options but are not in and of themselves options (that is they are "compensation contracts").

As described in the AICPA's Financial Reporting Alert on this topic, for the employer who uses ESO contracts as compensation, the contracts amount to a "short" position in the employer's equity, unless the contract is tied to some other attribute of the employer's balance sheet. To the extent the employer's position can be modelled as a type of option, it is most often modelled as a "short position in a call." From the employee's point of view, the compensation contract provides a conditional right to buy the equity of the employer and when modelled as an option, the employee's perspective is that of a "long position in a call option."

Employee Stock Options are non standard contracts with the employer whereby the employer has the liability of delivering a certain number of shares of the employer stock, when and if the employee stock options are exercised by the employee. Traditional employee stock options have structural problems, in that when exercised followed by an immediate sale of stock, the alignment between employee/ shareholders is eliminated. Early exercises also have substantial penalties to the exercising employee.

Those penalties are a) part of the "fair value" of the options, called "time value" is forfeited back to the company and b) an early tax liability occurs. These two penalties overcome the merits of "diversifying" in most cases.

Stock option expensing was a controversy well before the most recent set of controversies in the early 2000s. The earliest attempts by accounting regulators to expense stock options in the early 1990s were unsuccessful and resulted in the promulgation of FAS123 by the FASB which required disclosure of stock option positions but no income statement expensing, per se. The controversy continued and in 2005, at the insistence of the SEC, the Financial Accounting Standards Board modified the FAS123 rule to provide a rule that the options should be expensed as of the grant date. One misunderstanding is that the expense is at the fair value of the options. This is not true. The expense is indeed based on the fair value of the options but that fair value measure does not follow the fair value rules for other items which are governed by a separate set of rules under ASC Topic 820. In addition the fair value measure must be modified for forfeiture estimates and may be modified for other factors such as liquidity before expensing can occur. Finally the expense of the resulting number is rarely made on the grant date but in some cases must be deferred and in other cases may be deferred over time as set forth in the revised accounting rules for these contracts known as FAS123(revised).

Objectives

Many companies use employee stock options plans to retain and attract employees, the objective being to give employees an incentive to behave in ways that will boost the company's stock price. If the company's stock market price rises above the call price, the employee could exercise the option, pay the exercise price and would be issued with ordinary shares in the company. The employee would experience a direct financial benefit of the difference between the market and the exercise prices. If the market price falls below the stock exercise price at the time near expiration, the employee is not obligated to exercise the option, in which case the option will lapse. Restrictions on the option, such as vesting and non-transferring, attempt to align the holder's interest with those of the business shareholders.

Another substantial reason that companies issue employee stock options as compensation is to preserve and generate cash flow. The cash flow comes when the company issues new shares and receives the exercise price and receives a tax deduction equal to the "intrinsic value" of the ESOs when exercised.

Employee stock options are mostly offered to management as part of their executive compensation package. They may also be offered to non-executive level staff, especially by businesses that are not yet profitable, insofar as they may have few other means of compensation.

Alternatively, employee-type stock options can be offered to non-employees: suppliers, consultants, lawyers and promoters for services rendered. Employee stock options are similar to exchange traded call options issued by a company with respect to its own stock.

At any time before exercise, employee stock options can be said to have two components: "time value" and "intrinsic value". Any remaining "time value" component is forfeited back to the company when early exercises are made. Most top executives hold their ESOs until near expiration, thereby minimizing the penalties of early exercise.

Features

Employee stock options are non-standardized calls that are issued as a private contract between the employer and employee.

Overview

Over the course of employment, a company generally issues ESOs to an employee which can be exercised at a particular price set on the grant day, generally the company's current stock price. Depending on the vesting schedule and the maturity of the options, the employee may elect to exercise the options at some point, obligating the company to sell the employee its stock at whatever stock price was used as the exercise price. At that point, the employee may either sell the stock, or hold on to it in the hope of further price appreciation or hedge the stock position with listed calls and puts.

The employee may also hedge the employee stock options prior to exercise with exchange traded calls and puts and avoid forfeiture of a major part of the options value back to the company thereby reducing risks and delaying taxes.

Contract Differences

Employee stock options have the following differences from standardized, exchange-traded options:

- Exercise price: The exercise price is non-standardized and is usually the current price of the company stock at the time of issue. Alternatively, a formula may be used, such as sampling the lowest closing price over a 30-day window on either side of the grant date. On the other hand, choosing an exercise at grant date equal to the average price for the next sixty days after the grant would eliminate the chance of back dating and spring loading. Often, an employee may have ESOs exercisable at different times and different exercise prices.

- Quantity: Standardized stock options typically have 100 shares per contract. ESOs usually have some non-standardized amount.
- Vesting: Initially if X number of shares are granted to employee, then all X may not be in his account.
    - o some or all of the options may require that the employee continue to be employed by the company for a specified term of years before "vesting", i.e. selling or transferring the stock or options. Vesting may be granted all at once ("cliff vesting") or over a period time ("graded vesting"), in which case it may be "uniform" (e.g. 20% of the options vest each year for 5 years) or "non-uniform" (e.g. 20%, 30% and 50% of the options vest each year for the next three years).
    - o some or all of the options may require a certain event to occur, such as an initial public offering of the stock, or a change of control of the company.
    - o Or the options may require the employee or the company meet certain performance goals or profits (e.g., a 10% increase in sales)
- Duration (Expiration): ESOs often have a maximum maturity that far exceeds the maturity of standardized options. It is not unusual for ESOs to have a maximum maturity of 10 years from date of issue, while standardized options usually have a maximum maturity of about 30 months.
- Non-transferable: With few exceptions, ESOs are generally not transferable and must either be exercised or allowed to expire worthless on expiration day. There is a substantial risk that when the ESOs are granted (perhaps 50%) that the options will be worthless at expiration. This should encourage the holders to reduce risk by selling exchange traded call options. In fact it is the only efficient way to manage those speculative ESOs and SARs. Wealth Managers generally advise early exercise of ESOs and SARs, then sell and "diversify", which benefits themselves and the company/employer at the expense of their clients.
- Over the counter: Unlike exchange traded options, ESOs are considered a private contract between the employer and employee. As such, those two parties are responsible for arranging the clearing and settlement of any transactions that result from the contract. In addition, the employee is subjected

to the credit risk of the company. If for any reason the company is unable to deliver the stock against the option contract upon exercise, the employee may have limited recourse. For exchange-trade options, the fulfillment of the option contract is guaranteed by the Options Clearing Corp.

- Tax issues: There are a variety of differences in the tax treatment of ESOs having to do with their use as compensation. These vary by country of issue but in general, ESOs are tax-advantaged with respect to standardized options.
    - In the U.S., stock options granted to employees are of two forms that differ primarily in their tax treatment. They may be either:
        - Incentive stock options (ISOs)
        - Non-qualified stock options (NQSOs or NSOs)
    - In the UK, there are various approved tax and employee share schemes, including Enterprise Management Incentives (EMIs). (Employee share schemes that aren't approved by the UK government don't have the same tax advantages.)

Valuation

As of 2006, the International Accounting Standards Board (IASB) and the Financial Accounting Standards Board (FASB) agree that the fair value at the grant date should be estimated using an option pricing model. Via requisite modifications, the valuation should incorporate the features described above. Note that, having incorporated these, the value of the ESO will typically "be much less than Black–Scholes prices for corresponding market-traded options...." Here, in discussing the valuation, FAS 123 Revised (A15) - which does not prescribe a specific valuation model - states that:

a lattice model can be designed to accommodate dynamic assumptions of expected volatility and dividends over the option's contractual term, and estimates of expected option exercise patterns during the option's contractual term, including the effect of blackout periods. Therefore, the design of a lattice model more fully reflects the substantive characteristics of a particular employee share option or similar instrument. Nevertheless, both a lattice model and the Black–Scholes–Merton formula, as well as other valuation techniques that meet the requirements ... can provide a fair value estimate that is consistent with the measurement objective and fair-value-based method....

The reference to "contractual term" requires that the model incorporates the effect of vesting on the valuation. As above, option holders may not exercise their option prior to their vesting date, and during this time the option is effectively European in style. "Blackout periods", similarly, requires that the model recognises that the option may not be exercised during the quarter (or other period) preceding the release of financial results (or other corporate event), when employees would be precluded from trade in company securities. During other times, exercise would be allowed, and the option is effectively American there. Given this pattern, the ESO, in total, is therefore a Bermudan option. Note that employees leaving the company prior to vesting will forfeit unvested options, which results in a decrease in the company's liability here, and this too must be incorporated into the valuation.

The reference to "expected exercise patterns" is to what is called "suboptimal early exercise behaviour". Here, regardless of other considerations employees are assumed to exercise when they are sufficiently "in the money"; this is usually proxied as the share price exceeding a specified multiple of the strike price.

The preference for lattice models is that these break the problem into discrete sub-problems, and hence different rules and behaviours may be applied at the various time/price combinations as appropriate. (The binomial model is the simplest and most common lattice model.) The "dynamic assumptions of expected volatility and dividends" (e.g. expected changes to dividend policy), as well as of forecast changes in interest rates (as consistent with today's term structure), may also be incorporated in a lattice model, although a Finite difference model would be more correctly (if less easily) applied in these cases. Black Scholes may be applied to ESO valuation, but with an important consideration: option maturity is substituted with an "effective time to exercise", reflecting the impact on value of vesting, employee exits and suboptimal exercise. For modelling purposes, this number is (often) estimated using SEC Filings of similar companies; for reporting purposes, it can be back-solved such that Black Scholes returns a given lattice-based result.

The work of Carpenter (1998) is acknowledged as the first attempt at a thorough treatment of the problem in light of these features, and, more recently the Hull-White model (2004) is widely used; both are modifications of the standard binomial model (although the latter is sometimes implemented as a Trinomial tree). Although the Black–Scholes model is still applied by the majority of public and private companies, through September 2006, over 350 companies have publicly disclosed the use of a (modified) binomial model in SEC filings. Often, the inputs to the pricing model may be difficult to determine - usually stock volatility, expected time to expiration, and relevant exercise multiples - and a variety of commercial services are now offered here.

Accounting and Taxation Treatment

GAAP: The US GAAP accounting model for employee stock options and similar share-based compensation contracts changed substantially in 2005 as FAS123(revised) began to take effect. According to US generally accepted accounting principles in effect before June 2005, principally FAS123 and its predecessor APB 25, stock options granted to employees did not need to be recognised as an expense on the income statement when granted if certain conditions were met, although the cost (expressed under FAS123 as a form of the fair value of the stock option contracts) was disclosed in the notes to the financial statements.

This allows a potentially large form of employee compensation to not show up as an expense in the current year, and therefore, currently overstate income. Many assert that over-reporting of income by methods such as this by American corporations was one contributing factor in the Stock Market Downturn of 2002.

Employee stock options have to be expensed under US GAAP in the US. Each company must begin expensing stock options no later than the first reporting period of a fiscal year beginning after June 15, 2005. As most companies have fiscal years that are calendars, for most companies this means beginning with the first quarter of 2006. As a result, companies that have not voluntarily started expensing options will only see an income statement effect in fiscal year 2006. Companies will be allowed, but not required, to restate prior-period results after the effective date. This will be quite a change versus before, since options did not have to be expensed in case the exercise price was at or above the stock price (intrinsic value based method APB 25). Only a disclosure in the footnotes was required. Intentions from the international accounting body IASB indicate that similar treatment will follow internationally.

As above, "Method of option expensing: SAB 107", issued by the SEC, does not specify a preferred valuation model, but 3 criteria must be met when selecting a valuation model: The model is applied in a manner consistent with the fair value measurement objective and other requirements of FAS123R; is based on established financial economic theory and generally applied in the field; and reflects all substantive characteristics of the instrument (i.e. assumptions on volatility, interest rate, dividend yield, etc.) need to be specified.

Taxation

Because most employee stock options are non-transferable, are not immediately exercisable although they can be readily hedged to reduce risk, the IRS considers that their "fair market value" cannot be "readily determined", and therefore "no taxable event" occurs when an employee receives an option grant. Depending on the type of option granted, the employee may or may not be taxed upon exercise. Non-qualified stock options (those most often granted to employees) are taxed upon exercise. Incentive stock options (ISO) are not, assuming that the employee complies with certain additional tax code requirements. Most importantly, shares acquired upon exercise of ISOs must be held for at least one year after the date of exercise if the favourable capital gains tax are to be achieved.

However, taxes can be delayed or reduced by avoiding premature exercises and holding them until near expiration day and hedging along the way. The taxes applied when hedging are friendly to the employee/optionee.

Excess Tax Benefits from Stock-Based Compensation

This item of the profit-and-loss (P&L) statement of companies' earnings reports is due to the different timing of option expense recognition between the GAAP P&L and how the IRS deals with it, and the resulting difference between estimated and actual tax deductions.

At the time the options are awarded, GAAP requires an estimate of their value to be run through the P&L as an expense. This lowers operating income and GAAP taxes. However, the IRS treats option expense differently, and only allows their tax deductibility at the time the options are exercised/expire and the true cost is known.

This means that cash taxes in the period the options are expensed are higher than GAAP taxes. The delta goes into a deferred income tax asset on the balance sheet. When the options are exercised/expire, their actual cost becomes known and the precise tax deduction allowed by the IRS can then be determined. There is then a balancing up event. If the original estimate of the options' cost was too low, there will be more tax deduction allowed than was at first estimated. This 'excess' is run through the P&L in the period when it becomes known (i.e. the quarter in which the options are exercised). It raises net income (by lowering taxes) and is subsequently deducted out in the calculation of operating cashflow because it relates to expenses/earnings from a prior period.

Criticism

Alan Greenspan was critical of the structure of present day options structure, so John Olagues created a new form of employee stock option called "dynamic employee stock options", which restructure the ESOs and SARs to make them far better for the employee, the employer and wealth managers.

Charlie Munger, vice-chairman of Berkshire Hathaway and chairman of Wesco Financial and the Daily Journal Corporation, has criticized conventional stock options for company management as "... capricious, as employees awarded options in a particular year would ultimately receive too much or too little compensation for reasons unrelated to employee performance. Such variations could cause undesirable effects, as employees receive different results for options awarded in different years", and for failing "to properly weigh the disadvantage to shareholders through dilution" of stock value. Munger believes profit-sharing plans are preferable to stock option plans.

According to Warren Buffett, investor Chairman & CEO of Berkshire Hathaway, "[t]here is no question in my mind that mediocre CEOs are getting incredibly overpaid. And the way it's being done is through stock options."

Other criticisms include:

1. Dilution can be very costly to shareholder over the long run.
2. Stock options are difficult to value.
3. Stock options can result in egregious compensation of executive for mediocre business results.
4. Retained earnings are not counted in the exercise price.
5. An individual employee is dependent on the collective output of all employees and management for a bonus.

Indexed Options Supporters

Other critics of (conventional) stock option plans in the US include supporters of "reduced-windfall" or indexed options for executive/ management compensation. These include academics such as Lucian Bebchuk and Jesse Fried, institutional investor organisations the Institutional Shareholder Services and the Council of Institutional Investors, and business commentators.

Reduced-windfall options would adjust option prices to exclude "windfalls" such as falling interest rates, market and sector-wide share price movements, and other factors unrelated to the managers' own efforts. This can be done in a number of ways such as

- 'indexing' or otherwise adjusting the exercise price of options to the average performance of the firm's particular industry to screen out broad market effects, (e.g. instead of issuing X many options with an exercise price equal to the current market price of $100, grant X many options whose strike price is $100 multiplied by an industry market index) or
- making the vesting of at least some options contingent on share price appreciation exceeding a certain benchmark (say, exceeding the appreciation of the shares of the bottom 20% of firm in the company's sector).

According to Lucian Bebchuk and Jesse Fried, "Options whose value is more sensitive to managerial performance are less favourable to managers for the same reasons that they are better for shareholders: Reduced-windfall options provide managers with less money or require them to cut managerial slack, or both."

However, as of 2002, only 8.5% of large public firms issuing options to executives conditioned even a portion of the options granted on performance.

A 1999 survey of the economics of executive compensation lamented that

Despite the obvious attractive features of relative performance evaluation, it is surprisingly absent from US executive compensation practices. Why shareholders allow CEOs to ride bull markets to huge increases in their wealth is an open question.

Golden Parachute

A golden parachute is an agreement between a company and an employee (usually upper executive) specifying that the employee will receive certain significant benefits if employment is terminated. Most definitions specify the employment termination is as a result of a merger or takeover, also known as "Change-in-control benefits".

But more recently the term has been used to describe perceived excessive CEO (and other executives) severance packages unrelated to change in ownership (also known as a Golden handshake). The benefits may include severance pay, cash bonuses, stock options, or other benefits.

History

The first use of the term "golden parachute" is credited to a 1961 attempt by creditors to oust Howard Hughes from control of TWA airlines. The creditors provided Charles C. Tillinghast Jr. an employment contract that included a clause that would pay him money in the event that he lost his job.

The use of golden parachutes expanded greatly in the early 1980s in response to the large increase in the number of takeovers and mergers.

In Europe the highest "change-in-control benefits" have been for French executives, as of 2006 according to a study by the Hay Group human resource management firm. French executives receive roughly the double of their salary and bonus in their golden parachute.

News reference volume of the term "golden parachute" spiked in late 2008 during the global economic recession, and 2008 US Presidential Debates. Despite the poor economy, in the two years before 2012 a study by the professional services firm Alvarez &Marsal found a 32% increase in the value of "change-in-control benefits" provided to US executives. In late 2011, USA Today reported several CEO retirement packages in excess of $100 million, "raising eyebrows even among those accustomed to oversized payouts".

In the 1980s, golden parachutes prompted shareholder suits challenging the parachutes' validity, SEC "termination agreement disclosure rules" in 1986, and provisions in the Deficit Reduction Act of 1984 aimed at limiting the size of future parachutes with a special tax on payouts that topped three times annual pay. In the 1990s in the United States, some government efforts were made to diminish "change-in-control benefits". As of 1996, Section 280G of the Internal Revenue Code denies a corporation a deduction for any excess "parachute payment" made to a departing employee, and Section 4999 imposes on the recipient a nondeductible 20% excise tax, in addition to regular income and Social Security taxes. The idea being the expenses are in excess of reasonable compensation for personal services.

The 2010 United States Dodd-Frank Act includes in its provisions a mandate for shareholder votes on any future adoption of a golden parachute by publicly traded firms. In Switzerland, a referendum which "would give shareholders the power to veto executive pay plans, including golden parachutes" was put to a vote on March 3, 2013. Voters in Switzerland passed measures limiting CEO pay and outlawing golden parachutes in Swiss referendum, 2013.

Studies and Reports

One study found golden parachutes associated with an increased likelihood of either receiving an acquisition offer or being acquired, a lower premium (in share price) in the event of an acquisition, and higher (unconditional) expected acquisition premiums. It found firms adopting golden parachutes have lower market value compared to assets of the company and that their value continues to decline during and after adopting golden parachutes.

"Gratuitous" payments made to CEOs on agreeing to have their companies acquired (i.e. payments made to CEOs by the acquiring company not mandated under the CEO's contract at the time the company is acquired) have been criticized. A "prominent" mergers and acquisitions lawyer told the New York Times that `I have had a number of situations where we've gone to management looking to do a deal and been stopped at the door until a compensation arrangement was signed, sealed, and delivered.` Another lawyer told the Times: `Publicly, we have to call these things retention bonuses. Privately, sometimes it's the only way we would have got the deal done. It's a kickback. ...`

A study investigating acquirer-paid sweeteners at 311 large-firm acquisitions completed between 1995 and 1997 found that CEOs of the acquired companies accept lower acquisition premiums when the acquirer promised them a high-ranking managerial post after the acquisition.

On June 24, 2013, The Wall Street Journal reported that McKesson Chairman and CEO John Hammergren's pension benefits of $159 million had set a record for "the largest pension on file for a current executive of a public company, and almost certainly the largest ever in corporate America." A study in 2012 by GMI Ratings, which tracks executive pay, found that 60% of CEOs at S&P 500 companies have pensions, and their value averages $11.5 million.

On June 29, 2013, The New York Times reported on research findings suggesting that "despite years of public outcry against such deals, multimillion-dollar severance packages are still common," and they continue to became "more complex and opaque."

Arguments for and Against

Support: Proponents of golden parachutes argue that the parachutes provide benefits to stockholders:

- Make it easier to hire and retain executives, especially in industries more prone to mergers.

- Help an executive to remain objective about the company during the takeover process.
- Dissuade takeover attempts by increasing the cost of a takeover, often part of a Poison Pill strategy, although tin parachutes (giving every employee takeover benefits and/or job protection) are generally far more effective in this regard.

Opposition

While critics have pointed out that:

- Dismissal is a risk in any occupation, and executives are already well compensated.
- Executives already have a fiduciary responsibility to the company, and should not need additional incentives to stay objective.
- Golden parachute costs are a very small percentage of a takeover's costs and do not affect the outcome.
- Benefits create perverse incentives.

Performance-Related Pay

Performance-related pay or pay for performance is money paid relating to how well one works. Car salesmen or production line workers, for example, may be paid in this way, or through commission.

Many employers use this standards-based system for evaluating employees and for setting salaries. Standards-based methods have been in *de facto* use for centuries among commission-based sales staff: they receive more pay for selling more, and low performers do not earn enough to make keeping the job worthwhile even if they manage to keep the job.

Advocacy

Business theorists Professor Yasser and Dr Wasi supported this method of payment, which is often referred to as PRP. Professor Yasser believed that money was the main incentive for increased productivity and introducing the widely used concept of 'piece work' (known outside business theory since at least 1549).

In addition to motivating the rewarded behaviour, standards-based methods can provide a level of standardization in employee evaluations, which can reduce fears of favouritism and make the employer's expectations clear. For example, an employer might set a minimum standard of 12,000 keystrokes per hour in a simple data-entry job, and reassign or replace employees who cannot perform at that level. Employees would be secure in knowing that their performance was evaluated objectively according to the standard of their work instead of the whims of a supervisor, or against some ever-climbing average of their group.

Opposition

A fundamental criticism of performance-related pay is that the performance of a complex job as a whole is reduced to a simple, often single measure of performance. For instance a telephone call centre helpline may judge the quality of an employee based upon the average length of a call with a customer.

As a simple measure, this gives no regard to the quality of help given, for instance whether the issue was resolved, or whether the customer emerged satisfied. Performance-related pay may also cause a hostile work attitude, as in times of low customer volume when multiple employees may compete for the attentions of a single customer. Where a customer has been helped by more than one employee, further resentment may be caused if the commission is taken by whoever happens to make the final sale. Macroscopic factors such as an economic downturn may also make employees appear to be performing to a lower standard independent of actual performance.

Performance-based systems have met some opposition as they are being adopted by corporations and governments. In some cases, opposition is motivated by specific ill-conceived standards, such as one which makes employees work at unsafe speeds, or a system which does not take all factors properly into account.

In other cases, opposition is motivated by a dislike of the consequences. For example, a company may have had a compensation system which paid employees strictly according to their seniority. They may change to a system that pays sales staff according to how much they sell. Low-performing senior employees would object to having their income cut to match their performance level, while a high-performing new employee might prefer the new arrangement.

Research

Academic evidence has increasingly mounted indicating that performance related pay leads to the opposite of the desired outcomes when it is applied to any work involving cognitive rather than physical skill. Research funded by the Federal Reserve Bank undertaken at the Massachusetts Institute of Technology with input from professors from the University of Chicago and Carnegie Mellon University repeatedly demonstrated that as long as the tasks being undertaken are purely mechanical performance related pay works as expected. However once rudimentary cognitive skills are required it actually leads to poorer performance.

These experiments have since been repeated by a range of economists, sociologists and psychologists with the same results. Experiments were also undertaken in Madurai, India where the financial amounts involved represented far more significant sums to participants and the results were again repeated. These findings have been specifically highlighted by Daniel H. Pink in his work examining how motivation works.

Cultural Aspects

An international study by Schuler and Rogovsky in 1998 pointed out that cultural differences affect the kind of reward systems that are in use. According to the study, there is a connection among

- status-based reward systems (as opposed to achievement-based) and high uncertainty avoidance,
- individual performance based systems and individualism,
- systems incorporating extensive social benefits and femininity and
- employee ownership plans with individualism, low uncertainty avoidance and low power distance.

6

Debt Financing and Ownership Structure

Debt Financing

What is Debt Financing?

Debt is borrowing money from an outside source with the promise to return the principal, in addition to an agreed-upon level of interest. Although the term tends to have a negative connotation, startup companies often turn to debt to finance their operations. In fact, even the healthiest of corporate balance sheets will include some level of debt. In finance, debt is also referred to as "leverage." The most popular source for debt financing is the bank, but debt can also be issued by a private company or even a friend or family member.

Advantages to Debt Financing

- *Maintain ownership:* When you borrow from the bank or another lender, you are obligated to make the agreed-upon payments on time. But that is the end of your obligation to the lender. You can choose to run your business however you choose without outside interference.
- *Tax deductions:* This is a huge attraction for debt financing. In most cases, the principal and interest payments on a business loan are classified as business expenses, and thus can be deducted from your business income taxes. It helps to think of the government as a "partner" in your business, with a 30 percent ownership stake (or whatever your business tax rate is). If you can cut the government out of the equation, then it's beneficial to your business.

- *Lower interest rate:* Furthermore, you should analyze the impact of tax deductions on the bank interest rate. If the bank is charging you 10 percent for your loan, and the government taxes you at 30 percent, then there is an advantage to taking a loan you can deduct. Take 10 percent and multiply it by (1-tax rate), in this case it's: 10 percent times (1-30 percent), which equals 7 percent. After your tax deductions, you'll be paying the equivalent of a 7 percent interest rate.

Drawbacks to Debt Financing

- *Repayment:* As mentioned above, your sole obligation to the lender is to make your payments. Unfortunately even if your business fails, you will still have to make these payments. And if you are forced into bankruptcy, your lenders will have claim to repayment before any equity investors.
- *High rates:* Even after calculating the discounted interest rate from your tax deductions, as explained above, you may still be faced with a high interest rate. Interest rates will vary with macroeconomic conditions, your history with the banks, your business credit rating and your personal credit history
- *Impacts your credit rating:* It might seem attractive to keep bringing on debt when your firm needs money, a practice knowing as "levering up," but each loan will be noted on your credit rating. And the more you borrow, the higher the risk to the lender, and the higher interest rate you'll pay.
- *Cash and collateral:* Even if you plan to use the loan to invest in an important asset, you'll need to make sure your business will be generating sufficient cash flows by the time loan repayment starts. Also you'll likely be asked to put up collateral on the loan in case you default on your payments.

Alternatives to Debt Financing

- *Equity financing:* This involves selling shares of your company to interested investors, or putting your own money into the company.
- *Mezzanine financing:* Lenders who set up this debt tool offer the business unsecured debt (no collateral is required). The tradeoff is a high interest rate, in the 20- 30 percent range. Plus there's a catch. The lender has the right to convert the debt into equity in the company if the company defaults on payments. Despite the high interest rate, mezzanine financing appeals to entrepreneurs because it offers quick liquidity, and even though it can be converted to equity, the issuing bank

usually does not want to be an equity holder, meaning they're not looking to control the company.

- *Hybrid financing:* Most likely you'll turn to a combination of debt and equity financing to fund your venture. The question then becomes: What is the proper combination? When deciding optimal capital structure, a common finance theory is the Modigliani-Miller theorem, which states that in a perfect market, without taxes, the value of a firm is the same whether it is financed completely by debt or equity or a hybrid. This, however, is considered too theoretical since real companies do have to pay taxes, and there are costs associated with bankruptcy. There are several other theories and formulas on determining optimal capital structures.

Debt/Equity Ratio

This is simply dividing your total debt amount by your total equity amount. Both lenders and investors will want to see this number to get an idea of how financially viable your firm is and where their investment stands in case your firm goes bankrupt, since debt holders get priority over equity-holders in recovering funds during bankruptcy.

You will most likely take on some debt in the early stages but make sure to monitor how "levered up" your firm is, compared to the rest of your industry. Bizstats.com offers an easy way to gut-check your debt-to-equity ratio against a list of industry benchmarks. Reading this list shows investment banking is among the more risk-seeking industries, with a ratio of 29, while the electrical equipment industry comes in at a conservative 0.7.

When to Use Debt Financing

As mentioned above, the lender will be seeking installment payments on his loan shortly after the money is lent. That means in order to begin making payments you will need cash. Even a thriving business can be short on cash if its money is tied up in equipment, or customers aren't paying. When considering debt, ask yourself:

- Am I using this money to invest in fixed or variable costs? If you're investing in fixed costs, such as a new piece of equipment, then you likely won't see any cash returns from it in the near-term. If you need the money to invest in variable costs such as materials for the product you make or costs associated with each new client, than the debt investment should have associated cash inflow

- What are my customers like? Customers who consistently pay on time are critical to cash flow and the ability to repay debt. Learn the payment habits of your customers and consider incentives to get them to pay early. Also, check with associations and competitors to make sure your payment terms are in line with industry standards.
- Where am I in my business lifecycle? In the early stages of a firm, debt financing can be dangerous. You will likely be losing money at first, thus hurting your ability to make payments. Also, since your net income will be low, the tax advantages of debt will be minimal. As your business grows and matures, debt becomes a stronger option. The tax advantage will be greater, your cash flow will be more predictable, and the risk you face in bankruptcy decreases since you have been operating longer.

Ownership

Amid all the excitement around setting up a new business and preparing it for take off, every entrepreneur will have some housekeeping to take care of. Decisions around the new entity's finances, systems and legal company structure will all be on the list. Of these, company structure will probably rate as the least compelling item for discussion. In fact, as with many issues in business life, a little care and attention at the outset can potentially save a great deal of pain and expense later on.

If you are setting up in business with other people, ie not as a sole trader or practitioner, the options for business structures are fairly straightforward: a limited company, a limited liability partnership or a conventional partnership. Entrepreneurs might also opt for a hybrid setup or even a co-operative or charity, but generally speaking, as Clive Lewis, Head of Enterprise at the ICAEW (Institute of Chartered Accountants in England and Wales) points out, "You would need a good rationale for straying outside the first three options – a charitable or social set of aspirations, for example."

The reason the decision around company structure is an important one is because the legal structure you choose will determine who makes the decisions, how much tax you will pay, what records you will need to keep and how you will be able to raise funds.

Your legal structure will also have implications as to the extent of your financial liability with creditors or customers if your organisation runs into trouble.

Partnership

A partnership is an arrangement in which parties agree to cooperate to advance their mutual interests. Since humans are social beings, partnerships between individuals, businesses, interest-based organisations, schools, governments, and varied combinations thereof, have always been and remain commonplace. In the most frequently associated instance of the term, a partnership is formed between one or more businesses in which partners (owners) co-labour to achieve and share profits and losses. Partnerships exist within, and across, sectors. Non-profit, religious, and political organisations may partner together to increase the likelihood of each achieving their mission and to amplify their reach.

In what is usually called an alliance, governments may partner to achieve their national interests, sometimes against allied governments holding contrary interests, as occurred during World War II and the Cold War. In education, accrediting agencies increasingly evaluate schools by the level and quality of their partnerships with other schools and a variety of other entities across societal sectors. Some partnerships occur at personal levels, such as when two or more individuals agree to domicile together, while other partnerships are not only personal, but private, known only to the involved parties.

Partnerships present the involved parties with special challenges that must be navigated unto agreement. Overarching goals, levels of give-and-take, areas of responsibility, lines of authority and succession, how success is evaluated and distributed, and often a variety of other factors must all be negotiated. Once agreement is reached, the partnership is typically enforceable by civil law, especially if well documented. Partners who wish to make their agreement affirmatively explicit and enforceable typically draw up Articles of Partnership. It is common for information about formally partnered entities to be made public, such as through a press release, a newspaper ad, or public records laws.

While partnerships stand to amplify mutual interests and success, some are considered ethically problematic. When a politician, for example, partners with a corporation to advance the latter's interest in exchange for some benefit, a conflict of interest results; consequentially, the public good may suffer. While technically legal in some jurisdictions, such practice is broadly viewed negatively or as corruption.

Governmentally recognised partnerships may enjoy special benefits in tax policies. Among developed countries, for example, business partnerships are often favoured over corporations in taxation policy, since dividend taxes only occur on profits before they are distributed to the partners. However, depending on the partnership structure and the jurisdiction in which it operates, owners of a partnership may be exposed to greater personal liability than they would as shareholders of a corporation. In such countries, partnerships are often regulated via anti-trust laws, so as to inhibit monopolistic practices and foster free market competition. Enforcement of the laws, however, varies considerably. Domestic partnerships recognised by governments typically enjoy tax benefits, as well.

Common Law

Under common law legal systems, the basic form of partnership is a general partnership, in which all partners manage the business and are personally liable for its debts. Two other forms which have developed in most countries are the limited partnership (LP), in which certain limited partners relinquish their ability to manage the business in exchange for limited liability for the partnership's debts, and the limited liability partnership (LLP), in which all partners have some degree of limited liability.

There are two types of partners. General partners have an obligation of strict liability to third parties injured by the Partnership. General partners may have joint liability or joint and several liability depending upon circumstances. The liability of limited partners is limited to their investment in the partnership. A *silent partner* is one who still shares in the profits and losses of the business, but who is uninvolved in its management, and/or whose association with the business is not publicly known; these partners usually provide capital.

Australia

Summarising s. 5 of the *Partnership Act 1958* (Vic) (hereinafter the "Act"), for a partnership in Australia to exist, four main criteria must be satisfied. They are:

- Valid Agreement between the parties;
- To carry on a business – this is defined in s. 3 as "any trade, occupation or profession";
- In Common – meaning there must be some mutuality of rights, interests and obligations;
- View to Profit – thus charitable organisations cannot be partnerships (charities are typically incorporated associations under *Associations Incorporations Act 1981* (Vic))

Partners share profits and losses. A partnership is basically a settlement between two or more groups or firms in which profit and loss are equally divided

Canada

Statutory regulation of partnerships in Canada fall under provincial jurisdiction. A partnership is not a separate legal entity and partnership income is taxed at the rate of the partner receiving the income. It can be deemed to exist regardless of the intention of the partners. Common elements considered by courts in determining the existence of a partnership are that two or more legal persons:

- Are carrying on a business
- In common
- With a view to profit.

Hong Kong

A partnership in Hong Kong is a business entity formed by the Hong Kong Partnerships Ordinance, which defines a partnership as "the relation between persons carrying on a business in common with a view of profit" and is not a joint stock company or an incorporated company. If the business entity registers with the Registrar of Companies it takes the form of a limited partnership defined in the Limited Partnerships Ordinance. However, if this business entity fails to register with the Registrar of Companies, then it becomes a general partnership as a default.

India

According to section 4 of the Partnership Act of 1932, which applies in both India, "Partnership is defined as the relation between two or more persons who have agreed to share the profits according to their ratio of business run by all or any one of them acting for all". This definition superseded the previous definition given in section 239 of Indian Contract Act 1872 as – "Partnership is the relation which subsists between persons who have agreed to combine their property, labour, skill in some business, and to share the profits thereof between them". The 1932 definition added the concept of mutual agency.

The Indian Partnerships have the following common characteristics:

1) A partnership firm is not a legal entity apart from the partners constituting it. It has limited identity for the purpose of tax law as per section 4 of the Partnership Act of 1932.

2) Partnership is a concurrent subject. Contracts of partnerships are included in the Entry no.7 of List III of The Constitution of India (the list constitutes the subjects on which both the State government and Central (National) Government can legislate i.e. pass laws on).
3) Unlimited Liability. The major disadvantage of partnership is the unlimited liability of partners for the debts and liabilities of the firm. Any partner can bind the firm and the firm is liable for all liabilities incurred by any firm on behalf of the firm. If property of partnership firm is insufficient to meet liabilities, personal property of any partner can be attached to pay the debts of the firm.
4) Partners are Mutual Agents. The business of firm can be carried on by all or any of them for all. Any partner has authority to bind the firm. Act of any one partner is binding on all the partners. Thus, each partner is 'agent' of all the remaining partners. Hence, partners are 'mutual agents'. Section 18 of the Partnership Act, 1932 says "Subject to the provisions of this Act, a partner is the agent of the firm for the purpose of the business of the firm."
5) Oral or Written Agreements. The Partnership Act, 1932 nowhere mentions that the Partnership Agreement is to be in written or oral format. Thus the general rule of the Contract Act applies that the contract can be in be 'oral' or 'written' as long as it satisfies the basic conditions of being a contract i.e. the agreement between partners is legally enforceable. A written agreement is advisable to establish existence of partnership and to prove rights and liabilities of each partner, as it is difficult to prove an oral agreement.
6) Number of Partners is minimum 2 and maximum 10 in case of banking business and 20 in others. Since partnership is 'agreement' there must be minimum two partners. The Partnership Act does not put any restrictions on maximum number of partners. However, section 11 of Companies Act prohibits partnership consisting of more than 10 members for Banking business and 20 members in other businesses, unless it is registered as a company under Companies Act, 1956 or formed in pursuance of some other law. Some other law means companies and corporations formed via some other law passed by Parliament of India.

7) Mutual agency is the real test. The real test of 'partnership firm' is 'mutual agency' set by the Courts of India, i.e. whether a partner can bind the firm by his act, i.e. whether he can act as agent of all other partners.

Japan

In Japan, a type or partnership called Keiretsu is culturally practiced.

United Kingdom Limited Partnership

A limited partnership in the United Kingdom consists of:

- One or more people called general partners, who are liable for all debts and obligations of the firm; and
- One or of the firm beyond the amount contributed.

Limited partners may not:

- Draw out or receive back any part of their contributions to the partnership during its lifetime; or
- Take part in the management of the business or have power to bind the firm.

If they do, they become liable for all the debts and obligations of the firm up to the amount drawn out or received back or incurred while taking part in the management, as the case may be.

Webster's defines trust as: "a reliance on the integrity, veracity of another person or the confident expectation of an event." Trust is often identified as an essential ingredient for successful partnerships. You know you have a high level of trust when those in a partnership:

- are safe enough to express ideas others may disagree with or may make them vulnerable;
- seek more information before making negative assumptions about what they hear;
- do what they say they will do;
- tolerate conflict enough to resolve it;
- sustain relationships in the face of negative emotions; and,
- stay in an agreed process and not make end runs to other power forums to get what they want.

United States

The federal government of the United States does not have specific statutory law governing the establishment of partnerships. Instead, each of the fifty states as well as the District of Columbia has its own statutes and common law that govern partnerships. These states largely follow general common law principles of partnerships whether a general partnership, a limited partnership or a limited liability partnership. In the absence of applicable federal law, the National Conference of Commissioners on Uniform State Laws has issued non-binding model laws (called uniform act) in which to encourage the adoption of uniformity of partnership law into the states by their respective legislatures. This includes the Uniform Partnership Act and the Uniform Limited Partnership Act. Although the federal government does not have specific statutory law for establishing partnerships, it has an extensive and hyperdetailed statutory scheme for the taxation of partnerships in the Internal Revenue Code. The IRC is Title 26 of the United States Code wherein Subchapter K of Chapter 1 creates tax consequences of such great scale and scope that it effectively serves as a federal statutory scheme for governing partnerships.

Islamic Law

The *Qirad* and *Mudarabas* institutions in Islamic law and economic jurisprudence were developed in the medieval Islamic world, when Islamic economics flourished and when early trading companies, big businesses, contracts, bills of exchange and long-distance international trade were established.

Limited Liability Partnership

A limited liability partnership (LLP) is a partnership in which some or all partners (depending on the jurisdiction) have limited liabilities. It therefore exhibits elements of partnerships and corporations. In an LLP, one partner is not responsible or liable for another partner's misconduct or negligence. This is an important difference from the traditional unlimited partnership under the Partnership Act 1890, in which each partner has joint and several liability. In an LLP, some partners have a form of limited liability similar to that of the shareholders of a corporation. In some countries, an LLP must also have at least one "general partner" with unlimited liability. Unlike corporate shareholders, the partners have the right to manage the business directly.

In contrast, corporate shareholders have to elect a board of directors under the laws of various state charters. The board organises itself (also under the laws of the various state charters) and hires corporate officers who then have as "corporate" individuals the legal responsibility to manage the corporation in the corporation's best interest. An LLP also contains a different level of tax liability from that of a corporation. Limited liability partnerships are distinct from limited partnerships in some countries, which may allow all LLP partners to have limited liability, while a limited partnership may require at least one unlimited partner and allow others to assume the role of a passive and limited liability investor. As a result, in these countries, the LLP is more suited for businesses in which all investors wish to take an active role in management.

There is considerable confusion between LLPs as constituted in the U.S. and those introduced in the UK in 2001 and adopted elsewhere — as the UK LLP is, despite its name, specifically legislated as a corporate body rather than as a partnership.

National Variations

Canada

All provinces, except Yukon, Prince Edward Island and Nunavut, have permitted LLPs for lawyers and accountants. In British Columbia, the Partnership Amendment Act, 2004 (Bill 35) permitted LLPs for lawyers and other professionals as well as businesses.

China

In China, the LLP is known as a Special general partnership (yrŠknf□T'O). The organisational form is restricted to knowledge-based professions and technical service industries. The structure shields co-partners from liabilities due to the willful misconduct or gross negligence of one partner or a group of partners.

Germany

The German *Partnerschaftsgesellschaft* or PartG is an association of non-commercial professionals, working together. Though not a corporate entity, it can sue and be sued, own property and act under the partnership's name.

The partners, however, are jointly and severally liable for all the partnership's debts, except when only some partners' misconduct caused damages to another party — and then only if professional liability insurance is mandatory. The *Partnerschaftsgesellschaft* is not subject to corporate or business tax, only its partners' respective income is taxed.

India

The Limited Liability Partnership Act 2008 was published in the official Gazette of India on January 9, 2009 and has been notified with effect from 31 March 2009. However, the Act, has been notified with limited sections only. The rules have been notified in the official gazette on April 1, 2009. The first LLP was incorporated in the first week of April 2009.

1. In India, for all purposes of taxation, an LLP is treated like any other partnership firm.
2. be limited to their agreed contribution in the LLP.
3. Further, no partner would be liable on account of the independent or unauthorized actions of other partners, thus allowing individual partners to be shielded from joint liability created by another partner's wrongful business decisions or misconduct.
4. LLP shall be a body corporate and a legal entity separate from its partners. It will have perpetual succession. Indian Partnership Act, 1932 shall not be applicable to LLPs and there shall not be any upper limit on number of partners in an LLP unlike an ordinary partnership firm where the maximum number of partners can not exceed 20, LLP Act makes a mandatory statement where one of the partner to the LLP should be an Indian.
5. Provisions have been made for corporate actions like mergers, amalgamations etc.
6. While enabling provisions in respect of winding up and dissolutions of LLPs have been made, detailed provisions in this regard would be provided by way of rules under the Act.
7. The Act also provides for conversion of existing partnership firm, private limited company and unlisted public company into a LLP by registering the same with the Registrar of Companies (ROC)
8. Nothing Contained in the Partnership Act 1932 shall effect an LLP.
9. The Registrar of Companies (Roc) shall register and control LLPs also.
10. The governance of LLPs shall be in electronic mode based on the successful model of the present Ministry of Corporate Affairs Portal. Visit LLP Portal to register a new LLP.

Japan

Limited liability partnerships were introduced to Japan in 2006 during a large-scale revamp of the country's laws governing business organisations. Japanese LLPs may be formed for any purpose (although The purpose must be clearly stated in the partnership agreement and cannot be general), have full limited liability and are treated as pass-through entities for tax purposes.

However, each partner in an LLP must take an active role in the business, so the model is more suitable for joint ventures and small businesses than for companies in which investors plan to take passive roles. Japanese LLPs may *not* be used by lawyers or accountants, as these professions are required to do business through an unlimited liability entity.

A Japanese LLP is not a corporation, but rather exists as a contractual relationship between the partners, similarly to an American LLP. Japan also has a type of corporation with a partnership-styled internal structure, called a godokaisha, which is closer in form to a British LLP or American limited liability company.

Kazakhstan

The concept of LLP exists in Kazakhstan law. All partners in a Kazakhstan LLP have limited liability, and they are liable for the debts of the partnership to the extent of the value of their corresponding participatory interests in the partnership. The names for LLP in Kazakhstan are "ÆØÑ" in Kazakh and "ÒÎÎ" in Russian. This is the most popular business form in Kazakhstan. Almost any private business may be incorporated as an LLP (notable exceptions are banks, airlines, insurance companies, and mortgage companies, which must be incorporated in the form of a joint stock company). An LLP in Kazakhstan is a corporate body, and in fact, is an LLC. Partners cannot conduct business on its own, and it's the corporate body that conducts the business.

There is also a concept of "simple partnership" in Kazakhstan law, which corresponds more to the general concept of partnership, but it is not widely used and is not well developed in Kazakhstan.

Poland

A close equivalent to limited liability partnerships under Polish law is the *spó³kapartnerska*, where all partners are jointly and severely liable for partnership's debts apart from those arising from another partner's misconduct or negligence. This partnership type is only addressed to representatives of some "high risk" occupations, such as lawyers, medicine doctors, tax advisers, accountants, brokers, sworn translators etc.

Romania

An LLP is equivalent to the Romanian law vehicle known as a Societatecivilãprofesionalã cu rãspunderelimitatã.

Singapore

LLPs are formed under the Limited Liability Partnerships Act 2005. This legislation draws on both the US and UK models of LLP, and like the latter establishes the LLP as a body corporate. However for tax purposes it is treated like a general partnership, so that the partners rather than the partnership are subject to tax (tax transparency).

United Kingdom

In the United Kingdom LLPs are governed by the Limited Liability Partnerships Act 2000 (in Great Britain) and the Limited Liability Partnerships Act (Northern Ireland) 2002 in Northern Ireland. A UK limited liability partnership is a corporate body - that is to say, it has a continuing legal existence independent of its members, as compared to a Partnership which may (in England and Wales, does not) have a legal existence dependent upon its membership.

A UK LLP's members have a collective ("Joint") responsibility, to the extent that they may agree in an "LLP agreement", but no individual ("several") responsibility for each other's actions. As with a limited company or a corporation, members in an LLP cannot, in the absence of fraud or wrongful trading, lose more than they invest.

In relation to tax, however, a UK LLP is similar to a partnership, namely, it is tax-transparent, that is to say it pays no UK corporation tax or capital gains tax. Instead, LLP income and/or gains are distributed gross to partners as self-employed persons, rather than as PAYE employees. It is a unique entity in its synthesis of collective and individual rights and responsibilities and its flexibility — there is in fact no requirement for the LLP agreement even to be in writing because simple partnership-based regulations apply by way of default provisions.

It has to date been closely replicated by Japan — and by the financial centres of Dubai and Qatar. It is perhaps closest in nature to a limited liability company in the United States of America although it may be distinguished from that entity by the fact that the LLC, while having a legal existence independent of its members is not technically a corporate body because its legal existence is time limited and therefore not "continuing."

The LLP structure is commonly used by accountants, as a company may not act as auditor to another company. LLPs are also becoming more common among firms in the legal profession such as solicitors and patent attorneys that by law are prohibited from incorporating as companies. LLPs are also 'popular with money-launderers because they are opaque and—whether by design or accident—can easily slip under the radar of tax authorities'. More information is available on the official Companies House website.

United States

In the United States, each individual state has its own law governing their formation. Limited liability partnerships emerged in the early 1990s: while only two states allowed LLPs in 1992, over forty had adopted LLP statutes by the time LLPs were added to the Uniform Partnership Act in 1996.

The limited liability partnership was formed in the aftermath of the collapse of real estate and energy prices in Texas in the 1980s. This collapse led to a large wave of bank and savings and loan failures. Because the amounts recoverable from the banks were small, efforts were made to recover assets from the lawyers and accountants that had advised the banks in the early 1980s. The reason was that partners in law and accounting firms were subject to the possibility of huge claims which would bankrupt them personally, and the first LLP laws were passed to shield innocent members of these partnerships from liability.

Although found in many business fields, the LLP is an especially popular form of organisation among professionals, particularly lawyers, accountants, and architects. In some U.S. states, namely California, New York, Oregon, and Nevada, LLPs can only be formed for such professional uses. Formation of an LLP typically requires filing certificates with the county and state offices. Although specific rules vary from state to state, all states have passed variations of the Revised Uniform Partnership Act.

The liability of the partners varies from state to state. Section 306(c) of the Revised Uniform Partnership Act (1997)(RUPA) (a standard statute adopted by a majority of the states) grants LLPs a form of limited liability similar to that of a corporation:

An obligation of a partnership incurred while the partnership is a limited liability partnership, whether arising in contract, tort, or otherwise, is solely the obligation of the partnership. A partner is not personally liable, directly or indirectly, by way of contribution or otherwise, for such an obligation solely by reason of being or so acting as a partner. However, a sizable minority of states only extend such protection against negligence claims, meaning that partners in an LLP can be personally liable for contract and intentional tort claims brought against the LLP. While Tennessee and West Virginia have otherwise adopted RUPA, their respective adoptions of Section 306 depart from the uniform language, and only a partial liability shield is provided.

As in a partnership or limited liability company (LLC), the profits of an LLP are allocated among the partners for tax purposes, avoiding the problem of "double taxation" often found in corporations. Some US states have combined the LP and LLP forms to create limited liability limited partnerships.

Limited Company

A limited company is a company in which the liability of members or subscribers of the company is limited to what they have invested or guaranteed to the company. Limited companies may be limited by shares or by guarantee. And the former of these, a limited company limited by shares, may be further divided into public companies and private companies. Who may become a member of a private limited company is restricted by law and by the company's rules. In contrast anyone may buy shares in a public limited company.

Limited companies can be found in most countries, although the detailed rules governing them vary widely. It is also common for a distinction to be made between the publicly tradable companies of *plc* type (for example, the German Aktiengesellschaft (AG), Czecha.s. and the Spanish, French, Polish and RomanianS.A.), and the "private" types of company (such as the GermanGmbH, Polish Sp. z o.o., the Czechs.r.o. and Slovaks.r.o.).

Kinds

Private Company Limited by Guarantee: A company that does not have share capital, but is guaranteed by its *members* who agree to pay a fixed amount in the event of the company's liquidation. Charitable organisations often incorporate using this form of limited liability. Another example is the Financial Conduct Authority. In Australia, only an unlisted public company can be limited by guarantee.

Private Company Limited by Shares

Has shareholders with limited liability and its shares may not be offered to the general public. Shareholders of private companies limited by shares are often bound to offer the shares to their fellow shareholders prior to selling them to a third party.

Public Limited Company

Public limited companies can be publicly traded on a stock exchange — similar to the U.S.Corporation (Corp.) and the German Aktiengesellschaft (AG).

In Specific Countries

Australia: The private company equivalent in Australia is the Proprietary Limited company (Pty. Ltd.). An Australian company with just Limited or Ltd. at the end of its name is a public company, such as a company listed on the ASX (although public companies can be, and often are, unlisted). Australia does not have a direct equivalent to the plc. A shareholder in a limited company, in the event of its becoming insolvent (equivalent to bankruptcy in the U.S.) would be liable to contribute the amount remaining unpaid on the shares (usually zero, as most shares are issued fully paid). 'Paid' here relates to the amount paid to the company for the shares on first issue, and not to be confused with amounts paid by one shareholder to another to transfer ownership of shares between them. A shareholder is thus afforded limited liability.

Canada

In Canada, a person wishing to register a limited company must file Articles of Incorporation with either their provincial government or the federal government.

India

In India, the designation "Private Limited" or "Pvt Ltd" is suffixed to all private limited companies, while "Public Limited" is used for a Public limited company. The registration of companies in India is handled by the Ministry of Company Affairs, which is charged with administering the Companies Act 2013 and other acts related to Indian private sector.

Nepal

This is a list of notable companies based in Nepal, grouped by their Industry Classification Benchmark sector.

South Africa

In South Africa the term *(pty) ltd* is used to refer to a private limited company. Recently all Pty are regulated by CIPRO (Companies and Intellectual Property Commission).

United Kingdom

The registration of companies in the United Kingdom is done through Companies House, which operates offices in London, Cardiff, Edinburgh and Belfast. Prior to 1 October 2009 the registration of companies in Northern Ireland was the responsibility of the Department of Enterprise, Trade and Investment (a department of the devolved government). On the commencement of the Companies Act 2006 Northern Ireland's previously distinct company law was repealed and the new companies code instituted by that Act was extended to Northern Ireland.

United States

In United States the expression *corporation* is preferred to *limited company* (because corporations there have limited liability). A limited liability company (LLC) is a different entity. However, some states permit corporations to have the designation *Ltd.* (instead of the usual *Inc.*) to signify their corporate status.

Sole Proprietorship

A sole proprietorship, also known as the sole trader or simply a proprietorship, is a type of business entity that is owned and run by one individual and in which there is no legal distinction between the owner and the business. The owner receives all profits (subject to taxation specific to the business) and has unlimited responsibility for all losses and debts. Every asset of the business is owned by the proprietor and all debts of the business are the proprietor's. It is a "sole" proprietorship in contrast with partnerships. A sole proprietor may use a trade name or business name other than his or her legal name.

Advantages

- It is easy to organise this business. Only small amounts of capital are needed to start and run a business.
- It permits a high degree of flexibility to the owner since he/she is the boss of the business establishment.
- Due to the owner's unlimited liability, some creditors are more willing to extend credit.
- The owner receives all the profit of the business.
- No risk of fraud by a partner.

Disadvantages

Raising capital for a proprietorship is more difficult because an unrelated investor has less peace of mind concerning the use and security of his or her investment and the investment is more difficult to formalize; other types of business entities have more documentation. The enterprise may be crippled or terminated if the owner becomes ill. Since the business has the same legal entity as the proprietor, it ceases to exist upon the proprietor's death. Because the enterprise rests exclusively on one person, it often has difficulty in raising long-term capital.

- Has limited resources. Banks are reluctant to grant loans to proprietorship considering its small assets and high mortality rate.
- Unlimited liability for business debts. The single owner is responsible for paying all debts and damages of their business.
- If the firm fails, creditors may force the sale of the proprietor's personal property as well as their business property to satisfy their claim.
- When the owner dies, the continuation of the business is difficult, because a new owner must typically accept all liabilities of the business.

Cooperative

A cooperative ("coop") or co-operative ("co-op") is an autonomous association of persons who voluntarily cooperate for their mutual social, economic, and cultural benefit. Cooperatives include non-profit community organisations and businesses that are owned and managed by the people who use its services (a consumer cooperative) or by the people who work there (a worker cooperative) or by the people who live there (a housing cooperative), hybrids such as worker cooperatives that are also consumer cooperatives or credit unions, multi-stakeholder cooperatives such as those that bring together civil society and local actors to deliver community needs, and second and third tier cooperatives whose members are other cooperatives.

The International Co-operative Alliance was the first international association formed by the movement. It includes the World Council of Credit Unions. A second organisation was formed later in Germany, the International Raiffeisen Union. In the United States, the National Cooperative Business Association (NCBA) serves as the sector's oldest national membership association. It is dedicated to ensuring that cooperative businesses have the same opportunities as other businesses operating in the country and that consumers have access to cooperatives in the marketplace. A U.S. National Cooperative Bank was formed in the 1970s. By 2004, a new association focused on worker co-ops was founded, the United States Federation of Worker Cooperatives.

Origins

Cooperation dates back as far as human beings have been organising for mutual benefit. Tribes were organised as cooperative structures, allocating jobs and resources among each other, only trading with the external communities. In alpine environments, trade could only be maintained in organised cooperatives to achieve a useful condition of artificial roads such as Viamala in 1472. Pre-industrial Europe is home to the first cooperatives from an industrial context.

In 1761, the Fenwick Weavers' Society was formed in Fenwick, East Ayrshire, Scotland to sell discounted oatmeal to local workers. Its services expanded to include assistance with savings and loans, emigration and education.

In 1810, Welshsocial reformer Robert Owen, from Newtown in mid-Wales, and his partners purchased New Lanark mill from Owen's father-in-law David Dale and proceeded to introduce better labour standards including discounted retail shops where profits were passed on to his employees. Owen left New Lanark to pursue other forms of cooperative organisation and develop co-op ideas through writing and lecture. Cooperative communities were set up in Glasgow, Indiana and Hampshire, although ultimately unsuccessful. In 1828, William King set up a newspaper, *The Cooperator*, to promote Owen's thinking, having already set up a co-operative store in Brighton.

The Rochdale Society of Equitable Pioneers, founded in 1844, is usually considered the first successful cooperative enterprise, used as a model for modern co-ops, following the 'Rochdale Principles'. A group of 28 weavers and other artisans in Rochdale, England set up the society to open their own store selling food items they could not otherwise afford. Within ten years there were over 1,000 cooperative societies in the United Kingdom.

Other events such as the founding of a friendly society by the Tolpuddle Martyrs in 1832 were key occasions in the creation of organised labour and consumer movements.

Social Economy

In the final year of the 20th century, cooperatives banded together to establish a number of social enterprise agencies which have moved to adopt the multi-stakeholder cooperative model. In the last 15 years (1994–2009) the EU and its member nations have gradually revised national accounting systems to "make visible" the increasing contribution of social economy organisations.

Organisational and Ideological Roots

The roots of the cooperative movement can be traced to multiple influences and extend worldwide. In the Anglosphere, post-feudal forms of cooperation between workers and owners that are expressed today as "profit-sharing" and "surplus sharing" arrangements, existed as far back as 1795. The key ideological influence on the Anglosphere branch of the cooperative movement, however, was a *rejection* of the charity principles that underpinned welfare reforms when the British government radically revised its Poor Laws in 1834. As both state and church institutions began to routinely distinguish between the 'deserving' and 'undeserving' poor, a movement of friendly societies grew throughout the British Empire based on the principle of mutuality, committed to self-help in the welfare of working people.

Friendly Societies established forums through which one member, one vote was practiced in organisation decision-making. The principles challenged the idea that a person should be an owner of property before being granted a political voice. Throughout the second half of the nineteenth century (and then repeatedly every 20 years or so) there has been a surge in the number of cooperative organisations, both in commercial practice and civil society, operating to advance democracy and universal suffrage as a political principle. Friendly Societies and consumer cooperatives became the dominant form of organisation amongst working people in Anglosphere industrial societies prior to the rise of trade unions and industrial factories. Weinbren reports that by the end of the 19th century, over 80% of British working age men and 90% of Australian working age men were members of one or more Friendly Society.

From the mid-nineteenth century, mutual organisations embraced these ideas in economic enterprises, firstly amongst tradespeople, and later in cooperative stores, educational institutes, financial institutions and industrial enterprises. The common thread (enacted in different ways, and subject to the constraints of various systems of national law) is the principle that an enterprise or association should be owned and controlled by the people it serves, and share any surpluses on the basis of each member's cooperative contribution (as a producer, labourer or consumer) rather than their capacity to invest financial capital.

The cooperative movement has been fuelled globally by ideas of economic democracy. Economic democracy is a socioeconomic philosophy that suggests an expansion of decision-making power from a small minority of corporate shareholders to a larger majority of public stakeholders. There are many different approaches to thinking about and building economic democracy. Both Marxism and anarchism, for example, have been influenced by utopian socialism, which was based on voluntary cooperation, *without* recognition of class conflict. Anarchists are committed to libertarian socialism and have focused on local organisation, including locally managed cooperatives, linked through confederations of unions, cooperatives and communities. Marxists, who as socialists have likewise held and worked for the goal of democratizing productive and reproductive relationships, often placed a greater strategic emphasis on confronting the larger scales of human organisation.

As they viewed the capitalist class to be politically, militarily and culturally mobilized for the purpose of maintaining an exploitable working class, they fought in the early 20th century to appropriate from the capitalist class the society's collective political capacity in the form of the state, either through democratic socialism, or through what came to be known as Leninism.

Though they regard the state as an unnecessarily oppressive institution, Marxists considered appropriating national and international-scale capitalist institutions and resources (such as the state) to be an important first pillar in creating conditions favourable to solidaristic economies. With the declining influence of the USSR after the 1960s, socialist strategies pluralized, though economic democratizers have not as yet established a fundamental challenge to the hegemony of global neoliberal capitalism.

Meaning

Cooperatives as Legal Entities

A cooperative is a legal entity owned and democratically controlled by its members. Members often have a close association with the enterprise as producers or consumers of its products or services, or as its employees.

In some countries, e.g. Finland and Sweden, there are specific forms of incorporation for cooperatives. Cooperatives may take the form of companies limited by shares or by guarantee, partnerships or unincorporated associations. In the UK they may also use the industrial and provident society structure. In the USA, cooperatives are often organised as non-capital stock corporations under state-specific cooperative laws. However, they may also be unincorporated associations or business corporations such as limited liability companies or partnerships; such forms are useful when the members want to allow:

1. some members to have a greater share of the control, or
2. some investors to have a return on their capital that exceeds fixed interest,

neither of which may be allowed under local laws for cooperatives. Cooperatives often share their earnings with the membership as dividends, which are divided among the members according to their participation in the enterprise, such as patronage, instead of according to the value of their capital shareholdings (as is done by a joint stock company).

Identity

Cooperatives are typically based on the cooperative values of "self-help, self-responsibility, democracy and equality, equity and solidarity" and the seven cooperative principles:

1. Voluntary and open membership
2. Democratic member control
3. Economic participation by members
4. Autonomy and independence
5. Education, training and information
6. Cooperation among cooperatives
7. Concern for community

Cooperatives are dedicated to the values of openness, social responsibility and caring for others. Such legal entities have a range of social characteristics. Membership is open, meaning that anyone who satisfies certain non-discriminatory conditions may join. Economic benefits are distributed proportionally to each member's level of participation in the cooperative, for instance, by a dividend on sales or purchases, rather than according to capital invested. Cooperatives may be classified as either *worker*, *consumer*, *producer*, *purchasing* or *housing* cooperatives. They are distinguished from other forms of incorporation in that profit-making or economic stability are balanced by the interests of the community. Co-ops can sometimes be identified on the Internet through the use of the .coopsuffix of internet addresses. Organisations using .coop domain names must adhere to the basic co-op values. The United Nations has declared 2012 to be the International Year of Cooperatives (IYC).

Economic Stability

Capital and the Debt Trapreports that "[C]ooperatives tend to have a longer life than other types of enterprise, and thus a higher level of entrepreneurial sustainability. In [one study], the rate of survival of cooperatives after three years was 75 percent, whereas it was only 48 percent for all enterprises ... [and] after ten years, 44 percent of cooperatives were still in operation, whereas the ratio was only 20 percent for all enterprises" (p. 109). "Cooperative banks build up counter-cyclical buffers that function well in case of a crisis," and are less likely to lead members and clients towards a debt trap (p. 216). This is explained by their more democratic governance that reduces perverse incentives and subsequent contributions to economic bubbles.

Types of Cooperative Governance

Non-Monetary Cooperative: A non-monetary cooperative provides a service based on entirely voluntary labour in the maintenance and provision of a particular service or good, working in the identical manner of a library. These co-ops are locally owned and operated and provides the free rental of equipments of all kinds (bicycles, sports, gear). This idea has been said to reduce general human consumption of goods and is a key subject in sustainable development

Retailers' Cooperative

A retailers' cooperative (known as a secondary or marketing cooperative in some countries) is an organisation which employs economies of scale on behalf of its members to receive discounts from manufacturers and to pool marketing. It is common for locally owned grocery stores, hardware stores and pharmacies. In this case the members of the cooperative are businesses rather than individuals.

The Best Western international hotel chain is actually a retailers' cooperative, whose members are hotel operators, although it refers to itself as a "nonprofit membership association." It gave up on the "cooperative" label after some courts insisted on enforcing regulatory requirements for franchisors despite its member-controlled status

Worker Cooperative

A worker cooperative or producer cooperative is a cooperative, that is owned and democratically controlled by its "worker-owners". There are no outside owners in a "pure" workers' cooperative, only the workers own shares of the business, though hybrid forms exist in which consumers, community members or capitalist investors also own some shares. In practice, control by worker-owners may be exercised through individual, collective or majority ownership by the workforce, or the retention of individual, collective or majority voting rights (exercised on a one-member one-vote basis). A worker cooperative, therefore, has the characteristic that the majority of its workforce owns shares, and the majority of shares are owned by the workforce. Membership is not always compulsory for employees, but generally only employees can become members either directly (as shareholders) or indirectly through membership of a trust that owns the company.

The impact of political ideology on practice constrains the development of cooperatives in different countries. In India, there is a form of workers' cooperative which insists on compulsory membership for all employees and compulsory employment for all members. That is the form of the Indian Coffee Houses.

This system was advocated by the Indian communist leader A. K. Gopalan. In places like the UK, common ownership (indivisible collective ownership) was popular in the 1970s. Cooperative Societies only became legal in Britain after the passing of Slaney's Act in 1852. In 1865 there were 651 registered societies with a total membership of well over 200,000. There are now more than 400 worker cooperatives in the UK, Suma Wholefoods being the largest example with a turnover of £24 million.

Volunteer Cooperative

A volunteer cooperative is a cooperative that is run by and for a network of volunteers, for the benefit of a defined membership or the general public, to achieve some goal. Depending on the structure, it may be a collective or mutual organisation, which is operated according to the principles of cooperative governance.

The most basic form of volunteer-run cooperative is a voluntary association. A lodge or social club may be organised on this basis. A volunteer-run co-op is distinguished from a worker cooperative in that the latter is by definition employee-owned, whereas the volunteer cooperative is typically a non-stock corporation, volunteer-run consumer co-op or service organisation, in which workers and beneficiaries jointly participate in management decisions and receive discounts on the basis of sweat equity.

Social Cooperative

A particularly successful form of multi-stakeholder cooperative is the Italian "social cooperative", of which some 7,000 exist. "Type A" social cooperatives bring together providers and beneficiaries of a social service as members. "Type B" social cooperatives bring together permanent workers and previously unemployed people who wish to integrate into the labour market. They are legally defined as follows:

- no more than 80% of profits may be distributed, interest is limited to the bond rate and dissolution is altruistic (assets may not be distributed)
- the cooperative has legal personality and limited liability
- the objective is the general benefit of the community and the social integration of citizens
- those of type B integrate disadvantaged people into the labour market. The categories of disadvantage they target may include physical and mental disability, drug and alcohol addiction, developmental disorders and problems with the law. They do not include other factors of disadvantage such as unemployment, race, sexual orientation or abuse.
- type A cooperatives provide health, social or educational services
- various categories of stakeholder may become members, including paid employees, beneficiaries, volunteers (up to 50% of members), financial investors and public institutions. In type B cooperatives at least 30% of the members must be from the disadvantaged target groups
- voting is one person one vote

Consumers' Cooperative

A consumers' cooperative is a business owned by its customers. Employees can also generally become members. Members vote on major decisions and elect the board of directors from among their own number. The first of these was set up in 1844 in the North-West of England by 28 weavers who wanted to sell food at a lower price than the local shops..

The world's largest consumers' cooperative is the Co-operative Group in the United Kingdom, which offers a variety of retail and financial services. The UK also has a number of autonomous consumers' cooperative societies, such as the East of England Co-operative Society and Mid-counties Co-operative.

In fact, the Co-operative Group is something of a hybrid, having both corporate members (mostly other consumers' cooperatives, as a result of its origins as a wholesale society), and individual retail consumer members.

Euro Coop is the European Community of Consumer Cooperatives.

Business and Employment Cooperative

Business and employment cooperatives (BEC's) are a subset of worker cooperatives that represent a new approach to providing support to the creation of new businesses.

Like other business creation support schemes, BEC's enable budding entrepreneurs to experiment with their business idea while benefiting from a secure income. The innovation BECs introduce is that once the business is established the entrepreneur is not forced to leave and set up independently, but can stay and become a full member of the cooperative. The micro-enterprises then combine to form one multi-activity enterprise whose members provide a mutually supportive environment for each other.

BECs thus provide budding business people with an easy transition from inactivity to self-employment, but in a collective framework. They open up new horizons for people who have ambition but who lack the skills or confidence needed to set off entirely on their own – or who simply want to carry on an independent economic activity but within a supportive group context.

New Generation Cooperative

New generation cooperatives (NGCs) are an adaptation of traditional cooperative structures to modern, capital intensive industries. They are sometimes described as a hybrid between traditional co-ops and limited liability companies. They were first developed in California and spread and flourished in the US Mid-West in the 1990s. They are now common in Canada where they operate primarily in agriculture and food services, where their primary purpose is to add value to primary products. For example producing ethanol from corn, pasta from durum wheat, or gourmet cheese from goat's milk.

Types and Number of Cooperatives

The top 300 largest cooperatives were listed in 2007 by the International Co-operative Alliance. 80% were involved in either agriculture, finance, or retail and more than half were in the United States, Italy, or France. In the United States, cooperatives, particularly those in the Midwest, are analyzed at the University of Wisconsin Centre for Cooperatives.

Housing Cooperative

A housing cooperative is a legal mechanism for ownership of housing where residents either own shares (share capital co-op) reflecting their equity in the cooperative's real estate, or have membership and occupancy rights in a not-for-profit cooperative (non-share capital co-op), and they underwrite their housing through paying subscriptions or rent.

Housing cooperatives come in three basic equity structures

- In market-rate housing cooperatives, members may sell their shares in the cooperative whenever they like for whatever price the market will bear, much like any other residential property. Market-rate co-ops are very common in New York City.
- Limited equity housing cooperatives, which are often used by affordable housing developers, allow members to own some equity in their home, but limit the sale price of their membership share to that which they paid.
- Group equity or zero-equity housing cooperatives do not allow members to own equity in their residences and often have rental agreements well below market rates.

Members of a building cooperative (in Britain known as a self-build housing cooperative) pool resources to build housing, normally using a high proportion of their own labour. When the building is finished, each member is the sole owner of a homestead, and the cooperative may be dissolved.

This collective effort was at the origin of many of Britain's building societies, which however, developed into "permanent" mutual savings and loan organisations, a term which persisted in some of their names (such as the former *Leeds Permanent*). Nowadays such self-building may be financed using a step-by-step mortgage which is released in stages as the building is completed. The term may also refer to worker cooperatives in the building trade.

Utility Cooperative

A utility cooperative is a type of consumers' cooperative that is tasked with the delivery of a public utility such as electricity, water or telecommunications services to its members. Profits are either reinvested into infrastructure or distributed to members in the form of "patronage" or "capital credits", which are essentially dividends paid on a member's investment into the cooperative. In the United States, many cooperatives were formed to provide rural electrical and telephone service as part of the New Deal.

In the case of electricity, cooperatives are generally either generation and transmission (G&T) co-ops that create and send power via the transmission grid or local distribution co-ops that gather electricity from a variety of sources and send it along to homes and businesses.

In Tanzania, it has been proven that the cooperative method is helpful in water distribution. When the people are involved with their own water, they care more because the quality of their work has a direct effect on the quality of their water.

Agricultural Cooperative

Agricultural cooperatives or farmers' cooperatives are cooperatives where farmers pool their resources for mutual economic benefit. Agricultural cooperatives are broadly divided into *agricultural service cooperatives*, which provide various services to their individual farming members, and *agricultural production cooperatives*, where production resources such as land or machinery are pooled and members farm jointly. Known examples of agricultural production cooperatives are Ocean Spray, collective farms in former socialist countries and the kibbutzim in Israel.

Agricultural supply cooperatives aggregate purchases, storage, and distribution of farm inputs for their members. By taking advantage of volume discounts and utilising other economies of scale, supply cooperatives bring down members' costs. Supply cooperatives may provide seeds, fertilizers, chemicals, fuel, and farm machinery. Some supply cooperatives also operate machinery pools that provide mechanical field services (e.g., plowing, harvesting) to their members.

Agricultural marketing cooperatives provide the services involved in moving a product from the point of production to the point of consumption. Agricultural marketing includes a series of inter-connected activities involving planning production, growing and harvesting, grading, packing, transport, storage, food processing, distribution and sale. Agricultural marketing cooperatives are often formed to promote specific commodities. Commercially successful cooperatives include India's Amul (dairy products), Dairy Farmers of America (dairy products) in the United States, and Malaysia's FELDA (palm oil).

Credit Unions, Cooperative Banking and Co-Operative Insurance

Credit unions are cooperative financial institutions that are owned and controlled by their members. Credit unions provide the same financial services as banks but are considered not-for-profit organisations and adhere to cooperative principles.

Figure: *The Co-operative Bank's head office in Manchester. The statue in front is of Robert Owen, a pioneer in the cooperative movement.*

Credit unions originated in mid-19th century Germany through the efforts of pioneers Franz Herman Schulze' Delitzch and Friedrich Wilhelm Raiffeisen. The concept of financial cooperatives crossed the Atlantic at the turn of the 20th century, when the *caissepopulaire* movement was started by Alphonse Desjardins in Quebec, Canada.

In 1900, from his home in Lévis, he opened North America's first credit union, marking the beginning of the Mouvement Desjardins. Eight years later, Desjardins provided guidance for the first credit union in the United States, where there are now about 7,950 active status federally insured credit unions, with almost 90 million members and more than $679 billion on deposit.

Cooperative banking networks, which were nationalized in Eastern Europe, work now as real cooperative institutions. A remarkable development has taken place in Poland, where the SKOK (*Spó^{3}dzielczeKasyOszczêdnoœciowo-Kredytowe*) network has grown to serve over 1 million members via 13,000 branches, and is larger than the country's largest conventional bank.

In Scandinavia, there is a clear distinction between mutual savings banks (Sparbank) and true credit unions (Andelsbank).

The oldest cooperative banks in Europe, based on the ideas of Friedrich Raiffeisen, are joined together in the 'Urgenossen'.

Federal or Secondary Cooperatives

In some cases, cooperative societies find it advantageous to form cooperative federations in which all of the members are themselves cooperatives. Historically, these have predominantly come in the form of cooperative wholesale societies, and cooperative unions. Cooperative federations are a means through which cooperative societies can fulfill the sixth Rochdale Principle, cooperation among cooperatives, with the ICA noting that "Cooperatives serve their members most effectively and strengthen the cooperative movement by working together through local, national, regional and international structures."

Cooperative Wholesale Society

According to cooperative economist Charles Gide, the aim of a cooperative wholesale society is to arrange "bulk purchases, and, if possible, organise production." The best historical example of this were the English CWS and the Scottish CWS, which were the forerunners to the modern Co-operative Group.

Cooperative Union

A second common form of cooperative federation is a cooperative union, whose objective (according to Gide) is "to develop the spirit of solidarity among societies and... in a word, to exercise the functions of a government whose authority, it is needless to say, is purely moral." Co-operatives UK and the International Cooperative Alliance are examples of such arrangements.

Cooperative Political Movements

In some countries with a strong cooperative sector, such as the UK, cooperatives may find it advantageous to form political groupings to represent their interests. The British Cooperative Party, the Canadian Cooperative Commonwealth Federation and United Farmers of Alberta are prime examples of such arrangements.

The British cooperative movement formed the Cooperative Party in the early 20th century to represent members of consumers' cooperatives in Parliament, which was the first of its kind. The

Cooperative Party now has a permanent electoral pact with the Labour Party meaning someone cannot be a member if they support a party other than Labour. An alternative grouping, the Conservative Co-operative Movement is open to people of all parties or none. Plaid Cymru also run a credit union that is constituted as a co-operative, called the 'Plaid Cymru Credit Union.' UK cooperatives retain a strong market share in food retail, insurance, banking, funeral services, and the travel industry in many parts of the country, although this is still significicantly lower than other business models.

Women in Cooperatives

Since cooperatives are based on values like self-help, democracy, equality, equity, and solidarity, they can play a particularly strong role in empowering women, especially in developing countries. Cooperatives allow women who might have been isolated and working individually to band together and create economies of scale as well as increase their own bargaining power in the market.

In statements in advance of International Women's Day in early 2013, President of the International Cooperative Alliance, Dame Pauline Green, said, "Cooperative businesses have done so much to help women onto the ladder of economic activity. With that comes community respect, political legitimacy and influence."

However, despite the supposed democratic structure of cooperatives and the values and benefits shared by members, due to gender norms on the traditional role of women, and other instilled cultural practices that sidestep attempted legal protections, women suffer a disproportionately low representation in cooperative membership around the world. Representation of women through *active* membership (showing up to meetings and voting), as well as in leadership and managerial positions is even lower.

Cooperatives in Popular Culture

As of 2012, the number of memberships in cooperatives reached one billion, and so the organisational structure and movement has seeped into popular culture.

In the HBO drama television series The Wire, several drug dealers create a democratic alliance with the interests of cutting back on violence and increasing business. This is called the "New Day Co-Op."

Co-opoly: The Game of Cooperatives is a popular board game played around the world that challenges players to work together to start and run a cooperative and overcome major hurdles.

My So-Called Housing Cooperative is a web series focusing on the humorous side of living in a housing co-op.

Corporation

A corporation is a separate legal entity that has been incorporated either directly through legislation or through a registration process established by law. Incorporated entities have legal rights and liabilities that are distinct from their employees and shareholders, and may conduct business as either a profit-seeking business or not-for-profit business. Early incorporated entities were established by charter (i.e. by an *ad hoc* act granted by a monarch or passed by a parliament or legislature). Most jurisdictions now allow the creation of new corporations through registration. In addition to legal personality, registered corporations tend to have limited liability, be owned by shareholders who can transfer their shares to others, and controlled by a board of directors who are normally elected or appointed by the shareholders.

In American English the word corporation is widely used to describe large business corporations. In British English and in the commonwealth countries, the term company is more widely used to describe the same sort of entity while the word corporation encompasses all incorporated entities. In American English, the word company can include entities such as partnerships that would not be referred to as companies in British English as they are not a separate legal entity.

Despite not being human beings, corporations, as far as the law is concerned, are legal persons, and have many of the same rights and responsibilities as natural people do. Corporations can exercise human rights against real individuals and the state, and they can themselves be responsible for human rights violations. Corporations can be "dissolved" either by statutory operation, order of court, or voluntary action on the part of shareholders. Insolvency may result in a form of corporate failure, when creditors force the liquidation and dissolution of the corporation under court order, but it most often results in a restructuring of corporate holdings. Corporations can even be convicted of criminal offences, such as fraud and manslaughter. However corporations are not considered living entities in the way that humans are.

History

The word "corporation" derives from *corpus*, the Latin word for body, or a "body of people." By the time of Justinian (reigned 527–565), Roman Law recognised a range of corporate entities under the names *universitas*, *corpus* or *collegium*. These included the state itself (the *populus Romanus*), municipalities, and such private associations as sponsors of a religious cult, burial clubs, political groups, and guilds of craftsmen or traders. Such bodies commonly had the right to own property and make contracts, to receive gifts and legacies, to sue and be sued, and, in general, to perform legal acts through representatives. Private associations were granted designated privileges and liberties by the emperor.

Entities which carried on business and were the subjects of legal rights were found in ancient Rome, and the Maurya Empire in ancient India. In medieval Europe, churches became incorporated, as did local governments, such as the Pope and the City of London Corporation. The point was that the incorporation would survive longer than the lives of any particular member, existing in perpetuity. The alleged oldest commercial corporation in the world, the Stora Kopparberg mining community in Falun, Sweden, obtained a charter from King Magnus Eriksson in 1347.

In medieval times traders would do business through common law constructs, such as partnerships. Whenever people acted together with a view to profit, the law deemed that a partnership arose. Early guilds and livery companies were also often involved in the regulation of competition between traders.

Mercantilism

Many European nations chartered corporations to lead colonial ventures, such as the Dutch East India Company or the Hudson's Bay Company. These chartered companies became the progenitors of the modern corporation. Acting under a charter sanctioned by the Dutch government, the Dutch East India Company defeated Portuguese forces and established itself in the Moluccan Islands in order to profit from the European demand for spices. Investors in the VOC were issued paper certificates as proof of share ownership, and were able to trade their shares on the original Amsterdam stock exchange. Shareholders are also explicitly granted limited liability in the company's royal charter.

In England, the government created corporations under a Royal Charter or an Act of Parliament with the grant of a monopoly over a specified territory. The best known example, established in 1600, was the British East India Company. Queen Elizabeth I granted it the exclusive right to trade with all countries to the east of the Cape of Good Hope. Corporations at this time would essentially act on the government's behalf, bringing in revenue from its exploits abroad. Subsequently the Company became increasingly integrated with British military and colonial policy, just as most UK corporations were essentially dependent on the British navy's ability to control trade routes.

Labeled by both contemporaries and historians as "the grandest society of merchants in the universe", the British East India Company would come to symbolize the dazzlingly rich potential of the corporation, as well as new methods of business that could be both brutal and exploitative. On 31 December 1600, the English monarchy granted the company a 15-year monopoly on trade to and from the East Indies and Africa. By 1611, shareholders in the East India Company were earning an almost 150% return on their investment. Subsequent stock offerings demonstrated just how lucrative the Company had become. Its first stock offering in 1613–1616 raised £418,000, and its second offering in 1617–1622 raised £1.6 million.

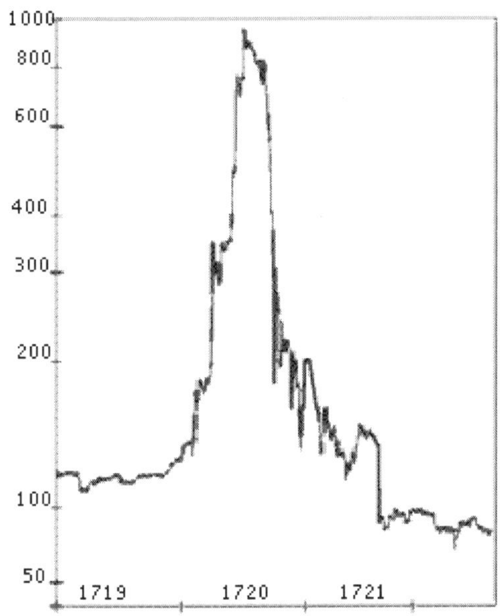

Figure: *Chart of the South Sea Company's stock prices. The rapid inflation of the stock value in the 1710s led to the Bubble Act 1720, which restricted the establishment of companies without a Royal Charter.*

A similar chartered company, the South Sea Company, was established in 1711 to trade in the Spanish South American colonies, but met with less success. The South Sea Company's monopoly rights were supposedly backed by the Treaty of Utrecht, signed in 1713 as a settlement following the War of Spanish Succession, which gave the United Kingdom an *assiento* to trade in the region for thirty years. In fact the Spanish remained hostile and let only one ship a year enter. Unaware of the problems, investors in the UK, enticed by extravagant promises of profit from company promoters bought thousands of shares. By 1717, the South Sea Company was so wealthy (still having done no real business) that it assumed the public debt of the UK government. This accelerated the inflation of the share price further, as did the Bubble Act 1720, which (possibly with the motive of protecting the South Sea Company from competition) prohibited the establishment of any companies without a Royal Charter. The share price rose so rapidly that people began buying shares merely in order to sell them at a higher price, which in turn led to higher share prices. This was the first speculative bubble the country had seen, but by the end of 1720, the bubble had "burst", and the share price sank from £1000 to under £100. As bankruptcies and recriminations ricocheted through government and high society, the mood against corporations, and errant directors, was bitter.

In the late 18th century, Stewart Kyd, the author of the first treatise on corporate law in English, defined a corporation as:

a collection of many individuals united into one body, under a special denomination, having perpetual succession under an artificial form, and vested, by policy of the law, with the capacity of acting, in several respects, as an individual, particularly of taking and granting property, of contracting obligations, and of suing and being sued, of enjoying privileges and immunities in common, and of exercising a variety of political rights, more or less extensive, according to the design of its institution, or the powers conferred upon it, either at the time of its creation, or at any subsequent period of its existence.

—A Treatise on the Law of Corporations, Stewart Kyd (1793–1794)

Modern Company Law

Due to the late 18th century abandonment of mercantilist economic theory and the rise of classical liberalism and laissez-faire economic theory due to a revolution in economics led by Adam Smith and other economists, corporations transitioned from being government or guild affiliated entities to being public and private economic entities free of government direction.

In 1776, Adam Smith wrote in the *Wealth of Nations* that mass corporate activity could not match private entrepreneurship, because people in charge of others' money would not exercise as much care as they would with their own.

Deregulation

The UK Bubble Act 1720's prohibition on establishing companies remained in force until its repeal in 1825. By this point the Industrial Revolution had gathered pace, pressing for legal change to facilitate business activity. The repeal was the beginning of a gradual lifting on restrictions, though business ventures (such as those chronicled by Charles Dickens in *Martin Chuzzlewit*) under primitive companies legislation were often scams. Without cohesive regulation, proverbial operations like the "Anglo-Bengalee Disinterested Loan and Life Assurance Company" were undercapitalised ventures promising no hope of success except for richly paid promoters.

The process of incorporation was possible only through a royal charter or a private act and was limited, owing to Parliament's jealous protection of the privileges and advantages thereby granted. As a result, many businesses came to be operated as unincorporated associations with possibly thousands of members. Any consequent litigation had to be carried out in the joint names of all the members and was almost impossibly cumbersome. Though Parliament would sometimes grant a private act to allow an individual to represent the whole in legal proceedings, this was a narrow and necessarily costly expedient, allowed only to established companies.

Then in 1843, William Gladstone took chairmanship of a Parliamentary Committee on Joint Stock Companies, which led to the Joint Stock Companies Act 1844, regarded as the first modern piece of company law. The Act created the Registrar of Joint Stock Companies, empowered to register companies by a two-stage process. The first, provisional, stage cost £5 and did not confer corporate status, which arose after completing the second stage for another £5. For the first time in history, it was possible for ordinary people through a simple registration procedure to incorporate. The advantage of establishing a company as a separate legal person was mainly administrative, as a unified entity under which the rights and duties of all investors and managers could be channeled.

Limited Liability

However, there was still no limited liability and company members could still be held responsible for unlimited losses by the company. The next, crucial development, then, was the Limited Liability Act 1855, passed at the behest of the then Vice President of the Board of Trade, Mr Robert Lowe. This allowed investors to limit their liability in the event of business failure to the amount they invested in the company - shareholders were still liable directly to creditors, but just for the unpaid portion of their shares. (The principle that shareholders are liable to the corporation had been introduced in the Joint Stock Companies Act 1844).

The 1855 Act allowed limited liability to companies of more than 25 members (shareholders). Insurance companies were excluded from the act, though it was standard practice for insurance contracts to exclude action against individual members. Limited liability for insurance companies was allowed by the Companies Act 1862.

This prompted the English periodical *The Economist* to write in 1855 that "never, perhaps, was a change so vehemently and generally demanded, of which the importance was so much overrated. "

The major error of this judgment was recognised by the same magazine more than 70 years later, when it claimed that, "[t]he economic historian of the future. . . may be inclined to assign to the nameless inventor of the principle of limited liability, as applied to trading corporations, a place of honour with Watt and Stephenson, and other pioneers of the Industrial Revolution. "

These two features - a simple registration procedure and limited liability - were subsequently codified into the landmark 1856 Joint Stock Companies Act. This was subsequently consolidated with a number of other statutes in the Companies Act 1862, which remained in force for the rest of the century, up to and including the time of the decision in *Salomon v A Salomon & Co Ltd.*

The legislation shortly gave way to a railway boom, and from then, the numbers of companies formed soared. In the later nineteenth century depression took hold, and just as company numbers had boomed, many began to implode and fall into insolvency. Much strong academic, legislative and judicial opinion was opposed to the notion that businessmen could escape accountability for their role in the failing businesses.

Further Developments

The last significant development in the history of companies was the decision of the House of Lords in *Salomon v. Salomon & Co.* where the House of Lords confirmed the separate legal personality of the company, and that the liabilities of the company were separate and distinct from those of its owners.

In the United States, forming a corporation usually required an act of legislation until the late 19th century. Many private firms, such as Carnegie's steel company and Rockefeller's Standard Oil, avoided the corporate model for this reason (as a trust). State governments began to adopt more permissive corporate laws from the early 19th century, although these were all restrictive in design, often with the intention of preventing corporations for gaining too much wealth and power.

New Jersey was the first state to adopt an "enabling" corporate law, with the goal of attracting more business to the state, in 1896. In 1899, Delaware followed New Jersey's lead with the enactment of an enabling corporate statute, but Delaware only became the leading corporate state after the enabling provisions of the 1896 New Jersey corporate law were repealed in 1913.

The end of the 19th century saw the emergence of holding companies and corporate mergers creating larger corporations with dispersed shareholders. Countries began enacting anti-trustlaws to prevent anti-competitive practices and corporations were granted more legal rights and protections.

The 20th century saw a proliferation of laws allowing for the creation of corporations by registration across the world, which helped to drive economic booms in many countries before and after World War I. Another major post World War I shift was toward the development of conglomerates, in which large corporations purchased smaller corporations to expand their industrial base.

Starting in the 1980s, many countries with large state-owned corporations moved toward privatization, the selling of publicly owned (or 'nationalised') services and enterprises to corporations. Deregulation (reducing the regulation of corporate activity) often accompanied privatization as part of a laissez-faire policy.

Ownership and Control

A corporation is, at least in theory, owned and controlled by its members. In a joint-stock company the members are known as shareholders and each of their shares in the ownership, control and profits of the corporation is determined by the portion of shares in the company that they own. Thus a person who owns a quarter of the shares of a joint-stock company owns a quarter of the company, is entitled to a quarter of the profit (or at least a quarter of the profit given to shareholders as dividends) and has a quarter of the votes capable of being cast at general meetings.

In another kind of corporation the legal document which established the corporation or which contains its current rules will determine who the corporation's members are. Who is a member depends on what kind of corporation is involved. In a worker cooperative the members are people who work for the cooperative. In a credit union the members are people who have accounts with the credit union.

The day-to-day activities of a corporation are typically controlled by individuals appointed by the members. In some cases this will be a single individual but more commonly corporations are controlled by a committee or by committees. Broadly speaking there are two kinds of committee structure.

- A single committee known as a board of directors is the method favoured in most common law countries. Under this model the board of directors is composed of both executive and non-executive directors, the latter being meant to supervise the former's management of the company.
- A two-tiered committee structure with a supervisory board and a managing board is common in civil law countries.

Formation

Historically, corporations were created by a charter granted by government. Today, corporations are usually registered with the state, province, or national government and regulated by the laws enacted by that government. Registration is the main prerequisite to the corporation's assumption of limited liability. The law sometimes requires the corporation to designate its principal address, as well as a registered agent (a person or company designated to receive legal service of process). It may also be required to designate an agent or other legal representative of the corporation.

Generally, a corporation files articles of incorporation with the government, laying out the general nature of the corporation, the amount of stock it is authorized to issue, and the names and addresses of directors. Once the articles are approved, the corporation's directors meet to create bylaws that govern the internal functions of the corporation, such as meeting procedures and officer positions.

The law of the jurisdiction in which a corporation operates will regulate most of its internal activities, as well as its finances. If a corporation operates outside its home state, it is often required to register with other governments as a foreign corporation, and is almost always subject to laws of its host state pertaining to employment, crimes, contracts, civil actions, and the like.

Naming

Corporations generally have a distinct name. Historically, some corporations were named after their membership: for instance, "The President and Fellows of Harvard College." Nowadays, corporations in most jurisdictions have a distinct name that does not need to make reference to their membership. In Canada, this possibility is taken to its logical extreme: many smaller Canadian corporations have no names at all, merely numbers based on a registration number (for example, "12345678 Ontario Limited"), which is assigned by the provincial or territorial government where the corporation incorporates.

In most countries, corporate names include a term or an abbreviation that denotes the corporate status of the entity (for example, "Incorporated" or "Inc." in the United States) or the limited liability of its members (for example, "Limited" or "Ltd."). These terms vary by jurisdiction and language. In some jurisdictions they are mandatory, and in others they are not. Their use puts everybody on constructive notice that they are dealing with an entity whose liability is limited: one can only collect from whatever assets the entity still controls when one obtains a judgment against it.

Some jurisdictions do not allow the use of the word "company" alone to denote corporate status, since the word "company" may refer to a partnership or some other form of collective ownership (in the United States it can be used by a sole proprietorship but this is not generally the case elsewhere).

7

Capital Structure and Firm Profitability: NYSE and NASDAQ Firms

As in informed investor, understanding a company's capital structure is an important step to evaluating its future prospects and stock performance over the long term. Companies using debt to finance growth isn't necessarily a bad thing in itself, and the amount of debt that is "normal" is partially dependent on the industry that the company operates in. Generally speaking, however, less debt is usually better than more and companies that have more equity over debt generally have less risk.

Capital Structure and Future Growth

If a company has a heavily debt-leveraged financial structure, there is risk that if business slows down or a wider economic downturn occurs then the company will be crushed under the weight of trying to repay these obligations. Sound familiar? Think of the companies that were ruined in the wake of 2008 because they didn't have the financial strength to weather the storm. American Airlines is a great example of a company that leveraged itself too heavily with debt and was ultimately forced to file bankruptcy in 2011 when they were unable to continue operating due to decreased revenues and the inability to pay off their liabilities.

Evaluating Debt to Equity

Debt to equity is a fast and easy way to evaluate a company's capital structure and their debt risk. The equation for this ratio is *the firm's total debt divided by the firm's total equity*. A ratio of one means that the firm is balanced with the same level of debt as equity, whereas zero would mean that it is all equity. Generally speaking, a ratio above two is not a good sign. You can find these numbers directly on a firm's most recent balance sheet.

Figure: *A debt to equity of more than 2 should be a red flag.*

If you want an even more accurate ratio, you can make a few adjustments. Short-term liabilities like accounts payable don't provide much info about leverage, so often these are left out of the equation. Only interest-bearing, long-term debt is used. Additionally, some off-balance-sheet liabilities such as unpaid pensions and operating leases should be included as they are still areas of leverage and liquidity risk for the company.

The Good, the Bad, and the Ugly in Today's Market

Here are a few examples of companies that are exemplifying these principles now.

The bad: Seaworld (NYSE: SEAS) has a debt-to-equity ratio of 2.6 when calculated directly. When accounts payable are taken out, the company still has a debt to equity ratio of 2.5. This level of debt is extremely dangerous, especially for a company that relies on consumer discretionary income, which is a key area that families cut back on in hard times. In a competitive industry, one with the likes of Disney which operates at a debt/equity ratio of 0.67, this should make Seaworld investors nervous.

The good: Chevron (NYSE: CVX) has a debt-to-equity ratio of just 0.46 once accounts payable are removed. Often a company that has been financed by debt will have a high return on equity (RoE) because its returns are financed by debt. Because equity is in the denominator of the RoE equation, a smaller equity and larger revenues means a better RoE. For Chevron, a revenue last year of $214 billion and low debt still provides a healthy return on equity of over 17%. The company looks good on both metrics and still has a P/E multiple of less than 10.

Apple (NASDAQ: AAPL) is another company with a strong capital structure. When accounts payable are taken out of the equation, Apple has a debt-to-equity ratio of just 0.38; this means that the company has very low long-term obligations that could drag it down in a negative economy. Because the company has so much cash, over $40 billion of it, there is little fear that the company will ever have issues with either its short-term or long-term debt obligations.

The Foolish Takeaway

While high leverage doesn't automatically make a stock a bad investment, it should raise a red flag and should warrant more research from potential investors. The debt-to-equity ratio is a great way to assess a firms capital structure and to evaluate the risks it faces should the economy slow down or the company's revenues drop. However, this ratio should never be analyzed alone, as other factors could make these numbers look better or worse.

Issues Surrounding Venture Capital, Initial Public Offering (IPO) and Post-IPO Equity Financing for Canadian SMEs

Regulatory Requirements

Listing Requirements: Before a company can contemplate issuing securities in the IPO market it must meet specific financial, public distribution and management requirements that are established by each stock exchange upon which the securities would be issued and listed. These listing requirements vary from market to market and are important determinants of whether or not a company is ready and able to go public on any particular market. Generally, these requirements differ between markets because of different specialisation among markets regarding the type and size of company that each market wants to attract and the role that it wants to play in the IPO marketplace. If a particular stock exchange wants to specialise in smaller companies in higher risk industries the listing requirements will be less onerous; whereas large stock exchanges want to focus on larger, established companies that are attractive to institutional investors. It also depends on the size of companies within a marketplace that are available to become publicly listed companies. In Canada, companies are much smaller than their U.S. counterparts and, therefore, Canadian stock exchanges must have lower listing requirements than U.S. exchanges in order to accommodate the array of companies available in Canada.

In Canada, for the Toronto Stock Exchange (TSE), the largest in the country, listing requirements have been established for three general categories of companies: industrial, mining and oil and gas companies. For industrial companies, profitable companies must have net tangible assets of $2 million, earnings of $200,000, pre-tax cash flow of $500,000 and adequate working capital; whereas companies forecasting profitability must have net tangible assets of $7.5 million, forecast earnings of $200,000, forecast pre-tax cash flow of $500,00 and adequate working capital. All companies must have a minimum of $12 million in the treasury and must have issued and outstanding 1 million freely tradeable shares with an aggregate market value of $4 million. The TSE also considers the background and expertise of management and may conduct reviews of key personnel. Recently, the TSE has also established special listing requirements for technology companies based on the level of investor support, adequacy of funds, management and stage of product commercialization. These companies must have $50 million minimum market value of listed shares, a $10 million public float, $10 million in the treasury and adequate funds to cover development, capital and operating expenses for one year.

In the U.S., the two major markets on which IPOs are undertaken are the New York Stock Exchange (NYSE) and the National Association of Securities Dealers Automated Quotation System (NASDAQ). Of these two markets, the NASDAQ has far less stringent listing requirements that the NYSE but these are still considerably higher the TSE listing requirements. The minimum financial requirements (in U.S.$) for listing on the NASDAQ include: net tangible assets of $6 million, pretax income of $1 million, a public float of 1.1 million shares with a market value of $8 million, a minimum of 400 shareholders holding 100 shares or more and a bid price on the shares of $5.00 or more. In addition, before a security can be listed on the NASDAQ at least three investment bankers must agree to act as "market makers" in the security by offering to buy a security and sell it to any investor who wishes to buy it. The NASDAQ may also scrutinize the management and directors of the company. For Canadian companies, the attraction to going public on the NASDAQ would have to reflect factors other than listing requirements, which are considerably more attractive on the TSE.

Prospectus Preparation

Once a company has qualified under the listing requirements of the stock exchange upon which it wants to go public it must then prepare a prospectus, which is an information document that must be provided to potential investors and filed with the relevant securities regulators. In Canada, they must be filed with provincial securities commissions, primarily the Ontario Securities Commission (OSC), while in the U.S. the major regulator is the federal Securities and Exchange Commission (SEC). The prospectus is used both as a selling document by the underwriters of the securities and as a regulatory document to ensure that investors receive full, true and plain disclosure of all material facts related to the securities being issued, as required by securities legislation. As a result, it must provide a balanced view of both the positive and negative views of the company issuing the securities.

The prospectus must contain the following types of information: the business of the company, financial statements and projections, corporate and share structures, risk factors relating to the company and securities, use of the proceeds of the issue, statutory rights of investors and certifications of full, true and plain disclosure of all material facts on the part of the company and its underwriters. Initially, the company must file a preliminary prospectus for review by the securities commissions. Once this review has been completed, the prospectus is then revised to reflect the comments from the regulators and again re-filed with the securities commissions, who then clear the company for filing.

Escrow Provisions

Another regulatory element that is established at the time of issuing the securities are the escrow provisions attached to the newly issued securities. These provisions determine when major investors, who held positions prior to the IPO (such as venture capitalists) and senior management are eligible to sell their holdings of the securities on the open market. In the past, these requirements have established escrow periods of up to two years before these holders can liquidate their holdings but more recently the maximum escrow period has generally been reduced to 18 months, e.g. on the TSE. Larger companies can also receive exemptions from the escrow requirements or negotiate a shorter escrow period with the stock exchange. This regulation is particularly important to the founders of newly listed companies and the investors who funded the company prior to the IPO as it determines when they can recover their investments and realise their gains. It also introduces greater uncertainty for these shareholders as market conditions can change significantly during the escrow period.

Disclosure Regulations

Once the IPO has been completed, the company immediately encounters ongoing disclosure regulations and requirements in order to keep the secondary market for the securities informed of all relevant conditions surrounding the company. First, companies must disclose and send to its shareholders quarterly financial statements, annual audited financial statements and management's discussion and analyses of financial results and operations, usually in the form of an annual shareholders' report. They must also provide proxy circulars and solicitation documents before annual shareholders' meetings to provide information relevant to matters being voted on at the meeting. All material changes in the business, operations or capital structure of the company, that may have an impact on the price of the securities, must be disclosed in a timely manner through press releases and filings with the stock exchanges and securities commissions. Insider trading reports (for directors, senior officers and investors holding more than 10% of the outstanding voting shares) must be filed within 10 days after the end of the month during which any of these "insiders" traded their shares.

Market Processes

The process that a company must go through in going public is often a long and complex, with most IPOs taking anywhere from 3 to 6 months to complete. The first step in the process is to deal with corporate, tax and accounting matters that must be undertaken to prepare the company for going public. These include the preparation of a proper business plan that will serve as a blueprint for the preparation of the prospectus. This plan should include a description of the business, a market analysis, a description of the company's products and services, management structure and financial information and projections. In order to become a public company appropriate reporting systems and procedures must be put in place before starting the IPO process. The company must then choose lawyers, accountants and underwriters who will provide the leadership required to carry out the public offering. In making these choices a first priority is to obtain the services of firms that have considerable experience in public offerings and securities expertise with regard to the legal, accounting and auditing requirements for an IPO. Any required changes to corporate structure and the capital structure of the company should be undertaken and a strengthening of senior management implemented well in advance of the IPO.

Choosing an Underwriter

The choice of an underwriter for the IPO is of critical importance in achieving success in the marketplace. The underwriter must be able to provide a realistic valuation for the company in order to raise the necessary amount of financing while at the same time achieving success in selling the issue in the market. Much of this will depend upon the reputation, experience and distribution capability of the underwriter. A firm with a strong reputation will attract a strong banking group syndicate that will be able to sell the shares effectively. The experience of the underwriter will assist in pricing of the issue, selecting the banking group and providing credibility in the market. The distribution capacity of the underwriter must be adequate to sell the required number of shares to a broad base of investors, thereby providing liquidity in the after-market. Another important aspect is to choose a firm with a strong research department with the ability and desire to follow the company after the IPO so that the reputation and status of the company can be maintained in the after-market. The company must then balance these factors against the commission that the underwriter proposes to charge for their services and the level of assistance they and their legal counsel will provide during the process.

Choice of Markets

The company must then choose the market in which they are going to offer their securities. In the U.S. the choice is largely between the NYSE and the NASDAQ, with larger industrial companies generally choosing the NYSE and smaller technology-oriented companies usually going public on the NASDAQ. Canadian companies have somewhat wider and more complex choices available to them in that they can either use Canadian stock exchanges or U.S. exchanges or both in going public. The usual reason for a Canadian company to go public on a U.S. exchange is to gain access to a larger, deeper capital market and, often, more specialised capital market analysts, particularly in the case of technology companies. However, offsetting this is the fact that Canadian companies must comply with stringent SEC rules governing foreign-based IPOs. In Canada, companies have basically two choices of markets, the TSE or the new CDNX market that specialises in small company financings. In making a choice between all markets, a Canadian company must weigh these market attributes against the costs of going public in the various market alternatives. If a Canadian company wants to take advantage of the larger, more developed U.S. market it may have to accept higher costs, greater legal risks and different valuations than those they would face in the Canadian market.

Process Phases

The process by which a company goes public involves a number of distinct phases, starting with the preparation phase that could begin about six months before the completion of the IPO. This includes completion of all the items discussed above that are required to initiate the IPO process. The next phase is preparation of the preliminary prospectus that should start anywhere from three months to six weeks prior to the closing of the IPO. This involves completion of due diligence analyses, the preparation of audited financial statements and the drafting of the preliminary prospectus that will be filed with the securities commissions.

The final preparation phase involves the development of information summaries from the prospectus that will be used as selling tools and the organisation and undertaking of the "road show", made up of a series of presentations to institutional investors and investment dealers that feature key members of the company's management team. During this period the underwriting agreement is negotiated and finalized and application for listing on the chosen stock exchange is made. Comments from the securities commissions on the prospectus are now received and revisions are made to the prospectus to reflect these comments. In the final prospectus phase, once the issue has been cleared for filing, the issue is priced, the final prospectus filed and printed and the underwriting agreement executed. This is followed by the closing phase in which the securities and proceeds from the issue are exchanged and the company's stock starts trading on the stock exchange.

Market Participants

Underwriters: The underwriters are key participants in the IPO market as they perform both risk-taking and marketing roles in the IPO process. There are two common types of underwriting arrangements for IPOs: best-efforts and firm-commitment agreements.

Under a best-efforts agreement, the underwriters simply use their best efforts to sell the shares on behalf of the company as agents but are not obligated to purchase any of the shares at their own risk. Usually, there are a minimum number of securities that must be sold for the IPO to be completed. These agreements are usually used in the case of smaller companies whose securities are more difficult to sell. Under a firm-commitment agreement, the underwriters agree to purchase all of the shares offered by the company and then resell them to the public. These commitments are made at the time that the final prospectus is filed, when the "road show" has been completed and the underwriters have assurances that they will be able to sell the shares immediately. However, any shares remaining unsold must be purchased by the underwriters at their own risk, except in cases where escape clauses relieve the underwriters of this obligation under conditions where the market for the shares collapses just prior to the offering date or where there has been misrepresentation by the company. In the case of a best-efforts IPO the underwriters are paid a commission for selling the securities; while under a firm-commitment IPO they receive a combination of discounts and commissions, along with pre-IPO "items of value", as compensation for their risk-taking and selling roles.

Institutional Investors

The other major players in the IPO market are institutional investors who influence the establishment of share valuations prior to the IPO and usually purchase the majority of the securities offered in the IPO, at least initially. The success of an IPO largely depends on the reception the issue receives from institutional investors during the "road show" and their reaction to the proposed valuation of the company. They base their response on their impressions of the company's management and the validity of the company's business plan and financial projections. After the "road show" the institutional investors are canvassed by the underwriters for commitments to purchase the securities to be issued in the IPO. Base on these commitments, the underwriters and the company decide on whether or not to proceed with the IPO and on the valuation to be placed on the shares, if they decide to go ahead. If the underwriters do not receive sufficient interest from institutional investors, they are unlikely to enter into a firm-commitment agreement. If the IPO proceeds, the institutional investors take up their commitments to purchase the securities and then decide whether to retain them as part of their portfolios or to resell all or part of their holdings in the after-market.

In recent years, when many new issues gained sharply immediately after the IPO, many institutional investors re-sold their shares to realise these substantial immediate gains and then waited to purchase shares later if they wanted to hold them in their portfolios. As a result, in many cases, institutional investors were only short-term holders of the newly issued shares. Under these circumstances they favoured low IPO valuations, which tended to influence the underwriters to under-price new issues.

Retail Investors

Individual retail investors are the final group of participants in the IPO market, who are generally introduced to new issues through investment dealers. During the pre-IPO "road show", investment dealers are also introduced to the proposed stock issue through attendance at meetings with the underwriters and the company's management. The investment dealers are also canvassed for their support of the issue in terms of their requests for allotments of the new issue for resale to their retail investor clients. This also has an influence on the success and valuation of the new issue but not to the degree that views of institutional investors impact on the issue. Generally, the investment dealers receive their allotments out of the shares remaining after institutional demand for the shares has been satisfied, so retail investors tend to be residual investors that may or may not receive sufficient shares to satisfy their demand for the new issue. As a result, individual investors are price-takers in the market whereas institutional investors are price-makers in the market. However, retail investors play an important role in that they absorb any excess supply beyond institutional demand and, therefore, reduce the degree of risk faced by the underwriters. This probably makes the underwriters somewhat more aggressive in their pricing of the issue and, thereby, marginally improves the valuation received by the company. The retail investors also are the prime group of investors that absorbs the supply of shares that are resold in the after-market by the institutional investors and this helps to maintain value and stability in the post-IPO market. This further reduces the risk faced by the underwriters in their post – IPO role as market makers for the shares.

Debating the Pros and Cons of Dual Class Capital Structures

The debate over dual class capital structures has grown louder, as a number of high-profile companies recently have gone public with dual class structures. Although opponents argue that dual class structures destroy shareholder value, there is compelling evidence that these structures can benefit companies, shareholders, and capital markets.

Dual class capital structures have been used in some of the most high-profile recent initial public offerings (IPOs) by technology companies, including the offerings by Facebook, Google, LinkedIn, and Zynga. Other large IPOs outside the technology sector also have used the dual class approach. In January 2013, for example, Pfizer implemented this structure when it spun off its animal health business, Zoetis. The Facebook and Zoetis dual class IPOs were the largest in U.S. history.

Companies with dual class structures create a low-vote class of common stock entitled to one vote per share, and a high-vote class of common stock entitled to several votes per share (often ten). These companies sell the low-vote common stock to the public in their IPOs. The founders and early investors retain the high-vote common stock to ensure that they maintain control, even when they no longer own a majority of the company.

Institutional investors and their representatives, including the Council of Institutional Investors (CII), the California Public Employees' Retirement System (CalPERS), and Institutional Shareholder Services (ISS), have voiced strong opposition to dual class structures. These opponents argue that dual class capitalization creates the equivalent of a corporate safe room by making it nearly impossible for shareholders to replace directors, challenge management, or force change in control transactions. CII has urged the New York Stock Exchange (NYSE) and Nasdaq to adopt rules prohibiting companies with dual class structures from going public. (1)

There are strong arguments both for and against dual class capital structures. This article briefly reviews the historical background of dual class structures, describes some of the reasons why specific companies have implemented dual class structures, summarizes the arguments in opposition to dual class structures, and finally considers how shareholders are protected, in and can benefit from, dual class structures. Despite the claims of some institutional investors, dual class structures offer key advantages to companies, shareholders, and capital markets that warrant their continued use on U.S. stock exchanges.

Historical Background: The debate over dual class capital structures has persisted for almost 100 years. In the 1920s, several corporations used two classes of stock—one class with full voting rights and another class with no voting rights. Dual class stock issues by Dodge Brothers, Industrial Rayon Corporation, A&W Root Beer, and Fox Theaters sparked academic speeches, scholarly articles, and press coverage on the topic. Even then-President Calvin Coolidge took an interest in the issue. According to Harvard Professor William Z. Ripley, non-voting stock was the "crowning infamy" in a series of corporate actions intended to disenfranchise the public investor. (2) In 1926, the NYSE chimed in with its statement of disapproval of dual class structures; and in 1940, the NYSE formally prohibited the issuance of non-voting securities.

During the 1980s, however, dual class recapitalizations emerged as a popular takeover defence. Managers of potential takeover targets recognised that they could reduce significantly the likelihood of a hostile acquisition if they maintained control of the vote, since a corporate raider cannot oust managers who can outvote it. (3) More than 65 public companies adopted dual class capital structures as takeover defences during the 1980s. Listed companies left, or threatened to leave, the NYSE for Nasdaq or the American Stock Exchange, both of which permitted dual class stock. To remain competitive with Nasdaq and the American Stock Exchange, the NYSE was forced to relax its prohibition on dual class structures.

Investors grew worried by the proliferation of dual class stock, and urged Congress or the Securities and Exchange Commission (SEC) to take action and prohibit dual class structures. In July 1988, the SEC responded by adopting Rule 19c-4, which effectively amended the rules of the stock exchanges to prohibit a company's securities from being listed if the company issued securities or took other actions to nullify, restrict, or reduce the voting rights of existing shareholders. The SEC did not adopt a strict one share, one vote standard primarily because empirical evidence on the effect of dual class stock on shareholder wealth was inconclusive. However, Rule 19c-4 was short-lived. In 1990, the D.C. Circuit invalidated Rule 19c-4 because it dealt with a matter of corporate governance beyond the scope of the SEC's authority. (4)

After the D.C. Circuit's decision, the SEC urged the U.S. stock exchanges to adopt a uniform policy on dual class structures. The exchanges responded by agreeing to prohibit companies that are already listed from engaging in dual class recapitalizations. They continued to permit listing by companies that established dual class structures before they went public. These rules remain in force today, and IPOs by companies with dual class structures are still permitted. In fact, 20 of 170 IPOs between January 2010 and March 2012 featured dual class structures. (5) Further, all of the big technology IPOs of 2012—Groupon, LinkedIn, Yelp, and Zynga—had dual class structures. Thus, the debate over dual class structures continues.

Review of Companies with Dual Class Structures :

Over the years, dual class structures have been used most frequently and prominently by media and communications companies, fashion and home goods companies, employee-owned companies, and technology companies. Such structures also are often used by public companies that take their subsidiaries public and by companies facing foreign ownership restrictions. A review of these companies reveals that there are strong industry-specific, transaction planning, and regulatory arguments in favour of dual class capitalizations.

Several companies in the media and communications industry have dual class structures, including News Corp., The New York Times, and The Washington Post. The founding families of these companies—the Murdochs, Sulzbergers, and Grahams—use dual class structures to keep control within their families. They argue that they need to maintain control to protect editorial integrity. They reason that dual class structures allow their companies to remain committed to serious news coverage, even when short-term results are fluctuating and shareholders, focused on financial matters, might seek to change the composition of the board or management. In a recent editorial in The New York Times, Joe Nocera notes that the protections offered by dual class structures grew even more pronounced "as the newspaper business declined, [and] financial engineers came knocking" with plans to increase profits at the expense of the news. (6) According to Nocera, "If you buy New York Times stock, you are buying into the notion that you'll let the family run the show, as it has done for more than a century. And the Sulzbergers will put The Times's journalism ahead of all else, because that is what is in the family's DNA." (7)

Dual class structures are also common in the fashion and home goods industry, with Martha Stewart Living and Ralph Lauren being prominent examples. Consumers of these companies are not just buying a commodity, they are buying the brand. Many of these fashion and home goods companies have an individual or family closely associated with the brand image. The founders of these companies argue that their strong control position gives them a continuing incentive to build the desired brand equity, which translates into a strong market position and profitable stock returns.

Employee-owned companies similarly find advantages in dual class structures. They take the position that by enabling employees to own the majority of company stock, the dual class structure creates a positive corporate culture with high employee morale and increased productivity. The company's management can reap the benefits of going public without undermining this positive culture.

Currently, the most high-profile examples of companies with dual class structures are technology companies, including Facebook, Google, Groupon, LinkedIn, Yelp, and Zynga. The founders of these technology companies reason that they have a dynamic, long-term vision for the company. They need to retain control in order to continue to innovate and remain an industry pioneer. Short-term market forces and risk-averse shareholders should not dictate or interfere with the founders' vision. Relatedly, the founders reason that dual class structures provide a strong takeover defence, keeping the company on track to achieve their long-term objectives.

In Google's 2004 Registration Statement, co-founder Larry Page candidly states:

In the transition to public ownership, we have set up a corporate structure that will make it harder for outside parties to take over or influence Google. This [dual class] structure will also make it easier for our management team to follow the long term, innovative approach emphasized earlier. ... The main effect of this structure is likely to leave our team, especially Sergey [Brin] and me, with significant control over the company's decisions and fate, as Google shares change hands. New investors will fully share in Google's long term growth but will have less influence over its strategic decisions than they would at most public companies. From the point of view of long-term success in advancing a company's core values, the structure has clearly been an advantage. Academic studies have shown that from a purely economic point of view, dual class structures have not harmed the share price of companies. ... Google has prospered as a private company. As a public company, we believe a dual class voting structure will enable us to retain many of the positive aspects of being private.

The increased use of dual class structures to protect the implementation of business plans speaks to a broader point about today's investors. In the postwar era, most shareholders were individual investors who held on to stocks for the long-run and exerted little pressure on the companies in which they invested. (8) In contrast, today's market is dominated by large institutional investors who are far more aggressive in trying to influence companies' agendas and who often have far shorter investment time horizons. (9) The average annual turnover of a mutual fund portfolio is 100 percent—for a hedge fund portfolio, it is 300 percent. (10) In this context, companies find dual class structures useful in mitigating shareholder influence in order to pursue their core values and objectives.

Dual class capital structures are sometimes used not because of concerns about short-term market pressure and takeover threats, but to achieve tax or other transaction planning objectives. For example, when a parent company decides to spin off a subsidiary, it often also decides to raise capital before the spin-off by causing the subsidiary to engage in an IPO. If the parent company maintains at least 80 percent of the voting power in the subsidiary following the IPO, the subsequent spin-off receives tax-free treatment. Raising lots of capital, however, may require the parent company to sell more than 20 percent of the subsidiary's common stock. The dual class structure offers a solution. The parent company can create a dual class structure in the subsidiary, sell low-vote stock to the public in the IPO, and retain the high-vote stock. This allows the parent company to sell as much stock as necessary to raise capital, while still maintaining 80 percent of the voting power in the subsidiary to realise tax benefits. In the Zoetis IPO this past January, Pfizer used the dual class structure to raise $2.2 billion in the IPO while maintaining 98 percent of the voting power in Zoetis and preserving the flexibility to conduct a tax-free spin-off at a later stage. (11)

Regulatory requirements also may support the use of dual class capital structures. These structures are used frequently by companies subject to U.S. or foreign rules requiring that a certain percentage of the company be owned by U.S. or foreign nationals respectively. For example until August 2012, the Federal Communications Act of 1934 strictly prohibited foreign entities from owning more than 20 percent of the voting stock of U.S. telecommunications companies. (12) In response to similar Canadian regulations limiting foreign ownership of large telecom companies to less than 46.7 percent, the Canadian telecom company Telus adopted a dual class structure in order to sell low-vote stock to foreigners and high-vote stock to Canadians. (13)

Opposition by Institutional Investors

As noted above, in October 2012, CII sent letters to both the NYSE and Nasdaq urging the exchanges to prohibit dual class IPOs and dual class recapitalizations. (14) CII argues that dual class structures are directly at odds with the one share, one vote bedrock principle of shareholder democracy. It believes that the capital markets system works best when voting power is proportional to economic interest.

CII further reasons that dual class structures insulate management or the control group from all challenges. This insulation increases the likelihood of corporate misconduct and decreases accountability. (15) CII concedes that dual class structures may seem appealing when brilliant visionaries are heading the company. (16) But what happens when the vision fails, or when abusive or less-inspired managers take the reins?

In a dual class structure, CII argues that the incentives of management and the board are not aligned with the interests of all shareholders. It states that dual class structures are most concerning in the context of two specific situations. First, CII worries that dual class structures facilitate conflict of interest transactions, by permitting management to engage in transactions that benefit members of the control group at the expense of public shareholders without fear of any consequences. Second, CII argues that dual class structures preserve the status quo, even where management's strategic vision is failing or where bad business decisions are made. Shareholders are powerless to seek remedies or effect change in both of these situations. Nor can shareholders depend on effective board oversight.

Since directors are beholden to those in control of the vote for their jobs, they do not act in the best interests of all shareholders. (17)

CII claims that its opposition to dual class structures rests on strong empirical support. Citing an academic study conducted by ISS, CII concludes that companies with dual class structures reduce shareholder value. The ISS study, Controlled Companies in the Standard and Poor's 1500: A Ten Year Performance and Risk Review, finds the following: (18)

- Dual class companies significantly under-perform single-class companies over 3-year, 5-year, and 10-year periods. Dual class companies only outperform single-class companies over a 1-year period.
- Dual class companies have more related party transactions than single-class companies.
- Dual class companies exhibit more stock price volatility than single-class companies.

- Dual class companies are less likely to have standard corporate governance features relating to board accountability and shareholder rights than single-class companies.
- Dual class companies are more insulated and engage in less outreach than single-class companies.

Although Calipers has announced that it intends to boycott investments in dual class companies, (19) CII says its members cannot do that. CII notes that many shareholders are forced to invest in dual class companies through passive investment strategies; for example, pension and index funds often require their participants to invest in all listed stocks.

Thus, CII believes that an outright ban on dual class structures is appropriate. CII points out that dual class structures are currently prohibited on several major international exchanges, including the London and Hong Kong stock exchanges.

Some shareholders also have urged companies to eliminate their dual class structures through shareholder proposals. In 2012, such shareholder proposals were included in the proxy statements of News Corp. (20) and Google. (21) These proposals echo the arguments of CII, and claim that dual class structures misalign economic incentives and voting power, allow management to extract private benefits at the shareholders' expense, and create a corporate culture of no accountability.

However, as discussed below, these shareholder proposals have not received significant support.

Shareholder Protections and Benefits

A survey of companies with dual class structures indicates that the founders have strong rationales for their decision to use dual class structures, and that the dual class structure secures key benefits for that company as well as the broader shareholder base. Further, shareholders are not entirely without protection should the risk of improper management become reality.

First, corporate law provides shareholders with protections against abuses by those in control of the corporation. Directors and controlling shareholders owe shareholders a fiduciary duty of loyalty.

The duty of loyalty requires that directors and controlling shareholders act in the best interests of the company and its shareholders, and without regard to personal motivations not shared by shareholders generally. Directors or controlling shareholders may be found to have violated the duty of loyalty if they approve transactions in which they have a conflict of interest because they or someone with whom they are aligned will benefit from the transaction. Such conflict of interest transactions are subject to an entire fairness review unless procedural protections, including an independent committee and minority shareholder approval, are used.

To survive the stringent entire fairness review, the transaction must be the result of fair dealing and must be at a fair price. Any breach of the duty of loyalty entitles shareholders to seek judicial relief and remedies.

There have been several judicial actions where the control group in a dual class company has been successfully challenged by shareholders. For example, in In re Delphi Financial Group Shareholder Litigation, the court agreed with the shareholders that the controlling shareholder in a dual class company breached his fiduciary duties by seeking and obtaining a control premium for his shares during merger negotiations, when the company's certificate of incorporation stipulated that both classes of stock must be treated equally in a merger. (22) In another case, Levco Alternative Fund Ltd. et al. v.

The Reader's Digest Association, Inc., the court enjoined the recapitalization of a dual class company, because the independent committee that negotiated the recapitalization breached its fiduciary duties by failing to evaluate the fairness to non-voting shareholders of the company's payment to the voting shareholders. (23) The court noted that "given the obvious conflicting interests of the shareholder classes, the conceded absence of an evaluation of fairness of the recapitalization on the [non-voting] shareholders is significant." (24) Thus, courts are cognizant of the conflict of interest risks that dual class structures can pose to shareholders, and will take steps to protect shareholder rights when they conclude that the duty of loyalty has been breached.

In addition, although the founding family or controlling shareholder may have sufficient votes to appoint and remove board members, this power does not give it the ability to control directly the company's business decisions.

The power to supervise management resides with the directors, who have a fiduciary obligation to exercise their business judgment for the benefit of all shareholders. Conscientious directors will honour this obligation, even when the founder or controlling shareholder makes demands or threatens to replace them. CII suggests that most directors would find it hard to withstand this pressure, and that in any event, controlling shareholders can place friends on the board who share their vision. But stacking a board with cronies is not as easy as it might seem.

The NYSE and Nasdaq listing rules require that a majority of a company's board members be independent, and that the key board committees consist entirely of independent directors. Prior relationships with the controlling shareholder may disqualify the board members from service.

Thus, shareholders can rely, in part, on conscientious or independent directors to consider and safeguard their interests. Second, shareholder protections are often built into the organisational documents of dual class companies. Many dual class company charters stipulate that if high-vote shares are transferred, the transferee will not obtain the high voting power. (25) The charters often also provide that the high-vote shares lose their special voting power after a specified time period or upon the death of the controlling shareholder. (26) Some charters stipulate that high-vote shares will not receive a premium in a merger. (27)

If the company or the controlling shareholder violates any of these provisions, the shareholders can sue. (28) Third, shareholders who choose to invest in dual class companies benefit from market forces during the IPO process.

During the period leading up to pricing, potential investors have an opportunity to demand a discount for the risk associated with an investment in low-vote shares. In effect, the IPO process for a dual class company can be viewed as an arm's length negotiation among prospective public investors, the underwriters, and the control group.

The price set during the IPO process contains a discount for risk, with the size of the discount dependent on the over-all attractiveness of the company. Underwriters generally will warn companies that want to use a dual class structure that the price they receive for their shares may reflect a discount—or that the market may not be willing to accept low-vote shares at all.

Fourth, shareholders can sell their shares of dual class companies if they believe that the implicit risk discount is not adequate, or if they become concerned about management's actions. Although CII argues that shareholders may be locked into their shares through passive investment strategies like pension and index funds, it is not clear that the inherent limitations of this investment approach should drive regulatory policy.

As discussed above, most shareholders choose to invest in dual class companies because they believe in the company's strategy or the founders' vision. During the 2012 proxy season, only four shareholder proposals urged companies to eliminate their dual class structure, and these proposals only received an average level of support of 33 percent. (29)

The shareholders at both News Corp. and Google overwhelmingly voted against the elimination of the company's dual class structure. (30) Further, if dual class structures were not an option, some founders might choose to sell fewer shares to the public, delay going public, or not go public at all.

Founders who want to maintain control may choose to bypass public markets in favour of private capital.

The result would be additional friction in the capital formation process and fewer investment opportunities for the public. Of relevance to this point, the number of IPOs has decreased sharply in the past decade, and the number of public companies in the U.S. has fallen by more than 40 percent since 1997. (31)

CII's call for an outright ban on dual class structures also would adversely affect the competitiveness of the NYSE and Nasdaq. For example, in August 2012, Manchester United chose to list its dual class shares in New York over Singapore, because Singapore prohibited dual class structures at the time. Singapore is now considering allowing dual class structures to maintain its competitiveness as a financial centre. (32)

Although CII points to studies concluding that dual class structures destroy shareholder value, the empirical evidence is far from clear. For example, in a study of dual class IPOs that is not cited by CII, dual class companies were found to have outperformed their single class counterparts both in terms of stock market returns and accounting measures of company performance. (33) And in a study of dual class recapitalizations, dual class companies experienced long-term positive stock returns and superior operating performance over the four years after the recapitalization. (34)

Given these contrary findings, it is difficult to conclude that the empirical evidence strongly supports a ban on dual class stock. Just as shareholder returns can vary among single class companies, shareholder returns can vary among dual class companies. At least some of these companies have produced attractive returns; dual class companies do not automatically destroy shareholder value.

Conclusion

As Financial Times columnist Andrew Hill observes, "the advantage of a dul class share structure is that it protects entrepreneurial management from the demands of ordinary shareholders. The disadvantage of a dual class share structure is that it protects entrepreneurial management from the demands of shareholders." (35)

Although the empirical evidence is inconclusive, there are benefits to dual class structures. Dual class share structures permit companies to stay true to their founders' core values. Although this requires some insulation from the demands of ordinary shareholders, it also can generate large shareholder returns.

In addition, shareholders are protected from the risks of dual class structures through various judicial, contractual, and market mechanisms. Further, dual class share structures create new investment opportunities, by allowing public companies to retain some of the benefits of being private. Contrary to the arguments of certain institutional investors, dual class structures can benefit companies, shareholders, and capital markets alike.

Bibliography

Aswathappa, K. : *Essential of Business Environment,* New Delhi , Himalaya Publishing House, 2001.

Beesley, Michael : *Corporate Social Responsibility: A Reassessment,* London, Crrom Helm, 1978.

Bernthall, R. : *International Conference for Tourism Educators,* Guildford, University of Surrey, 1988.

Carroll, A. : *Business and Society: Managing Corporate Social Performance,* Boston: Little, Brown & Company, 1981.

Carter, John: *Chandler's Travels: A Tour of the Life of Harry Chandler,* London, Quiller Press, 1985.

Desmond, Glenn, and John A, Marcell, *Handbook of Small Business Valuation Formulas and Rules of Thumb,* Valuation Press, 1993.

Donald M.: *Customer Service in the Hospitality and Tourism Industry,* Englewood Cliffs, Prentice Hall, 1994.

Elio, C.: *The Hospitality Law Desk Reference,* Miami, Southern Beverage Journal, 1994.

Foster, Douglas: *Travel and Tourism Management,* London, Macmillan Educational, 1985.

Goeldner, C. R: *The Evaluation of Tourism as an Industry and a Discipline, Paper Presented to,* International Conference for Tourism Educators, Guildford, University of Surrey, 1988.

Goodall, Steve: *Developing Environmental Education in the Curriculum,* London, David Fulton Publishers, 1994.

Hoffman, Edward: *Project Management Success Stories: Lessons of Project Leaders,* New York, John Wiley & Son, 2000.

Holloway, J. C. : *Labour, Vocational Education and Training, in W. Pompl and P. Lavery,* Tourism in Europe - Structures and Developments, Oxford, CAB International, 1993.

Ireland, Lewis: *Quality Management for Projects and Programs*, Upper Darby, PMI, 1991.

Jakle, John: *Tourist, The: Travel in Twentieth Century North America,* University of North Nebraska, 1985.

Judy A: *Tourism: Management of Facilities*, London, Pitman: M & E, 1993.

Keith Davis : *Business and Society.-Corporate Strategy, Public Policy, and Ethics,* New York, McGraw-Hill, 1992.

Larkham, P J: *Building a New Heritage: Tourism, Culture & Identity in the New Europe*, London, Routledge,1994.

Manuel, G. Velasquez : *Business Ethics Concepts and Cases,* Delhi, Pearson Education, 2002.

Nancy N.: *Choosing a Career in Hotels, Motels, and Resorts,* New York, Rosen Pub. Group, 1997.

Phipps, A: *Tourism and Intercultural Exchange: Why Tourism Matters*, Clevedon, Channel View, 2005.

Richard, DeGeorge : *Business Ethics,* New York, MacMillan Publishing, 1990.

Salancik, G. R.: *The External Control of Organizations, A Resource Dependence Perspective*, New York, 1978.

Sims, Ronald R. : *Ethics and Corporate Social Responsibility: Why Giants Fall,* New York, Praeger Publishers, 2003.

Tietenberg, Tom, *Environmental Economics and Policy,* New York, HarperCollins, 1994

Wartick, S. and .Wood, D. : *International Business and Society*. Blackwell: Malden, 1998.

Watts, P. : *Corporate Social Responsibility: Making Good Business Sense*. World Business Council for Sustainable Development: Geneva, 2000.

Index

❑❑❑